Paddy Hopkirk says:

'Sooner or later, every car owner faces the ruinous cost of servicing, maintaining and repairing his car. That's why more and more car owners are turning to DIY methods as the only way of slashing motoring costs.

PITMAN'S ALL-IN-ONE motoring books are written by professional motoring writers who understand car owners' needs.
The books have been specially designed to give all the information needed, in clear diagrams, trouble-shooting charts, photographs and easy-to-follow text, making it easy for DIY car owners to keep costs of motoring at rock bottom.

Whatever the car owner's approach to home servicing - whether as a novice or an expert - PITMAN'S ALL-IN-ONE motoring books offer him for the first time a combined maintenance handbook and workshop manual - all the DIY car owner needs to get the best out of his car.'

A 1976 Renault 4 TL. This has improved trim, a heated rear window, an alternator and a restyled radiator grille

This earlier Renault 4 is typical of the range, including most of the later cars up to 1975

All-in-one book of the Renault 4

Staton Abbey

A maintenance, fault-tracing and home workshop manual

Covering the Renault 4 from October 1965 onwards
R1123: de Luxe, L and TL models

Pitman Publishing

First published 1976

UK
Pitman Publishing Ltd
Pitman House, 39 Parker Street, London, WC2B 5PB

Pitman Medical Publishing Co Ltd
42 Camden Road, Tunbridge Wells, Kent, TN1 2QD

Focal Press Ltd
31 Fitzroy Square, London, W1P 6BH

Pitman Publishing Corporation
Fearon Publishers Inc
6 Davis Drive, Belmont, California 94002

AUSTRALIA
Pitman Publishing Pty Ltd
Pitman House, 158 Bouverie Street, Carlton, Victoria 3053

CANADA
Pitman Publishing
Copp Clark Publishing
517 Wellington Street West, Toronto, M5V 1GL

EAST AFRICA
Sir Isaac Pitman and Sons Ltd
Banda Street, PO Box 46038, Nairobi, Kenya

SOUTH AFRICA
Pitman Publishing Co (SA) Pty Ltd
Craighall Mews, Jan Smuts Avenue, Craighall Park,
Johannesburg 2001

ISBN 0 273 01003 4

4714:19

Designed by DP Press Ltd
Set in Univers light by Lyth Engraving Ltd
Printed in England by the Pitman Press, Bath

Contents

Acknowledgements

Special thanks are due to Renault Ltd for providing information and advice during the preparation of this book, and also to the parent company at Billancourt in France for permission to use drawings in the official workshop manuals as the basis of many of the illustrations

Among other firms to whom thanks are due are –

Champion Sparking Plug Company Ltd
AE Edmunds Walker Ltd
Holt Products Ltd

The greatest care has been taken to check and cross-check the information and servicing data, but liability cannot be accepted for errors or omissions, or for changes in specifications that are sometimes introduced by a manufacturer during the production run of a model

An underbonnet view. This is typical of all but the earliest models

1 Air cleaner and carburettor
2 Water pump
3 Exhaust pipe
4 Gearchange control
5 Radiator filler
6 Gearbox
7 Stowage for jack
8 Alternator (shown) or dynamo
9 Expansion-tank filler cap
10 Battery master switch
11 Battery
12 Petrol pump
13 Ignition distributor
14 Engine oil filler
15 Fuse box (when fitted)

Part one

1 Before you begin
How this series was planned

Are you a dedicated do-it-yourself enthusiast – or an owner with only limited practical experience, forced by continually rising costs to maintain and repair your car at home?

Whatever your approach to home servicing – whether as a novice or as an expert – the handbooks in this series have been tailored to meet your needs and abilities. Each forms a combined, all-in-one maintenance handbook and home workshop manual, with the emphasis solidly on the practical aspects of the work.

We introduce you to your car, advise you how to vet a used example, tell you how to get it through the Ministry test and take you progressively through preventive maintenance, trouble-shooting, servicing, repairs and overhauls.

We have made the workshop manual chapters as comprehensive as possible, while bearing in mind the less than ideal conditions under which the average owner must usually carry out repairs and overhauls. But it must be accepted that some jobs are outside the province of the home mechanic; they call for the use of special workshop tools and equipment and – in many cases – for special skills.

Botched-up repairs can be dangerous and we feel strongly that owners should not be encouraged to do work which might entail safety risks.

How this book is arranged

In Part One you will find an in-depth study of the models covered, together with information on servicing and preventive maintenance. We take the logical view that it is better to avoid trouble than to try to put it right after it has developed.

Even the most meticulous maintenance, however, cannot guarantee freedom from faults, so we have included in Part Two a comprehensive set of trouble-tracing charts which should enable you to pin-point a trouble quickly and accurately.

If your car is due for the Ministry test, the tips that we give should enable it to pass with flying colours. Many cars fail quite unnecessarily, due to faults which could have been put right by a practical owner.

While still on the theme of putting your car in tip-top condition, we tell you how to tackle rust and bodywork blemishes and how to restore a showroom shine.

The remainder of the book forms a concise home workshop manual, covering all the jobs that can be safely tackled without the need for elaborate equipment, and supported by comprehensive specifications and data tables.

The practical aspects

We have tried to anticipate your difficulties and to give practical pointers and advice where necessary. For example, would it be quicker and cheaper to fit a new or fully-reconditioned part instead of stripping and repairing a worn component? When should the help of a specialist repair firm be enlisted? We give you the pros and cons (and the economics) of these problems, to help you to make the correct decision.

Time is often a vital factor and we have included in the workshop manual chapters what we think are some realistic times for the more important jobs and major operations. We have erred on the generous side, bearing in mind the needs of the novice, but it would be wise to allow an additional safety margin to take care of unexpected snags. The times that we suggest, therefore, will not necessarily agree with those that may be quoted by a dealer, who has a well-equipped workshop and racks full of expensive special tools.

Finally, we have broken down the servicing and overhaul instructions into simple step-by-step sequences which are exceptionally easy to follow and should give a beginner the confidence to tackle fairly ambitious work.

Where there are snags, we don't hesitate to say so. And where special service tools and other equipment are needed, we list them.

As for the work itself, that is – literally – in your hands. We hope that we shall have helped to make it a little easier.

2 Getting to know your car
Facts and figures

The French are said to be a logical race, and this is a trait which shows in the design of most of their family cars. When the Renault R4 was first introduced in 1961, therefore, it was perhaps predictable that it would be versatile, practical and adaptable – and above all, economical to run.

A very comfortable four-seater family saloon, the new model was also an uncomplaining work-horse when converted into a utility or estate car. While lacking any pretensions to styling or elaborate trim, the lines of the cleverly designed, functional package did not date, and the combination of comfort and economy made the car a best-seller all over the world.

Although the general design of the car has been unchanged over the years, there have been some noticeable improvements from time to time. The earliest models, for example, which had 747 cc engines based on the earlier Renault 4 CV power units, were seriously underpowered. They had very leisurely acceleration and a top speed which seldom exceeded 55 mph – although it may be remarked in passing that the pedestrian performance of these cars might almost be described as sparkling when compared with the 600 cc models which were available for a time in France!

The car that has sold in the greatest numbers in the UK, however, is the 845 cc model first introduced in 1963 and further refined in October 1965, when the name was changed from the Renault R4 and R4L to the Renault 4, and it is with these cars, from October 1965 onwards, that we are concerned in this book.

The engine

The four-cylinder engine has overhead valves operated by short push-rods, removable 'wet' cylinder liners and a three-bearing crankshhaft. The use of a light-alloy cylinder head and detachable cylinder barrels which are partly surrounded by coolant, means that care must be taken when removing and refitting the head if distortion of the head, gasket troubles and internal water leakage are to be prevented. Regular checks must also be made on the tightness of the cylinder-head bolts.

Nevertheless, when properly looked after these engines are not temperamental and present no difficulties in maintenance and overhaul as far as a practical owner is concerned.

An excellent feature is that matched sets of new pistons and cylinder barrels can be installed, and the connecting-rod bearings and oil pump can be serviced, without removing the engine from the car, although major overhauls are, of course, more conveniently carried out with the engine out.

The cooling system is sealed, and the coolant, a mixture of water, glycol and rust inhibitor, need be changed only at three-yearly intervals, or after about 2700 miles have been covered.

Although the engine size and power output are modest, the Renault 4 is capable of keeping up with the traffic stream and can be cruised at an indicated 60–65 mph without strain.

Even when heavily laden, calling for the use of full throttle for fairly long periods, the car will return excellent petrol consumption figures, bettering 40 mpg without difficulty on a give-and-take run. This economical running is enhanced by the fact that the cheapest grades of petrol can be used without the risk of pinking. A fuel with an octane rating 90–92 is quite sufficient and no advantage will be gained by using a higher-grade petrol.

The transmission

The gearbox and final-drive gears are mounted ahead of the engine, the power unit being, in effect, turned round in the car as compared with a conventional rear-wheel-drive layout. The gear lever projects from the fascia and has a push-pull and twist action, operating the vertical selector rod on the gearbox through a horizontal shaft mounted above the engine and giving, in spite of its unusual operation, quick, precise changes.

The front wheels are driven through universally-jointed shafts which – as is the case with all front-wheel-drive cars – call for periodical checks on the condition of the universal joints and their sealing gaiters. We have more to say about this aspect of a used car in Chapter 3.

Suspension and steering

The suspension, by means of torsion bars at front and rear, is very soft, with a long wheel travel that gives an extremely good ride, plus the ability to soak-up rough surfaces and pot-holes without the need to slacken speed – all typically French, in fact.

Also typically French is its tendency to allow considerable initial roll when cornering fast. This can be disconcerting at first, especially to a passenger, but one soon realizes that once the car has taken up its initial roll angle it is immensely stable and the ability of the soft springs to keep all four wheels on the ground results in exceptional roadholding.

The other aspect of the steering that takes a little getting used to, is that it is somewhat heavier than some more recent front-wheel-drive designs; the amount of effort needed at the wheel builds up as the steering lock or the speed is increased. Renault 4s do, however, tend to vary in this respect, some having noticeably lighter steering than others.

The torsion bars seldom – if ever – need attention, unless they have suffered accidental damage. The riding height of the car can be set by adjustable mountings at the fixed ends of the bars and if this adjustment is inadequate the bars can be moved around to the extent of one spline. As we emphasize in Chapter 14, however, this sort of work should normally be left to a Renault dealer.

The brakes

Lockheed drum brakes are fitted at the front and rear, with a pressure-limiting valve in the rear-brake pipe-line to reduce the tendency of the rear wheels to lock-up under heavy braking. The front wheels, however, may lock if the brakes are applied hard on a wet or greasy road.

Although no servo assistance is provided, the pedal pressure required for a quick stop is – or should be – quite modest. The handbrake operates the front brake shoes through a mechanical linkage and is particularly powerful, providing a reassuring grip on a steep hill and also giving useful emergency stopping power if the hydraulic system should fail.

The bodywork

The versatility of the seating and load-carrying arrangements has already been emphasized. The Renault 4, in fact, probably has more usable passenger and luggage accommodation than any other car of similar size and price.

The interior trim is functional rather than decorative, but the spartan treatment does not extend to the seats, which are exceptionally comfortable. The sit-up-and-beg driving position seems to suit most drivers, whether the bench-type front seat or individual front seats are fitted.

The chassis, bodyshell, wings and wing valances are bolted together and can be easily removed and replaced, which considerably reduces the cost of repairing accident damage or renewing rusty components on an older car – although this does not necessarily imply that the Renault 4 is particularly subject to corrosion, as we mention in Chapter 3.

Model line-up

Now for a list of the most important changes in the development of the Renault 4, including, as a matter of interest, the earlier R4 models not covered by this book –

Background to the Renault 4: the earlier R4 models

1961, October. Renault R4 and R4L models first introduced in UK with 747 cc engines and three-speed gearboxes, without synchromesh on bottom gear.
1962, October. Estate-car version, fitted with 845 cc engine and all-synchromesh three-speed gearbox offered in UK.
1963, October. 845 cc engine fitted to saloon models and manual choke fitted to carburettor instead of electrically-operated choke.
1965, July. Saloon model no longer imported. Bench-type seats fitted to estate car, with individual front seats offered as optional extra.

Renault 4 models covered by this book

1965, October. Renault 4 introduced, the name R4 being discontinued. This model is the first of the range covered by this book.
1966, September. Fascia redesigned, with rocker switches; optional individual front seats; rear seat improved; fresh-air vents; Sofica heater; childproof locks. Larger front brakes, diameter increased from 7 in. to 8 in.
1967, September. Four-speed all-synchromesh gearbox fitted. Bonnet and front grille redesigned with headlamps in grille. Stronger bumpers with rubber over-riders fitted. Tailgate counterbalanced instead of being supported by manual prop. Standard and de Luxe versions offered.
1970, September. 12-volt electrical system fitted. Hinged rear folding parcel shelf provided and key-operated lock on passenger door.
1971, September. 1972 models do not have a hole in the front bumper to take a starting handle.
1972, February. Starting handle dog no longer fitted to gearbox.
1972, August. Black, non-reflective fascia and steering wheel with padded centre fitted. Universally-jointed steering column.
1973, August. Anti-pollution engine (type 800–05) fitted in place of the previous 800–01 engine. New gearbox introduced – type 354, as fitted to Renault 5 TL. Individual reclining front seats offered as optional extra.
1974, August. Larger, 7½ gal. petrol tank fitted. Wipers changed to self-parking type. Improved seats on de Luxe model. New front grille.
1975, January. Restyled radiator grille.
1975, October. Slightly higher gear ratios introduced to give better fuel economy. Alternator and voltmeter fitted as standard. Heated rear window on de Luxe model. Renault 4 becomes 4L and 4 de Luxe the 4TL.

3 Vetting a used car
How to detect or forestall trouble

Unlike many other 'foreign' cars, Renault 4 models are usually accepted quite readily in part-exchange by non-Renault dealers – which is, perhaps, the best evidence that although they are strongly individualistic designs, they have proved to be very reliable in service and are free from any potentially expensive troubles.

Buying any used car, however, must always be something of a gamble, and to reduce the risk of acquiring an expensive liability it is advisable to carry out a really thorough check on the lines suggested in this chapter before concluding the deal.

It is always dangerous to generalize when discussing used cars, but experience suggests that a critical point in the life of the average Renault 4 is around the 30 000 mile mark. The brake linings, clutch, shock absorbers, universal joints and the tyres all seem to need replacement at about this mileage. When buying a used car, therefore, it would probably be safer to look for one with a considerably lower or a slightly higher mileage, or to check that the critical parts have been replaced.

Another point to bear in mind is that earlier models have 6-volt electrical systems, which are much more prone to suffer from the effects of voltage-drop due to poor connections, than the 12-volt systems introduced in September 1970.

If you have already bought a used model, give it a similar vetting to that described in this chapter before deciding what work will be needed to put it in really good condition.

As each check is completed, fill-in a detailed inspection record (see page 18). The time will be well repaid later, when summing-up the overall condition of the car and planning the work to be done.

Begin with the bodywork

Rust is always likely to be a problem when a car is a few years old, and although the Renault 4 is treated against corrosion on the production line, it will pay to check one or two vulnerable spots on an older model.

Examine the main chassis members and the floor panel, which can rust through if water penetrates the spot-welded seams. The box sections in front of the driver's and passenger's feet should also be carefully checked. If water should leak past the windscreen seal, the floor will rust from the inside along the seams beneath the heater.

On a car first registered between late 1968 and mid 1970, check the areas mentioned carefully as the anti-corrosion treatment of the floor pan and underbody was not fully up to standard on these models.

As was mentioned in Chapter 2, other bodywork panels which may be subject to rust or accidental damage, including the doors, wings and bonnet, are bolted together and can be renewed easily and relatively cheaply.

Don't forget to check the exhaust system. As with many cars today, rust can set in quite early in its life.

If possible, have the vehicle raised on a lift at some stage during the inspection, or at least on wheel ramps or axle stands, so that the underside can be carefully inspected. Apart from checking for rust, also pay special attention to the safety points mentioned on page 12.

During the test run, listen for any abnormal noises, such as door rattles, squeaks and knocks from beneath the car. Wear in the bushes or the bearings which carry the rear-suspension arms, for example, will cause knocks and clonks and renewal of the worn parts may not be within the scope of a practical owner. Also be suspicious if the suspension appears to be sloppy.

As mentioned earlier, new shock absorbers may be needed if the car has covered about 30 000 miles. But bear in mind that the suspension is very flexible, although the car should feel under control at all times. The comments that we make under the heading 'Suspension and steering' may help you to form a judgement.

Checking engine condition

Even with the 845 cc engine the Renault 4 is no road-burner, but a properly tuned engine is a very willing and flexible power unit, with good pulling power from low speeds.

These Renault 4 engines wear well and it is unlikely that a used example should need any major attention before it has covered about 60 000–80 000 miles and then, as indicated in Chapters 8 and 9, essential repairs are well within the scope of a practical owner, with a certain amount of help from specialist firms.

Some engines develop slight piston slap – evidenced by a light tapping from the crankcase area – after moderate mileages have been covered but experience has shown that this does no harm and that the engine will continue to run for a long time in this condition.

A noisy timing chain, however, cannot be dealt with easily. Since the engine is, in effect, turned round in the chassis with the gearbox ahead of it, fitting a new chain and tensioner entails removing the engine and transmission and taking off the cylinder head and sump.

This in turn means that the front suspension must be disconnected to allow the drive shafts to be withdrawn and the steering gear must also be taken off before the engine and gearbox can be lifted out as a unit – so don't allow a plausible salesman to persuade you that a noisy timing chain is nothing much to worry about!

Fortunately, however, experts seem to agree that the timing chain and the tensioner will normally last the life of the engine between major overhauls.

Any engine which has covered a high mileage will, of course, have been subject to the usual wear and tear, so check for such obvious pointers as oil or water leaks, smoke from the exhaust, suspicious noises when the engine is revved up – with the engine both hot and cold – followed by as extensive a test as possible, during which any misfiring, knocking or lack of power should be evident.

Transmission checks

If the clutch does not free cleanly or slips on taking-up the drive, one must first suspect that the cable is sticking or incorrectly adjusted. Otherwise the trouble must lie in the clutch, and renewing this unit can be a fairly expensive item unless you are prepared to do the work yourself.

When you have changed up or down through the gears once or twice, the unusual action of the gear lever will seem quite natural. The movement of the lever should be smooth and positive, but the mechanism is so simple that any stiffness or sloppiness can easily be put right.

On any high-mileage car it is not unusual for the synchromesh to be weak on second or third gear and a badly worn gearbox may show signs of jumping out of these gears on the overrun. Obviously such a car should be avoided, or allowance should be made for the cost of fitting a reconditioned gearbox.

If oil leakage develops at the point at which the drive shafts are connected to the gearbox or transmission, renewal of the seals is normally a dealer job – so make a careful check for leaks here. It is reassuring to know, however, that this fault is fairly rare.

As with all front-wheel-drive models, it pays to check the drive-shaft joints for wear. Several different types have been used, and some of the earlier outer universal joints needed replacement after about 20 000–25 000 miles. The later pattern has proved relatively trouble-free, but shafts fitted with this type of joint cannot be substituted for the earlier pattern without also changing the lower suspension arms. In any event, when the joints are worn, usually the only cure is to fit a complete new drive-shaft assembly.

Suspension and steering

The suspension is very soft, but although anyone new to the car may find that it heels over alarmingly when cornering fast, it quickly becomes apparent that this movement is controlled and does not affect the steering or roadholding. It is likely, in fact, that the driver's courage will run out before the Michelin tyres show any sign of relinquishing their grip on the road!

Take an unsurfaced, rough track at speed, and the ability of the soft springs to soak up bad bumps and pot-holes without protest is astonishing when compared with conventionally-sprung cars.

Check for any sign of grease leakage from the front hubs and the suspension ball joints. Also make sure that the rubber boots on the joints in the steering linkage are in good condition.

The braking system

When testing the brakes bear in mind that they are adequate, rather than outstanding. They should be smooth and progressive, but a panic stop will call for a moderately heavy pressure on the brake pedal. If the brakes lack power under ordinary driving conditions or the steering pulls to one side, Chart 9 will help to pinpoint the most likely causes. Remember, however, that the brakes need regular adjustment and servicing. Check these points, as described in Chapter 15, before assuming that more serious faults necessarily exist in the system.

Performance tests

We give below some typical performance figures for the various models. Of these, the acceleration times are the most useful in providing an indication of the overall efficiency of the car.

As far as fuel consumption is concerned, it is difficult to suggest an acceptable figure, since this will depend on road and traffic conditions, the load carried and, above all, on the way in which the car is driven. To be realistic, the figures quoted (like all the performance figures) should be regarded as only representative averages and should not be interpreted too strictly.

Typical performance figures

Maximum speed in top gear	68–70 mph
Acceleration, top gear – 20–40 mph	12.5–13 seconds
Fuel consumption	36–46 mpg

4 Planned servicing
Preventive maintenance

In this and other chapters, we emphasize the importance of *preventive* maintenance – the avoidance of trouble before it becomes serious, or can result in a roadside breakdown.

The official Renault diagnostic-maintenance scheme calls for a visit to the lubrication bay once in every 3000 miles, or at least once in every six months, and a very thorough diagnostic check-up at between 6000 and 9000 miles, or at least once a year.

The full diagnostic routine, however, would probably take the average owner, using only the limited facilities available in the home garage, the better part of a week-end to complete.

The home-servicing scheme outlined in the following pages has therefore been adapted from the official maintenance schedule so as to spread the work-load as much as possible. It also has the advantage of introducing more frequent checks on some items – particularly those associated with safety – than would be the case if a full diagnostic-maintenance check were to be deferred for the maximum recommended interval of one year or 9000 miles.

A question that often arises is whether one should service on a mileage or a time basis.

If the car is used mostly for shopping and for an occasional week-end run into the country, of course, the mileage will not accumulate very quickly. While the car is standing idle the contact-breaker gap or the tappet clearances will not be increasing, the brake shoes or pads will not be wearing away and other parts will not require the checks and adjustments called for in the maintenance schedule.

In such cases servicing according to the mileage intervals quoted makes sense. There are cases, however, which justify – for some items – servicing on a time basis rather than by the mileage covered. For example, the engine oil will deteriorate much more quickly when short runs and frequent starts from cold cause excessive condensation of water and acids in the cylinders and sump and will require more frequent changing. The tyres will probably lose pressure whether the car is running or standing unused and the battery will be subject to slow self-discharge.

The brake fluid slowly absorbs moisture from the air, due to 'breathing' through the vent in the fluid-reservoir filler cap and through slightly porous hoses and the wheel cylinder seals. It will need to be changed after 12–24 months to avoid the risk of brake failure due to the fluid boiling in the wheel cylinders after a spell of hard braking.

The maintenance schedule must therefore be approached in a certain spirit of compromise, depending on the sort of use that the car receives.

Vital checks

A major drawback of do-it-yourself servicing in the home garage is the tendency of most owners to ignore the underside of the car: a case of out of sight, out of mind, perhaps?

Don't be tempted to crawl under the car when it is supported only by a jack or by a pile of bricks, however. A pair of drive-on wheel ramps will usually give enough clearance, or the car can be taken to your neighbourhood dealer at least twice a year to be put on a lift or over a pit so that the whole of the underside can be thoroughly inspected at leisure. It is well worthwhile to pay for this service, if necessary, or to hire a self-service bay if a garage is operating this scheme in your district.

If the underside is coated with mud and filth, it will obviously pay to hose it down thoroughly, or better still to have it steam-cleaned, before starting work. Garages which service commercial vehicles usually have steam-cleaning equipment, but the cost of the work, although well worthwhile, is not cheap.

Now for the vital check points:

First go over the whole of the underside of the car for any signs of flaking paint, peeling underbody coating, if this has been applied, and the beginning of rust. Pay particular attention to the sub-frame and the areas around the suspension mountings.

Check the brake pipes inch by inch for any signs of chafing, rust or pitting. A small corrosion pit can eat through a new pipe within two years, causing a pin-hole leak which may result in complete loss of brake fluid.

Check the flexible brake hoses for perishing, chafing and leakage from the unions.

There will probably have been some oil leakage from the engine and transmission units, but a heavy leak obviously calls for investigation.

Examine the inner walls of the tyres for cuts or splits. It is surprising how often accidental damage occurs on the inside wall of a tyre, rather than on the outside, where it would be immediately visible. While checking the tyres, look for any signs of rubbing against the body when the springs are fully compressed or when the front wheels are turned to full lock.

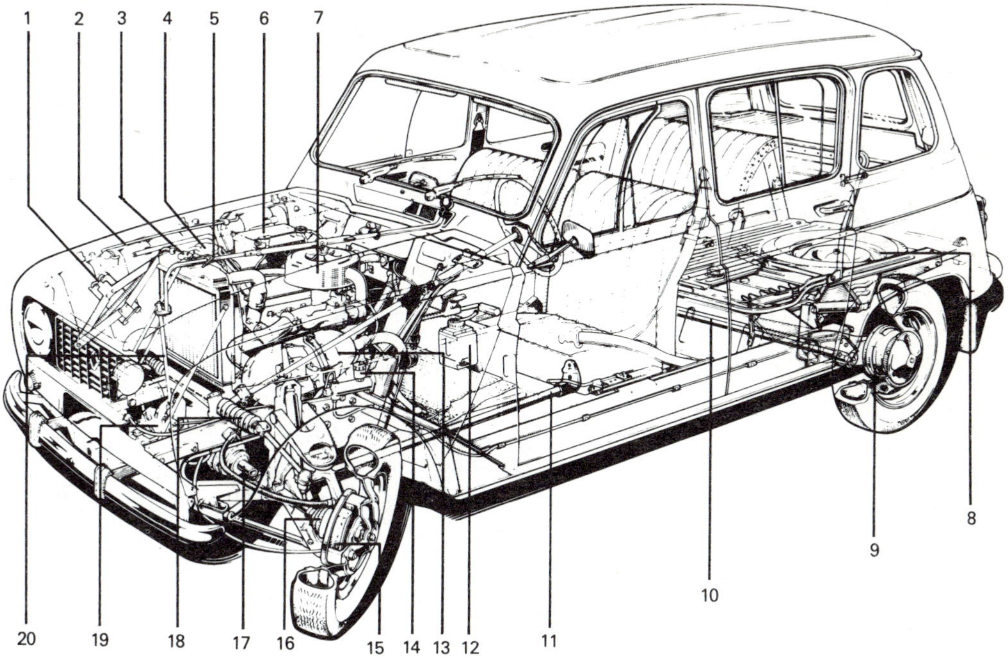

1 Jack stowage
2 Starting handle
3 Radiator filler plug
4 Expansion-bottle filler
5 Gearchange rod
6 Battery
7 Air cleaner and carburettor
8 Spare wheel
9 Rear brake and hub assembly
10 Rear torsion bar
11 Front torsion bar
12 Windscreen washer reservoir
13 Silencer
14 Brake master cylinder reservoir
15 Front brake and hub assembly
16 Steering tie-rod ball joint
17 Drive shaft
18 Steering gear
19 Gearbox
20 Gear lever

Fig. 4.1 A cut-away view of a typical model. Although this is a left-hand-drive car, the right-hand-drive versions are similar, apart from some items such as the steering column and brake master cylinder being transferred to the other side of the car

Maintenance summary

This chart has been arranged to show at a glance the frequency with which the various jobs must be done. The items which make up a complete service can thus be identified and the work spread over several week-ends, if necessary. Remember that the columns are cumulative: the 3000 mile jobs must be repeated at 6000 and 9000 miles, the 6000 mile service at 12 000 miles (plus the jobs in the 12 000 mile column), and so on

	Weekly or before a long journey	Every 3000 miles (5000 km) or 3 months	Every 6000 miles (10 000 km) or 6 months	Every 12 000 miles (20 000 km) or 12 months	Every 27 000 miles (45 000 km) or 3 years
Vital safety checks					
Wheels and Tyres Check tyre pressures when cold. Watch for signs of uneven wear. Check tightness of wheel nuts	●				
Brake Fluid Reservoir Check level of fluid (this is a precautionary check only – topping-up should be required only at long intervals, unless a leak has developed in system)	●				
Brakes Check pedal travel; adjust brakes if necessary. Inspect brake pipes and hoses for leakage		●			
Brakes – Preventive Check Check thickness of linings. Check operating cylinders for leakage. Blow out dust. Check handbrake adjustment. Check pipes and flexible hoses for chafing. Renew all flexible hoses and rubber seals in braking system after 40 000 miles (65 000 km) or 3 years in service			●		
Wheels Remove road wheels, wash and examine for possible damage			●		
Exhaust System Check for corrosion, leakage and security of attachments			●		
Lighting System Check headlamp beam alignment, lamp glasses for cracks, side, tail and indicator lamps for blackened bulbs, rusty contacts and water in lampholders		●			
Lubrication					
Engine Check oil-level and top-up if necessary (check daily if engine is worn and also when refilling with fuel on long run)	●				
Engine Drain oil and re-fill sump. Renew oil-filter element when external filter is fitted			●		
Ignition Distributor Lubricate			●		
Dynamo (when fitted) Lubricate end bearing when lubricator is fitted. Add several drops of engine oil			●		
Gearbox Check oil level			●		
Oil-can Lubrication Apply a few drops of oil to throttle linkage, handbrake linkage, door, boot and bonnet locks and hinges			●		
Speedometer Cable Lubricate inner cable with grease					●

Servicing and adjustments

Cooling System Expansion Tank Check water-level and top-up if necessary	●				
Cooling System Check condition of hoses, and for leaks. Check tension of fan/generator driving belts			●		
Cooling System De-scale, flush and refill. Check operation of thermostat					●
Battery Check level of liquid in cells	●				
Windscreen Washer Reservoir Check level of fluid. Add special anti-freeze solvent in winter	●				
Engine Check valve-rocker clearances. Adjust if necessary			●		
Engine Service crankcase breather system			●		
Engine Clean the gauze filter in oil filter cap, when fitted			●		
Carburettor Check slow-running adjustments		●			
Carburettor Air-cleaner Renew pleated-paper element			●		
Carburettor Clean float chamber and jets			●		
Fuel Pump Check pump and clean filter if necessary			●		
Sparking Plugs Clean; check gaps and re-set if necessary			●		
Ignition System Fit new sparking plugs and new contact-breaker points. Preferably do this at 10 000 miles (16 000 km)				●	
Ignition Distributor Clean or renew contact points and adjust gap. Clean distributor rotor and cap. Check timing. Preferably have system checked with electronic test-tune equipment			●		
Clutch Check cable adjustment			●		
Steering and Front Suspension Check bellows on rack-and-pinion unit for splits or leakage. Check steering and suspension for damaged grease-retaining gaiters and wear			●		
Steering and Front Suspension Have front-wheel alignment and steering geometry checked with special equipment			●		
Front and Rear Wheel Bearings Check for leakage of grease, excessive end-play and noise when wheel is rotated				●	
Wheels Change from side to side at front and rear. Grease wheel studs. Have wheel balance checked			●		
Braking System Drain fluid from system, flush, refill and bleed-off air. This should be done every 2 years if mileage is less than 27 000 miles (45 000 km) in this period (see also **Vital safety checks** above)					●
Electrical System Clean and tighten battery terminals. Check operation of charging system, starter motor, lights and instruments			●		
Dynamo (when fitted) Check condition of brushes and commutator					●
Starter Motor Check condition of brushes, commutator and pinion drive assembly					●
Road Test Give car a thorough road test and carry out any adjustments required. If possible, have final check made with electronic test-tune equipment and check compression in cylinders. After test, check for oil, fuel, fluid or grease leaks at all plugs, flanges, joints and unions			●		

Check the exhaust system for rust, damage and leakage and make sure that the supports are sound.

Finally, push, pull and shake all suspension and steering components vigorously, to show up any wear or loose attachments.

Your basic tool kit

The items listed below will be needed for routine servicing. More specialized tools can be added, as necessary, when repairs and overhauls are undertaken and a list of these is given at the beginning of each workshop manual section.

Special tools tend to be rather expensive, but you may be able to hire them from your local Renault dealer. The most frequently needed items, such as extractors, however, can normally be purchased from car accessory shops and these are usually cheaper than the 'official' service tools. Alternatively, there may be a shop in your neighbourhood which hires-out tools at reasonable charges.

A basic tool kit for routine servicing and minor repairs should include –

Set of open-ended or ring, or combination spanners, in metric sizes
Set of socket spanners with extensions and preferably a universal joint
Selection of screwdrivers, including two sizes for cross-head screws
Large and small adjustable spanners
Self-locking adjustable spanner (Mole wrench type)
Side-cutting and pointed-nose 6 in. pliers
Set of feeler gauges
Sparking plug gap-setting tool
Tyre-pressure gauge
Tyre tread-depth gauge
Engineer's hammer (ball pane)
Soft-faced hammer (with hide, plastic or copper faces)
Fine carborundum stone
Wire brush
Centre-punch, scriber and marking paint
Inspection lamp

A good tyre-pressure gauge is essential. Garage pressure gauges are not always as accurate as they should be: and pressures should always be checked with the tyres *cold*, which is obviously impossible if the car has to be driven to a garage or if pressures are checked during the course of a journey.

A tyre tread-depth gauge is an inexpensive item which will enable you to keep a check on the rate of wear of the tyres and will also indicate when they are due for replacement. The official regulation in Britain calls for 1 mm of tread over three-quarters of the width of the tread pattern, around the complete circumference of the tyre, but it is much safer to change the tyres when the treads are worn down to a depth of 2 mm.

A workbench will be needed for any jobs that are done on components that have been removed from the car, but it is quite possible to make do with a stout kitchen table, which can often be picked up inexpensively at an auction. If any but elementary servicing is carried out, a vice will be needed. This can often be obtained quite cheaply from a shop which deals in Ministry surplus equipment.

Turning the engine when making adjustments

When the crankshaft has a starting handle dog the easiest way to turn the engine is, of course, to use the handle.

In the case of a later car which does not have a starting handle, either engage top gear and push the car backwards and forwards, or jack-up one front wheel and turn the wheel with top gear engaged. *In both cases make sure that the ignition is switched off or the ignition distributor cap removed, to prevent the engine starting with the gear engaged.*

Some garage mechanics become adept at turning the engine by operating the starter motor for a few seconds at a time, but this method is only justifiable as a timesaver to obtain approximately the correct position of the flywheel. Final adjustment must be made by one of the methods just described, since accuracy is essential when setting the ignition timing, or adjusting the valve-clearances.

Working beneath the car

If an inspection pit is not available, a pair of drive-on wheel ramps will also be needed. A cheaper alternative is a pair of adjustable axle stands. These have the advantage of leaving the wheels free to rotate. On the other hand, it takes only a minute or two to drive the front or rear wheels on to a pair of ramps, whereas both sides of the car must be jacked-up to allow stands to be placed below the jacking points.

For obvious reasons, ramps or axle-stands which lift only one end of the car must not be used when checking the oil-levels.

Finally, never be tempted to work beneath the car when it is supported only by the jack or by an insecure pile of bricks.

Part two

5 Trouble-shooting
Systematic diagnosis

The risk of an unexpected breakdown must obviously be greatly reduced by regular servicing. The work described in Chapter 4 can therefore be described as *preventive* maintenance in the best sense of the word; it aims at detecting or forestalling trouble before it becomes serious. Most faults, in fact, can be traced back to neglect at some stage. Dirt, lack of lubrication or incorrect adjustment are the most frequent culprits.

When devising the special trouble-shooting charts in this section, we had in mind mainly the practical owner, who often has to trace a fault without the benefit of a voltmeter, an ammeter, a vacuum gauge, a cylinder compression-pressure gauge or a simple stethoscope. These useful aids to diagnosis are usually conspicuous by their absence when the car breaks down miles from the home base!

The aim has been to produce a set of charts which will encourage a logical process of elimination. Inspired guesswork (intelligent intuition?) will sometimes get results, but systematic investigation will usually be less time-consuming in tracking-down obscure faults—although there are, of course, occasions on which the possibility of a particular fault can be assumed with a fair amount of certainty.

Take the case of a normally well-behaved engine that refuses to fire from cold after the car has been parked in the open during a spell of damp, misty weather, for example. Condensation on the high-tension leads, ignition coil, distributor, and sparking-plug insulators is almost a certainty, and a spray with one of the water-repelling aerosol fluids, or a wipe with a dry cloth, will usually be all that is needed to restore normal starting.

Similarly, if an engine runs well, but is a brute to start from cold, suspect too weak a starting mixture. Make sure that the mixture control is operating properly and that the petrol pump is delivering plenty of fuel. If the engine is reluctant to start when hot, on the other hand, check for an over-rich mixture. In either case, if the carburation seems to be satisfactory, the ignition system should be checked-over, following the step-by-step charts in this chapter.

Now a word as to how to use the trouble-tracing charts.

By reading vertically down the column, under the various symptoms, the most likely causes of the trouble can be picked out and eliminated one by one. Alternatively, by reading horizontally across the chart, a combination of different symptoms will often point pretty conclusively to one particular fault which is causing the trouble.

In some cases, these charts cover alternative types of equipment. To find out which items apply to your model, consult the Specifications and Overhaul Data at the end of this book.

Preventing trouble and restoring performance

There is a great deal to be said for carrying out a systematic inspection of the car at regular intervals—say, every 5000-6000 miles—in order to detect any incipient trouble and to correct any faults which may exist.

A ten-point check and tune-up to restore engine efficiency is outlined on page 19. A suggested routine for a more thorough check of the whole car is given in the fault-tracing and condition report sheet. If these checks are conscientiously carried out and any necessary adjustments are made, they will restore 'new car' performance on a vehicle that is in reasonably good mechanical condition. Any major faults which are present, such as loss of engine compression, and transmission or similar troubles, will, of course, require attention as soon as possible.

An inspection record of this type has, in itself, a number of advantages. Not only does it ensure that no item is overlooked, but it also enables the general condition of the car to be assessed at a glance. If completed systematically at each inspection period and filed for reference purposes, it will serve as a guide to the reconditioning required and as a check on the performance of each item.

When made out for the first time, as with a newly-purchased used car, the chart is almost certain to reveal defects that might otherwise have been unsuspected and that might have developed into major troubles.

Inspection record

Vehicle make and year ____________________
Capacity or horse power ____________________
Reg. number ____________________
Speedometer reading ____________________
Date of inspection ____________________

Engine and accessories

Compression

Tappets: clearance; noise

Valve gear: noise; cover gaskets

Timing gears or chain: noise; backlash

Cylinder head: nuts; gaskets

Manifolds: securing nuts; gaskets; air or gas leaks

Driving belts: fan; dynamo; accessories

Water pump: leakage; effectiveness

Radiator: water level; leakage; filler cap; condition of core; shutters; relief valve; overflow pipe

Oil leaks: crankcase; pipes and unions; timing covers; main bearings; drain plugs

Oil filters

Engine mountings

Carburettor and fuel pump

Jets

Float chamber level

Cold starting device: interconnecting linkage thermostat; dashboard control

Fuel pump: effectiveness; delivery pressure

Filters: carburettor; petrol pump; air cleaner

Ignition system

Contact breaker points: gap; condition

Rotor: condition

Distributor cap: cleanliness; cracks; tracking

Timing control: manual; centrifugal; suction operated

Coil and wiring: efficiency; condition of high and low tension wiring; support

Sparking plugs: gap at points; condition of points and insulators; washers

Electrical system

Dynamo or alternator: charging rate

Dynamo brushes and commutator: burning or pitting; chatter and sparking

Dynamo or alternator drive: condition of belt, tension

Voltage regulator

Ammeter: accuracy

Battery: acid level; specific gravity; voltage of each cell; connections; corrosion

Lights

Headlamps: focus and alignment; condition of reflectors

Side lamps

Tail lamps

Stop lamp

Other lamps: ignition warning; interior; trafficators

Switches and fuses

Electrical accessories

Windscreen wipers: efficiency; noise; condition of blades

Indicators

Starter: efficiency; condition of pinion and fly-wheel teeth

Horns

Interior heater

Defroster

Radio

Steering

Lost motion

Stiffness

Front axle alignment: toe-in; castor and camber angles

Swivels and bushes

Front hub bearings

Steering linkage and joints

Suspension

Springs: condition

Shock absorbers: effectiveness; fluid leaks; security of attachments

Torque reaction rods or cables: adjustment; security of attachment

Brakes

Pedal travel

Condition of rods or cables

Hydraulic system: fluid level; leakage from pipe lines, choked pipes, air in system

Handbrake: adjustment; condition of ratchet

Servo mechanism: vacuum servo; pipe lines

Bodywork

General appearance

Windows: winding controls; glass; channels

Doors: alignment; buffers; locks; check straps

Sunshine roof: operation; water leaks

Seats: condition of springs; adjustments

Bumpers: condition; attachments

Tool kit

Fire extinguisher, safety belts

Transmission

Clutch: adjustment

Backlash: in universal joints; in back axle; in gearbox

Rear axle: leakage

Wheels

Rims: buckling; rust

Wheel nuts: tightness; condition of studs; splines on knock-off wheels

Tyres

Pressures

Tread wear

Condition of sidewalls

Valves and caps

Road test

Engine

Ease of starting
Oil pressure when hot
Idling
Acceleration
Maximum speed
Fuel consumption
Oil consumption
Engine temperature
Exhaust: noise, restriction; smoke
General noise, fumes

Clutch

Slip
Fierceness
Spinning
Unusual noises

Propeller shaft

Vibration
Noise

Gearbox

Noisy gears
Synchromesh operation
Preselector operation
Vibration on gear lever
Gears jumping out of mesh

Instruments

Functioning
Accuracy

Suspension

Comfort
Roll on corners

Brakes

Power
Balance
Smoothness
Judder or squeal
Binding

Back axle

Noise on drive
Noise on overrun
Noise on corners

Steering

Positiveness
Castor action
Wander
Road shocks at steering wheel

Ten-point engine check and tune-up

The ten-point check on engine efficiency described in this section carries the principle of preventive maintenance, already outlined in Part 1, a stage further.

The object of an engine tune-up at an intermediate stage is to check deterioration: to restore the keen edge of engine efficiency, with a bonus in the form of improved performance and better fuel consumption. A good time to carry it out would be between the 5000-6000 miles services.

1 Electrical check

The effectiveness of the ignition system depends on sound electrical connections throughout the low-tension and high-tension wiring. Check them systematically, starting at the battery terminals and the earthing strap, and working via the ignition switch to the low-tension terminals on the ignition coil, and from there to the terminal on the side of the ignition distributor.

Check the security of the high-tension leads in the distributor cap and coil by lightly tugging them. Bear in mind that modern carbon-trace ignition cables usually have a. life of about two years. After that, misfiring is increasingly likely. A new set of leads will often rejuvenate an engine.

2 Check carburettor and manifold flange nuts

The nuts must not be loose but must never be overtightened—particularly the carburettor flange nuts—owing to the risk of distorting or cracking the flanges, a fault which is a common cause of air leakage into the induction system, resulting in a weak mixture, misfiring and difficult starting.

3 Clean the carburettor filter (when fitted) and the float chamber

Traces of sediment or water in the float chamber can upset the carburation and cause misfiring.

4 Fuel pump check

If the fuel pump does not deliver its maximum output when the engine is operating under full-throttle, continuous high-speed conditions, fuel starvation may cause severe exhaust-valve burning and possibly piston failure. If in doubt, have the pump checked by a garage, using a special flow-test rig.

5 Check the ignition distributor and contact-breaker

Peak efficiency cannot be expected if the contact-breaker points are dirty, badly pitted or incorrectly gapped. Distributor checks are covered in the section dealing with the ignition system.

6 Check the ignition timing

Again refer to the section dealing with the ignition system. The correct ignition timing is critical, affecting both performance and fuel consumption.

7 Remove and check the sparking plugs

The plugs are a good guide to running conditions, as shown by the colour illustrations in this chapter. Clean them if necessary and re-set the gaps. Carry out a compression check (below) before refitting them.

8 Compression test

The compression check gives a reliable indication of the efficiency of the valves, piston rings and cylinder bores. A compression gauge is not expensive. The simple type which combines a compression gauge with a tyre-pressure gauge will give reliable readings.

Bring the engine to normal running temperature. Remove all the sparking plugs and wedge or tie the throttle fully open. The compressions should be recorded at normal cranking speed which must remain constant throughout the test, so the battery must be well charged.

Make a note of the number of pulsations required to obtain a maximum gauge reading for the first cylinder tested. The same number of crankshaft revs should be used when testing the other cylinders.

When the first set of readings has been recorded, repeat the tests with approximately a tablespoonful of engine oil injected into each cylinder. Higher readings may now be obtained on some or all of the cylinders, indicating that the oil has sealed any leakage past the piston rings that was occurring during the first tests.

Any remaining differences between the maximum pressures recorded for the individual cylinder which exceed about 10lb per sq. in. are probably due to leakage past the valves (possibly due to wrong valve clearances). It is also possible that the cylinder head gasket is leaking, but this would normally cause overheating and, in some case, misfiring.

9 Check carburettor idling adjustments

Refit the plugs and adjust the carburettor idling speed and mixture strength. These adjustments are fully described in the chapter dealing with the carburettor and fuel system.

10 Road test

Carry out a thorough road test as described in the section which deals with vetting a used car. Record the figures and file them for reference when the next tune-up is carried out. 'Before and after' comparisons will then quickly show up any loss of efficiency and indicate the need for further action.

At-a-glance trouble-shooting chart 1

Engine faults - key chart

Symptoms

	Engine will not start	Starts but will not keep running	Stalls during normal running	Poor idling	Misfiring at all speeds	Not giving full power or revs	Fuel consumption excessive	Oil consumption excessive	Pinking or detonation	Over-heating, pre-ignition, running-on	Unusual noises
Carburation and Fuel System Chart 5	●	●	●	●	●	●	●		●	●	
Ignition System Chart 4	●	●	●	●	●	●	●		●	●	
Electrical System Chart 10	●										
Mechanical Faults Chart 2	●	●	●	●	●	●	●	●	●	●	●
Cooling System Chart 3						●	●	●	●	●	

First - Check your plugs

Normal
Nose lightly coated with grey brown deposits. Electrodes not burning unduly – gap increasing about .001 in. per 1000 miles. Plugs ideally suited to engine.

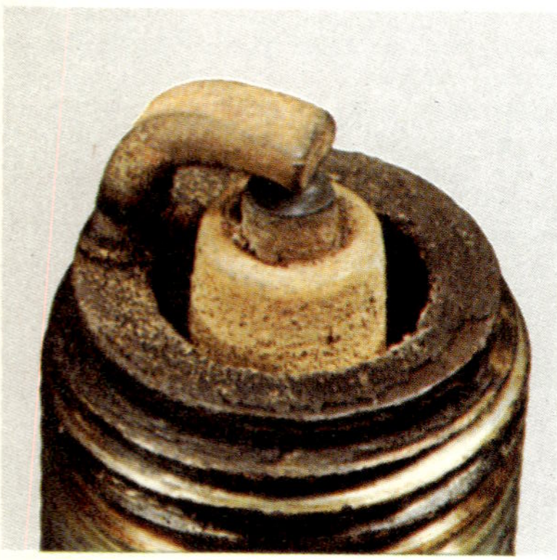

Carbon fouling
Deposits can short circuit the firing end. If recommended plug is fitted check for over-rich mixture, faulty choke mechanism or clogged air cleaner.

Oil fouling
Deposits can short circuit the firing end and this weakens or eliminates the spark. May be caused by worn valve guides, bores or piston rings or by running in an overhauled engine.

Overheating
Likely causes are overadvanced ignition timing, wrong grade of plug, use of too low octane fuel, weak mixture, or cooling system troubles.

At-a-glance trouble-shooting chart 2

Engine: mechanical faults and noise

Running conditions and probable causes	Tapping or clicking	Knock, tapping or light clatter	Clatter or knocking	Light clatter or chattering	High-pitched metallic tapping	Scraping noise	Knocking, rumbling or thumping	Lashing, rattling or grinding noise	Squeaks or whistles
Apparent source	Cylinder head or block	Cylinder head or top of block	Crankcase or front of engine	Cylinder head	Audible when accelerating	Cylinder block	Crankcase	Timing chain cover	Front of engine or near manifolds
Engine cold—worn pistons, rings, cylinder bores (piston slap)[1]		●							
Engine hot—worn little-end bearings[1]		●							
Engine hot, more evident when idling—worn camshaft bearings			●						
Valve-rocker clearances too great, worn valve-operating mechanism, bent push-rod	●			●					
Broken piston rings[2]	●					●			
Engine under load or when revved in neutral—big-end bearing wear[3]			●						
Engine under load and hot—'pinking' caused by pre-ignition or detonation[4]					●				
Crankcase, engine under load—main-bearing and/or crankshaft journal wear[3]							●		
Loose flywheel							●		
Occurring at high revs—valve-bounce (possibly weak valve springs)				●					
Loose or broken engine mounting							●		
Worn timing chain (when fitted). Defective chain tensioner								●	
Front of engine— loose crankshaft pulley or worn pulley key (can be mistaken for big-end bearing wear)			●						
Front of engine—worn, glazed or slipping fan belt. Worn or dry generator or fan bearings. Noisy water pump bearing or seal									●
Vicinity of inlet and exhaust manifolds—loose manifold bolts or nuts, or defective gaskets									●

1 Noise can be reduced or eliminated by shorting-out appropriate sparking plug

2 Badly-worn rings and grooves in pistons may also cause clicking

3 Usually accompanied by low oil pressure

4 Check that correct grade of fuel is in use. Also see Chart 1

At-a-glance trouble-shooting chart 3

Cooling system

This is a general chart covering water-cooled and air-cooled engines. All the items apply to water-cooled systems but only those marked with an asterisk affect air-cooled engines

Symptoms: * Overheating at normal atmospheric temperatures	* Overheating in very cold weather	* Engine slow to warm-up	* Engine does not reach normal running temperature	* Radiator needs frequent topping-up	Probable causes
●	●				* Fan belt – not correctly tensioned or broken
●				●	Radiator filler cap – not sealing properly, or wrong pressure rating
●	●	●	●		Thermostat – faulty or wrong rating
●	●				* Radiator or cooling fins – water or air passages clogged
●	●				Water passages in cylinder head or block – choked by deposits of lime, rust or sludge
	●				Radiator – frozen at base (no anti-freeze, or too low a concentration)
●	●				Water pump – inefficient or inoperative
●	●			●	Air-lock – in cooling system or heater
				●	Water hoses – leaking (check with engine revved-up)
●					Water hoses – perished, collapsed or obstructed by disintegrated linings
●	●			●	Internal water or gas leakage – caused by faulty cylinder-head gasket, cracked head or cylinder block
●	●			●	Local boiling in cylinder head – rust and lime deposits, filler cap pressure rating too low, or cap leaking
●					* Ignition faults – retarded timing, pre-ignition or detonation (see Chart 4)
●					* Carburation – faults causing weak mixture (see Chart 5)
●	●				* Brakes – binding (see Chart 9)
●					* Exhaust system – choked or damaged, restricting flow of gas
●	●				* Engine – assembled too tightly after overhaul

At-a-glance trouble-shooting chart 4

Ignition system faults

The faults in this chart are confined to the ignition system. Some of the symptoms may be caused by carburation, mechanical or cooling system faults. These are dealt with in Charts 2, 3, 5

Engine running symptoms

Engine will not start	Starts but will not keep running	Stalls during normal running	Poor idling	Mis-firing at all speeds	Mis-firing at high speed	Not giving full power or revs	Fuel con-sumption excessive	Pinking or detonation	Overheating, pre-ignition, running-on	**Probable causes**
●										Battery voltage too low – discharged or defective battery, resulting in heavy 'coil robbing' due to current drain by starter
●										Cold-start coil circuit (when fitted) defective
●	●	●	●	●	●	●	●			Low-tension circuit – faulty ignition switch, loose connections, faulty earthing strap (engine or battery to frame)
●	●	●	●	●	●	●	●	●	●	Sparking plugs – wrong gap, dirty or worn-out
			●	●	●	●	●	●	●	Sparking plugs – wrong type fitted
●	●	●	●	●	●	●	●	●	●	Contact-breaker points – dirty or pitted, wrong gap, incorrectly assembled, sticking open
			●	●	●	●	●			Contact-breaker – weak contact spring
●										Contact-breaker – broken spring
●	●	●	●	●	●	●	●			High-tension circuit – current leakage across coil, distributor cap or rotor: insulation cracked, dirty or damp
●	●	●	●	●	●	●	●			High-tension leads – poor contact at terminals, breaks in internal conductors, leads shorting to earth or to each other, faulty suppressors (when fitted)
●	●		●	●						Sparking plug leads – connected in wrong sequence
			●	●	●	●	●			High-tension polarity incorrect – ignition to coil low tension connections reversed
●	●	●	●	●	●	●	●			Distributor cap centre contact broken or sticking
●	●	●	●	●	●	●	●			Coil or condenser – open-circuit, short-circuit, intermittent faults
●			●	●	●	●	●	●	●	Static ignition timing – incorrect
			●	●	●	●	●	●		Centrifugal timing mechanism – not functioning correctly
							●	●		Vacuum timing mechanism – not functioning correctly
			●	●	●	●	●	●		Distributor – shaft bearing worn
				●	●	●	●	●	●	Distributor – wrong type fitted

At-a-glance trouble-shooting chart 5

Carburettor and fuel system

The faults in this chart are confined to the carburettor and fuel system. Some of the symptoms may be caused by other faults, which are dealt with in Charts 2, 3, 4.

Engine will not start	Starts but will not keep running	Stalls during normal running	Poor idling	Misfiring at all speeds	Not giving full power or revs	Fuel consumption excessive	Pinking or detonation	Overheating, pre-ignition, running-on	Probable causes
									Carburettor(s)
●		●							No petrol in float chamber – petrol tank empty, float needle valve sticking faulty fuel pump, filter clogged, petrol pipe obstructed, pipe union loose (see *Petrol Pump, Pipes and Tank*)
●	●								Mixture (choke) control not lowering jet fully (S.U. carburettor)
	●	●	●	●		●			Mixture (choke) control not returning to 'off' position
				●	●	●			Hydraulic damper needs topping-up (S.U. carburettor)
●	●	●	●	●	●	●	●	●	Carburettor suction piston sticking (S.U. carburettor). Choked jets (Zenith, Solex, Weber carburettors)
●	●	●	●	●	●	●			Carburettor flooding – float needle valve not seating, fuel pump pressure too high
●	●	●	●		●		●	●	Air leakage past carburettor or manifold flanges
●		●	●	●	●		●	●	Water or sediment in float chamber
	●	●	●	●	●	●			Idling speed and mixture adjustments incorrect
			●	●	●	●		●	Twin carburettors not properly synchronized
				●	●	●	●	●	Wrong jet needle, jet or piston spring fitted (S.U. and Stromberg carburettors). Wrong size of jet, faulty acceleration pump (Zenith, Solex, Weber carburettors)
	●	●		●	●				Carburettor icing-up internally (normal running restored when carburettor warms-up). See also *Air Cleaner*
									Petrol pump, pipes and tank
●		●		●	●		●	●	Electric pump – dirty filter, poor electrical connections, dirty contacts
●		●		●	●		●	●	Mechanical pump – dirty filter, air leak at filter cover flange
●	●	●	●	●		●			Electrical or mechanical pump – delivery pressure excessive
●	●	●	●	●	●				Fuel pipes – clogged, loose unions, vapour-lock in fuel pipe
●	●	●							Petrol tank – empty (fuel gauge may be giving wrong reading)
●	●	●	●	●	●				Petrol tank – air-vent obstructed, internal filter clogged
									Air cleaner
					●	●			Filter clogged, overdue for renewal
					●	●			Air intake not correctly positioned for summer or winter use or thermostatically-controlled flap not functioning properly (may cause carburettor icing in winter – see *Carburettor icing-up*)

At-a-glance trouble-shooting chart 6

Clutch and transmission

This chart deals only with manual transmissions. Automatic transmission torque converters and gearboxes are complex units and special test equipment, which is held by authorized dealers, must be used to diagnose faults in them

Clutch slip	Clutch judder or snatch	Rattle, knock or squeal from clutch	Difficulty in engaging gear	Jumping out of gear	Noisy gearbox	Rattle or buzz from gear lever	Rattle from transmission when idling	Knocking or clicking from front of car when cornering	**Probable causes**
			●						Air in clutch hydraulic operating system – needs bleeding (hydraulically-operated clutches)
●			●						Clutch adjustment incorrect
●									Clutch driven plate – worn, or oil on friction lining
		●							Clutch release bearing dry and due for renewal
	●								Clutch driven plate buckled during assembly
		●	●						Clutch release mechanism worn
	●	●							Clutch hub splines worn
				●	●		●		Gears and/or bearings worn
					●				Gear teeth chipped
			●	●		●			Selector linkage worn or damaged
						●			Gear lever pivot and linkage worn or needs lubrication
			●	●					Synchromesh mechanism worn
							●		Noise caused by transfer-gears on some front-wheel drive models – difficult to cure at idling speed, but careful carburettor adjustment helps
								●	Universal joints at outer ends of driving shafts worn and due for renewal (front-wheel drive cars only)

At-a-glance trouble-shooting chart 7

Suspension

This is a general trouble-shooting chart, applicable to most suspension systems using leaf springs, coil springs, torsion bars and also hydro-pneumatic systems (eg British Leyland Hydrolastics, Hydragas and other pressurized systems using gas and hydraulic fluid)

Symptoms: 'Bouncy' ride – insufficient damping	Car too low at front and/or rear	Car sags to one side	Groaning or grunting from suspension	Squeak from front or rear suspension	Knock from front suspension	Knock from rear suspension	Rumble or whine from front or rear suspension	**Probable causes**
●	●	●						Weak or broken springs. Incorrect pressure in hydro-pneumatic system or loss of fluid
					●	●		Weak springs allowing suspension to hit bump stops
			●					Noisy damper valves in hydro-pneumatic system
						●		Broken check strap
●								Faulty shock absorbers or hydro-pneumatic unit
					●	●		Worn shock absorber bushes or loose mountings
				●				Squeak from rubber components – to cure, spray with silicone fluid or brush on brake fluid (*not* mineral oil)
						●		Worn bushes in radius arms or links
					●			Worn bushes in tie-bars, suspension arms or linkage
				●	●	●		Worn or incorrectly adjusted wheel bearings
							●	Worn, unlubricated or incorrectly adjusted wheel bearings

At-a-glance trouble-shooting chart 8

Steering and controlability

Excessive free movement at steering wheel	Car wanders, or 'oversteers' excessively	Car pulls to one side	Heavy steering	Wheel wobble or vibration at steering wheel	Rattle or knock from beneath front floor near passenger's feet	Knock from base of steering column	Probable causes
	●	●	●	●			Incorrect tyre pressures
	●						Rear tyre pressures too low
	●	●		●			Incorrect steering geometry and/or front-wheel alignment
				●			Tyres 'out of round,' or unbalanced tyres and wheels – have front and rear wheels balanced regularly
●	●	●		●			Worn or incorrectly adjusted steering and suspension joints and/or wheel hub bearings
●		●	●				Worn or incorrectly adjusted steering rack-and-pinion
			●				Distortion of column or rack-and-pinion unit caused by incorrect fitting
●	●			●	●		Loose bolts holding rack-and-pinion unit to bulkhead
●	●			●		●	Loose clamping bolt on steering column clamp or universal joint
					●		Worn bush in rack-and-pinion unit
			●		●		Lack of oil in rack-and-pinion unit – check condition of telescopic gaiters
	●	●	●				Accidental damage – have suspension and steering units checked by authorized dealer
		●		●			Braking system faults – brakes unevenly adjusted, faulty hydraulic system, oil or grease on linings, brake discs running out-of-true. See Chart 9
	●	●					Suspension faults causing insufficient damping, sagging to one side or incorrect suspension height at front or rear – see Chart 7

At-a-glance trouble-shooting chart 9

Braking system

This chart covers the most common faults in the full range of braking systems – all-drum, disc-and-drum and servo-assisted installations. When disc brakes or a servo are not fitted, the relevant items in the chart do not, of course, apply

Excessive pedal travel	Pedal feels spongy	Brakes lack power	Brakes bind or fail to release fully	Unbalanced braking – locking or pulling to one side	Brake judder	Brake squeal	Rapid wear of linings	Probable causes
●		●	●	●			●	Brakes incorrectly adjusted
	●	●						Fluid level in reservoir too low
	●	●	●	●			●	Rubber seals in hydraulic cylinders swollen
		●	●	●			●	Wheel cylinder or caliper piston seized
●	●	●		●				Leakage past seals in main or wheel cylinders, or from pipeline
	●							Internal fluid leak in servo (level in reservoir falls without visible external leak)
		●			●	●		Accumulation of brake dust in drums
		●		●			●	Badly-scored discs or drums
●					●	●		Worn wheel bearings
		●		●	●	●	●	Wrong type of friction linings fitted
●		●						Brakes 'fading' due to excessive use or wrong grade of linings
●		●						Brake fluid boiling in wheel cylinders – pump all fluid out of system, refill with correct fluid and bleed brakes
		●		●	●	●		Master-cylinder, wheel cylinder or caliper bolts loose
	●	●						Air in system – requires bleeding
	●	●						New linings or pads not bedded-in
●					●			Disc running out of true or drums distorted
		●		●	●	●		Water, oil or brake fluid on linings
		●	●					Servo defective
		●						Servo vacuum hose leaking or non-return valve faulty
			●				●	Pedal push-rod incorrectly adjusted
			●				●	Handbrake operating levers or cable guides seized with rust or mud – brakes remain on or partly applied
				●				Faulty rear-brake pressure-regulating valve
				●	●			Worn steering and suspension parts – see Charts 7 and 8

At-a-glance trouble-shooting chart 10

Electrical equipment

It has been possible to deal only with the broader aspects of electrical fault-tracing in this chart. Detailed diagnosis calls for the use of accurate instruments and a good deal of electrical know-how. It is best left to a qualified auto-electrician

Symptoms

Battery and Charging system				Starter motor		Lamps				
Battery cells need frequent topping-up with water	Battery apparently not receiving sufficient charge	Battery will not hold charge	Starter does not turn engine, or rotates it slowly	Starter runs but pinion does not engage with flywheel gear	Starter pinion jams in mesh of flywheel gear	Headlamps give poor illumination when correctly aligned	Brightness of lights varies noticeably with engine speed	Lights flicker	Bulbs or light units burn out frequently	**Probable causes**
			●	●		●	●			Battery discharged
	●	●								Battery electrolyte level too low or of wrong specific gravity
		●	●	●		●	●			Defective battery – sulphated or buckled plates
	●						●			Generator driving belt slipping
	●						●			Faulty generator
●	●						●		●	Charging regulator defective or incorrectly adjusted. Charging rate too high or too low
							●		●	Loose or high-resistance connections in charging circuit
						●		●		Loose or high-resistance connections in lighting circuits
	●		●	●			●	●	●	Corroded or loose battery terminals
			●	●		●		●		Poor earth-return connections
		●								Leakage of current in car wiring
			●							Faulty starter switch
			●	●						Poor connections in starter circuit
				●	●					Dirty or faulty starter pinion drive
					●					Worn starter pinion teeth on flywheel ring gear
			●							Faulty starter motor

6 Bodywork Defects
Dealing with dents, scratches and rust

One of the recurring themes in this book is 'Prevention is better than cure'. In Chapter 3 we emphasize the importance of making a careful check for rust. Here we are concerned with minimizing its effects. Neglect even a minor blemish, and you will find that rust can spread with alarming rapidity under the surrounding paintwork.

1 Dealing with scratches and chips

As shown in the first photograph, it is best to use a fine brush for touching-in small blemishes. If an aerosol paint spray is used it is difficult to confine the spray to a very small area. We give some notes on spraying larger areas at the end of this section.

Scrape any loose paint and rust from the area with the tip of a penknife blade, apply a rust-preventive, such as Zinc Plate, to the bright metal and then knife-on a thin layer of cellulose stopping, building up the level to slightly above the surrounding paintwork.

When the stopping is dry, rub it down with very fine wet-or-dry paper, used wet; with a smear of soap to prevent clogging. Then touch-in the area with the correct colour to match the surrounding finish.

Alternatively, your accessory shop may sell a card of special paint transfers which, when applied on a clean surface and rubbed down, produce an almost indetectable repair to a scratch or chip.

2 Removing dents

The second picture shows the sort of dent that can be dealt with at home by filling it with glass-fibre resin paste.

Rub down to bare metal, extending to about 2 in. beyond the edge of the dent, using 80 grit paper. Score the base and sides of the dent with a file or screwdriver to provide a key for the body filler, and apply this with a plastic spatula as illustrated until the level is above the surrounding metal.

If the dent is localized, it is usually a mistake to attempt to tap it out. The metal has probably been stretched, and too enthusiastic attempts at amateur panel-beating will turn the dent into a bulge—which must then be tapped back again so that the hollow can be built-up with body filler!

In the case of a large, shallow dent, however, the metal may simply have bulged inwards and can be persuaded to spring out again by applying pressure to the inside of the panel. When the inner side cannot be reached—for example in a double-skinned section of the body—the simplest plan is to drill a hole at the centre of the dent, insert a self-tapping screw and pull the dent out by gripping the head of the screw with a pair of pliers, a self-locking wrench, or a claw hammer. The hole can then be filled with stopper, sanded down and touched-in. Another ploy that has proved successful is to ease a deflated football bladder between the two skins of the bodywork, pump it up and pop the dent out.

3 Rubbing down the filler

Here the filler is being rubbed down with progressively finer paper, after the paste has hardened, until a good finish is obtained, to prepare the surface for spraying as described in Sections 8 and 9.

4 Dealing with badly-rusted panels

The corroded metal must be ruthlessly cut away until sound, bright metal is reached. When rust has attacked the back of a panel this may mean that an innocuous-looking pimpled area is converted into a fairly large hole with ragged edges, as shown in the photograph. These must be tapped back with a hammer to about ¼ in. below the level of the surrounding paintwork.

5 Glass-fibre repairs

A typical glass-fibre kit is shown in this photograph. It contains a supply of glass-fibre mat, which is used to cover the damaged area, tissue and ribbon to repair smaller areas, resin, hardener and filler powder, and often a stippling brush, a stirring rod and a mixing bowl.

If the damaged area is a load-bearing one, the only safe repair is to have a patch welded in by a garage. You can then save money by filling and spraying the repaired area at home. If the part is unstressed, however, the sound edges should be tapped in until they are about ¼ in. below the surface of the surrounding metal and a glass-fibre patch can be applied.

6 Applying the glass-fibre mat

Here we show a piece of glass-fibre mat being applied to the damaged area. It is essential to follow the instructions which are supplied with each kit. The principle is to cut a suitably sized piece of mat, mix some resin and catalyst in the correct proportions, stipple the resin generously over the damaged area, apply the glass mat, thoroughly soak this with resin, and repeat the operation with a second layer of mat.

If the damage is fairly extensive, a sheet of perforated zinc can be used to reinforce the glass-fibre. When repairing a rusty hollow section, a self-foaming plastic can be poured into the cavity until it overflows from the

hole, quickly setting into a sufficiently rigid mass to provide a good support for the glass-fibre mat.

7 Preparing for spraying

When the resin has hardened, build up the external surface with the filler paste as shown in the picture.

Use coarse emery paper, an emery disc in an electric drill, or a Surform file to obtain the correct profile. Then rub down the surface with 180 grade wet-or-dry emery paper, used wet, to blend the repair into the surrounding paintwork, followed by light rubbing with 400 grade, again used wet, and preferably with a trace of soap, until a silky smooth surface can be felt.

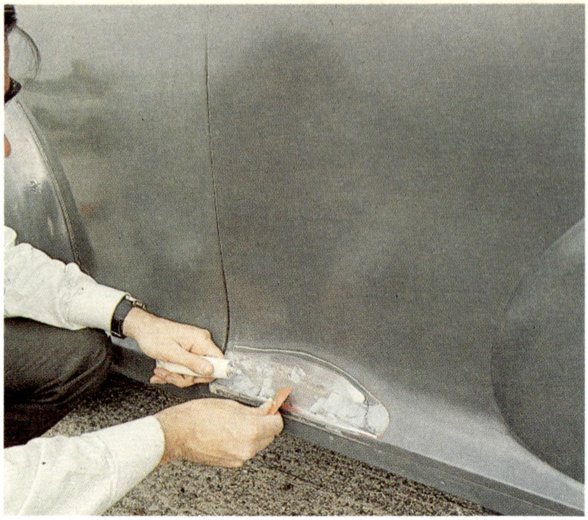

8 Masking-off and spraying

Special masking tape can be obtained from garages and accessory shops. Never use ordinary cellulose tape, which will lift during spraying. Tape around the area to be sprayed, and attach sheets of newspaper to this tape with a second strip of tape, as shown.

Allow sufficient space to blend-in the new paint gradually. If you spray right up to the masking tape, the paint will build up along the edge of the tape and leave a ridge when it is removed.

Aerosol paint spray cans are ideal for small jobs, but first practise spraying on a sheet of metal or hardboard. Spray guns are more expensive and call for experience to obtain really good results.

Wash the prepared surface and allow it to dry before applying at least two coats of primer. Keep the spraying nozzle about 6-9 in. away from the surface, as shown in the photograph. Rub down each coat with 400 grade paper. The first colour coat can then be sprayed on, again followed by a light rub down, before the next coat is applied. Apply further light coats until a good finish is obtained.

Blend the spray into the surrounding paintwork. The colour of the new paint will usually change slightly as it dries and the true colour may not be obtained until a day or so has elapsed.

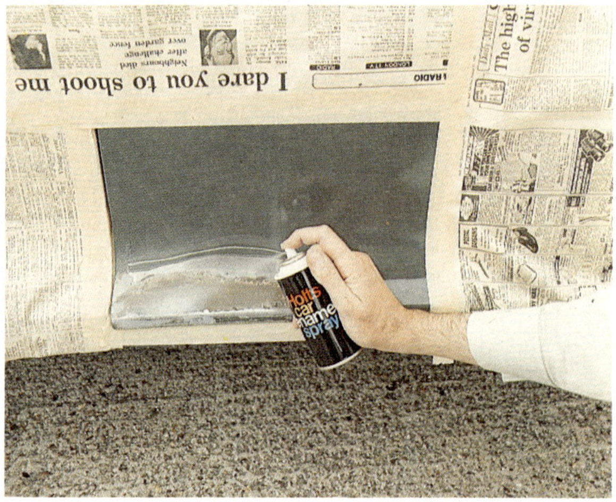

9 Blending and polishing

After the new paint has hardened thoroughly – allow at least a week for this – the surface can be polished and blended in with the old paintwork by using a mild abrasive compound. Liquid metal polish, or one of the 'cleaners' sold by the car polish firms for removing the stale outer film from the paintwork (such as Colour Cut) will produce a good finish.

7 The Ministry test
Will your car pass or fail?

When you submit your car for the DoE test, the chances are about one in three that it will fail at the first attempt.

This is, of course, an average failure rate for all the cars tested in Great Britain. A more encouraging aspect is that an experienced tester will tell you that in many cases these failures need never have occurred. The faults could have been detected by a practical owner and should have been put right before the car was taken to the testing station.

The value of the test is that it is essentially a safety check. Think of it, if you like, as an expert second opinion on the efficiency of your servicing during the past twelve months, covering such vital points as the brakes, steering, tyres, seat belts and the lighting system. Approach it in this spirit, and you will give your car the best chance of passing with flying colours.

In the space available here it is not possible to give a detailed, point-by-point summary of the requirements laid down in the comprehensive Ministry tester's manual (which is revised from time to time to include additional items) but it *is* possible to provide an overall picture of the sort of checks that you can carry out at home.

A surprisingly large number of cars do not get even as far as a detailed inspection. The tester may refuse to carry out the test, for example, if he considers that the car is unsafe to drive.

Faults such as a badly-rusted exhaust system which allows fumes to enter the car, shock absorbers which are so worn as to affect the controllability of the vehicle, windscreen wipers and washers, direction indicators or horns, which refuse to work, loose or broken seat mountings, a faulty door lock or bonnet catch, or leaving loosely-stowed luggage or packages inside the car which might be a risk during a braking test on the road, are all valid reasons for the issue of a 'fail' certificate.

Before going further, you might ask yourself, 'If this were a car belonging to a stranger, would I be completely happy to drive it?'.

It is also reasonable to expect a refusal if the underside of the car is so caked with mud and grime that the tester cannot easily examine it, or if you cannot produce a previous test certificate or the vehicle registration book as evidence of the age of the car.

If you have carried out the checks described in Chapter 3, however, and have, preferably, filled in a condition report sheet on the lines suggested in Chapter 5, and have conscientiously carried out the regular servicing outlined in Chapter 4, you should be able to face the test with confidence and we can now turn to some of the detailed checks which can be carried out at home. These form, in effect, a 'dummy run' for the actual test itself.

Checking the braking system

Begin by checking the 'feel' of the brake pedal, with the engine running if a servo is fitted. A 'spongy' pedal, or the need to pump it to take up excessive travel, will call for immediate investigation. Refer to Chart No. 9 to diagnose the most likely causes and turn to Chapter 15 for advice on how to put them right.

Next get under the car, and with an inspection lamp go over the flexible hoses, every inch of the rigid pipelines and the unions. Look for cracks in the hoses, corrosion of the pipelines and seepage of fluid from the unions. Make sure that there is no risk of the hoses being rubbed by the front wheels on full lock and that none of the rigid pipes is in danger of being chafed where it passes close to the underframe or through an opening. Pay particular attention to the handbrake operating cables and rods, looking for frayed cables, worn pivots and clevis pins, and any signs of binding in the mechanism.

Seepage of brake fluid or grease from the wheel bearings on to the brake drums, backplates, discs and calipers will immediately be obvious and would be an equally immediate cause for failing the car.

Check the handbrake for excessive travel and make sure that the ratchet holds securely.

The tester will pay particular attention to all these points before carrying out a brake test, you will not be able to measure the efficiency of the brakes – the minimum is 50% for the foot brake and 25% for the handbrake – but by testing the brakes at about 30 mph on a smoooth-surfaced, traffic-free road you should be able to detect any lack of efficiency or a tendency to pull to one side or the other, or to lock one wheel prematurely.

A final point: before handing the car over to the tester, make sure that the brake fluid reservoir has been topped-up to the correct level.

Steering checks

It is reasonable to suppose that you would not allow your car to go for test if there was an obvious fault such as excessive lost motion at the steering wheel, tight steering, poor self-centring, a tendency to pull to one side or wheel-wobble. Apart from steering faults, one cannot rule out poor roadholding due to weak dampers or a generally tired suspension system.

Check through the symptoms listed in Chart No. 8 and then turn to Chapters 14 and 15 for the corrective action.

The Ministry inspection is not confined to the road test. The tester will raise the car on a lift, or place it over a pit and with front wheels supported clear of the ground, will push, pull and tug at all the steering connections in order to detect worn joints or loose mountings.

You can forestall him by jacking up each wheel in turn, grasping it at top and bottom and rocking it to show up excess play in the wheel bearings and in the hub-carrier swivel joints. There should be just perceptible end-play in the wheel bearings. Any excessive movement calls for investigation. Next spin the wheel and listen for grinding or rubbing noises which would indicate that the bearings are badly worn or are breaking up.

With both wheels lowered to the ground, get under the car and ask a friend to tug the steering wheel towards each lock in turn and release it, while you closely watch the steering joints for any signs of wear.

Nowadays, the joints are of the self-adjusting type, except where rubber bushes are used. It used to be said that if any slackness could be felt when the upper part of the joint was levered away from the lower part, replacement was indicated. Many modern joints, however, have a small amount of 'lift' when new, in order to increase their service life. With this type of joint, if the lower half can be raised by more than about 0.01in. by exerting pressure with a lever pivoted against the inside of the wheel rim, renewal is probably necessary.

You may find that an eccentric type joint is fitted, however, which must be checked for wear by levering it *sideways* in relation to the ball-pin.

Obviously, accurate assessment of the amount of wear which is present calls for experience and that is why we recommend that the best check is to watch the joints while the steering wheel is tugged towards each lock and released. Sloppy joints will immediately show up under this treatment.

If the protective rubber boot on a joint is found to be damaged or displaced, the joint should be renewed as a safety precaution. The tester will probably condemn it, anyway.

The tyres

It should be obvious that tyres which are worn below the legal minimum of 1 mm of tread depth across at least three-quarters of the width of the tread, and around the whole of the circumference of the tyre, are potentially lethal. Damaged wheel rims will also be a cause of failure.

Not so obvious, however, are cuts or bulges on the inner walls of the tyres, especially on the inner sides of rear tyres which often escape routine inspection. The tester will also look for uneven tread wear, which suggests steering or braking defects, and will immediately fail the car if he discovers an illegal mixture of cross-ply and radial-ply covers. If the tyres are of different types, the radials must always be fitted to the rear wheels. Obviously it is best to avoid any mixture and stick to cross-plies or radials throughout.

Remember to check the spare wheel. The tester must assume that if you carry a spare you intend to use it if a puncture occurs, and it is therefore logical to fail the car if the spare wheel is fitted with a badly-worn or otherwise defective tyre, or one of the wrong type.

Bodywork condition

The tester will pay particular attention to the underside of the vehicle. Vital components in this respect are underframes, stressed body sills, suspension mountings and the floor pans, especially where the seat mountings and seat belt attachments are bolted through.

Never be tempted to try to camouflage badly-rusted, stressed areas by glass-fibre repairs. An experienced tester will spot this immediately and will refuse to pass the car until a proper repair has been made by welding-in new sections.

The lighting system

The requirements laid down in the tester's manual can be summed-up in a few words: all the lights on the car which are required by the Construction and Use Regulations must be working properly and the headlamps must be correctly aligned so that they do not dazzle other drivers when dipped.

So far as the standard lighting system is concerned, therefore, all that you have to do is to check for a 'blown' bulb, a wiring fault, a poor earth contact or a faulty switch which prevents a light functioning, a cracked or missing lamp glass or a badly-rusted reflector.

It is not really practical to attempt to adjust the lamp beams by aiming them at marks on a wall. There are too many sources of error and a proper check can be carried out so much more accurately by a garage, using an optical beam setter. If you have any doubts, have this check made before submitting the car for the test.

The seat belts

Finally, don't forget to check the seat belts and their mountings. The tester is justified in failing a car if he finds a loose or insecure mounting or a badly-frayed belt.

Part three

8 Strip, repair or replace?
Practical notes on overhauls

'Whip it off and fit a new one!' says the garage mechanic or a knowledgeable friend dogmatically when a fault develops in a component which calls for more than a minor repair – and with high labour charges in mind you may feel inclined to agree with him.

But is he giving you good advice? Does it always make economic sense, for example, to fit a service-exchange starter motor? The answer is probably 'No,' if all that is required is a set of new brushes and cleaning up the commutator – but the works-reconditioned component has been fully overhauled and *does* carry a guarantee!

In the case of an alternator, on the other hand, it is almost certainly best to fit an exchange unit. It is possible to change the alternator brushes, but testing the diodes and the charging regulator should be left to a qualified auto-electrician.

Where safety is involved we think it better to renew all doubtful items. The hydraulic components in the braking system should be replaced as complete assemblies, for example, instead of trying to salvage them by fitting new rubber parts from an overhaul kit. New rubbers in scored or corroded bores can have very short lives! The same principle applies to steering gear parts.

Again, where the clutch is concerned, renew everything that can wear – in this case as a matter of sound economics. It is much too time-consuming to remove and strip the clutch later should a worn part fail.

Similarly, when you strip a worn gearbox you will probably end up by replacing most of the parts, so there may not be much difference between the cost of these and the price of a reconditioned exchange unit.

In subsequent chapters, and in the notes on engine overhaul which follow, we deal with this subject more fully, indicating those jobs which are likely to be beyond the skill or the resources of the beginner, and suggesting 'repair by replacement' where this is likely to be more economical or more satisfactory.

A final point to bear in mind is that if special service tools will be needed to carry out an overhaul properly, the expense of these – assuming that they cannot be borrowed or hired – will seldom be justified for a one-off job.

Practical aspects of engine overhauls

It is possible to tackle virtually any degree of engine wear in the home garage by dividing the work into three stages and taking advantage of the replacement or reconditioned part or assemblies which are available from specialist firms. The practical aspects of the work are fully covered in Chapter 9, so we can confine ourselves here to a brief discussion of the pros and cons of the various stages of overhaul, which can be summarized as follows –

Stage 1 Fitting new piston rings, including special oil-control rings, to the existing pistons.

Stage 2. Partial overhaul, including new special pistons with rings and gudgeon pins, fitting new connecting-rod bearings, exhaust valves, valve springs and timing chain.

Stage 3. Full overhaul, including fitting a new set of cylinder barrels, complete with a matched set of piston rings and gudgeon pins, together with a reground crankshaft, new bearing shells, a new flywheel, and a new camshaft, camshaft bearings, followers, timing chain and tensioner, plus any other auxiliaries which need to be replaced. Alternatively, a 'half-engine', 'short motor' or 'pin up' (these terms will be described later) or a reconditioned, exchange engine.

Even if you are a novice, you should be able to tackle Stages 1 and 2 with every prospect of success. If you have had some experience of working on engines, there is no reason why you should not carry out the more ambitious Stage 3 overhaul, provided that you are able to borrow or hire lifting tackle to remove and refit the engine (don't rely on the roof beam of a prefabricated garage to carry the weight of the engine) and can call on the assistance of a friend when an extra pair of hands is needed.

Bearing in mind these points, a brief run through the pros and cons of the different reconditioning methods may help you to come to the right decision.

Fitting new piston rings (Stage 1)

A set of special piston rings can deal successfully with bore wear up to a maximum of about 0.003–0.004 in. for each inch of cylinder diameter, but their effectiveness depends on correct fitting.

It is usually necessary to send the pistons to the firm that supplies the rings so that the worn grooves can be machined to match the new rings. Since the connecting-rod eyes must be heated and special tools used when removing and refitting the gudgeon pins, it would probably be better to negotiate the whole deal with your Renault dealer.

Never be tempted to fit a set of oil-control rings to

worn pistons without enlisting the help of a specialist supplier. At best, the result may be disappointing; at worst, ring breakage may occur, scoring the cylinder walls and rendering a rebore essential.

Oil consumption should remain within reasonable limits for about 10 000 miles after a Stage 1 overhaul. If it is proposed to sell or exchange the car within this mileage, therefore, the fitting of special rings alone may well be an economic proposition.

Stage 2 overhaul

If you intend to keep the car for a longer period, however, and it has not covered more than about 40 000–60 000 miles, serious consideration should be given to a Stage 2 overhaul.

Most of the work entailed will be the same as that required when fitting new rings alone but the replacement of the pistons and the connecting-rod bearings, combined with a top-overhaul and the fitting of new exhaust valves, and a set of valve springs, will give the engine a new lease of life.

'Intermediate engine overhaul' kits are available from specialist firms such as AE Edmunds Walker and can be ordered through your garage. They contain everything that is needed for a Stage 2 overhaul – pistons and rings, bearing shells, exhaust valves, valve springs, gaskets, jointing compound and even an oil filter and a piston-ring clamp.

Renault recommend, however, that if the cylinder bore ovality or taper wear exceeds about 0.006 in. (0.15 mm) a new set of cylinder barrels and pistons should be fitted. In practice, however, cylinder wear is often negligible even after high mileages. It is the rings which wear and cause loss of compression and high oil consumption.

Stage 3 overhaul

The simplest solution is to lift the engine out and install a reconditioned unit; or you can go to the other extreme and strip it right down, fit new or reconditioned parts as necessary and rebuild it.

If you decide to fit a 'recon' engine, you again have the choice of ordering a factory-rebuilt unit from your local dealer, or shopping around for a rebuilt engine at a lower price, among the smaller engineering firms which specialize in this work. The advertisements in the practical motoring papers will provide a list of prospects.

Owing to the specialized construction of these engines and the use of aluminium-alloy components, it would be wise to deal only with a reputable firm – say, one which is a member of the Federation of Engine Remanufacturers.

Reputable engine rebuilding firms usually offer a worthwhile guarantee, however. In such cases their units should be just as satisfactory as factory-rebuilt units.

Although these are known in the trade as 'full' engines, they are not in fact complete. You will have to remove the carburettor, manifolds, ignition distributor, starter, fuel pump, dipstick and ignition timing pointer from your engine and fit them to the new unit – after suitably reconditioning them, of course.

It will probably be necessary also to remove and keep the securing studs, bolts and nuts for these items, which will not be supplied with the new unit. In some cases you may have to fit your own flywheel and valve cover, so check carefully just what is offered.

A cheaper proposition is the 'half engine' or 'short motor'. This consists of a cylinder block with new barrels and pistons, fitted with a reground crankshaft in new main bearings complete with reconditioned connecting rods, a reground camshaft, new or refaced cam followers and new timing sprockets. To this you add your own reconditioned cylinder head, the auxiliaries already mentioned and the other bits and pieces that go to make up the complete engine.

A short engine obviously entails a good deal more work on your part, but with a corresponding saving in expense. Few, if any, special tools are required and all the skilled work has been done for you.

Finally, the cheapest proposition is that known in the trade as a 'pin-up' – which sounds interesting, but in fact means simply that the parts supplied are limited to a reconditioned crankcase, cylinder barrels, pistons, crankshaft and connecting rods, ready-assembled for you to build into a complete engine, using your own new and reconditioned parts for the remaining items.

The time factor

If this is to be your first attempt at carrying out, say a partial engine overhaul, make sure that you allow plenty of time, plus a safety margin for unexpected delays. If you begin work on a Thursday evening, it should be possible to complete the preliminary dismantling on the cylinder head that night, so that any replacements that are found to be necessary and are not included in the intermediate engine overhaul kit referred to earlier can be obtained on Friday morning.

By making an early start on Friday it should be possible to lift the engine out, withdraw the connecting rods and pistons, have the old pistons removed and the replacements fitted by your Renault dealer, if necessary, reassemble the pistons and connecting rods (fitted with new bearing shells) and the cylinder barrels and finally turn your attention to decarbonizing the cylinder head and grinding-in the valves.

The whole of Saturday will probably be occupied in finishing off the bottom half of the engine, fitting a new filter, refitting the cylinder head, manifolds and carburettor, reinstalling the engine and making adjustments, followed by a short test run.

9 The engine

In Chapter 8 we have explained how a do-it-yourself enthusiast can successfully tackle quite an ambitious engine overhaul without the need for special skills or an impressive array of workshop equipment.

The secret, of course, is to confine oneself, as far as possible, to straightforward stripping and assembly, leaving the trickier jobs to the experts.

The engine repairs and adjustments that can be tackled without the use of special tools and equipment are mainly influenced by the design of the cylinder head and valve-operating gear and, in the case of major overhauls, by the pistons, cylinder barrels, crankshaft and the crankcase components. Notes on the practical aspects of these components are given in the sections which deal with the individual units.

Briefly, the jobs that can be undertaken by a practical owner without removing the engine from the car (in addition to the usual maintenance tasks) are: valve clearance checks and adjustments; removing the cylinder head for decarbonizing and a top-overhaul; changing the pistons and cylinder barrels; checking the oil pump, suction filter and pressure-release valve; and renewing the connecting rod big-end bearings – but not the main bearings, one of which cannot be removed with the engine *in situ*.

For other jobs the engine must be lifted out, complete with the gearbox.

The type numbers of the engines covered by this book are given below and we have used these to identify the different units where necessary.

800–01 845 cc engine fitted to models before October 1973.

800–05 Detoxed (anti-pollution) engine fitted to 1974 and later models (October 1973 onwards). Similar to 800–01, apart from anti-pollution carburettor and air filter, aluminium-tin main

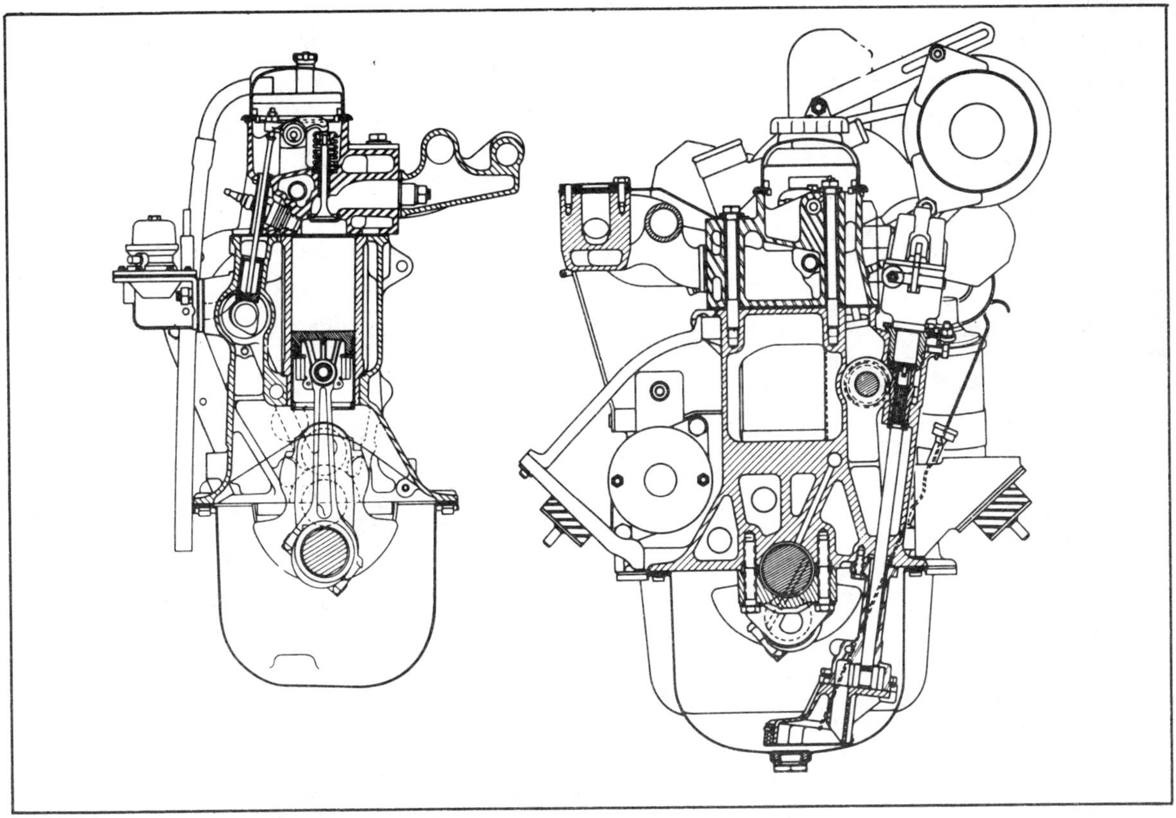

Fig. 9.1 Sections through the engine

and big-end bearing shells, the fitting of an external oil filter and larger cooling system capacity.

Routine engine maintenance

The jobs described in the following sections are those listed in the maintenance schedule. Engine maintenance of course, also includes a certain amount of work on the cooling system, the carburettor and petrol pump and the ignition system. These jobs are dealt with in Chapters 10, 11 and 12.

9.1 Engine lubrication and oil changes

The engine oil has been aptly described as the life-blood of the engine. It therefore pays to use a first-class multi-grade oil. The correct grades are given in Chapter 17.

Here are some important practical tips –

1 The intervals between oil changes recommended in the maintenance schedule *apply only when a multigrade oil is used, under favourable conditions.* Change the oil more frequently when most of the driving is done in cold weather, or when the car is used for short runs and frequent starts are made from cold, or in hot, dusty conditions. In such cases it is best to change the oil after 2000 miles, or, in extreme cases, as frequently as every 1000 miles.

2 The correct oil pressure is given in Chapter 17. If the pressure is appreciably below this figure at normal speeds in top gear, with the engine thoroughly warmed-up, investigation is called for. Running the engine with too low a pressure can result in expensive damage to the crankshaft, main and connecting-rod bearings and other components. Some causes of low oil pressure are discussed in Section 9.17.

3 An oil-pressure gauge is not provided but the combined oil pressure and water pump warning lamp in the instrument panel will glow if the oil pressure should fall below a safe minimum figure. If the lamp does not light up when the ignition is switched on or does not go out when the engine is running, check the switch on the cylinder block, which is operated by the oil pressure. Either fit a replacement switch, or ask a garage to check the oil pressure by temporarily connecting a gauge to the switch union.

4 The sump should be drained when the car has just come in from a run, when the oil is hot and fluid. The system should *not* be flushed out after draining the oil. The drain plug has a 10 mm square recess in it. The squared end of the special Renault combination spanner B.Vi 380–01 fits the recess and the socket at the other end of the spanner can be used to undo the gearbox drain and level plugs.

However, a practical owner could make a spanner from a length of 10 mm square steel bar, or file a square on the end of a bolt and use a spanner to turn the bolt. Since the gearbox plugs can be undone with an adjustable spanner, the Renault tool is not essential, but is worth having.

9.2 Changing the oil filter element

An external oil filter is provided only on the 800–05 engines. This must be renewed after it has been in use for 6000 miles. Carbon, sludge and grit accumulate in the filter, and if the element becomes clogged, a safety valve opens in order to maintain adequate oil circulation to the engine – *but this oil will not be filtered.*

After September 1970 a modified cylinder block having a mounting base for this type of filter was fitted to the 800–01 engines but the mounting base was blanked off. It is possible to fit the modern type of oil filter to these engines, however, by removing the blanking plug and screwing in a threaded union 48 mm (1⅞ in.) long. Your Renault dealer should be able to carry out this conversion for you.

The rubber seal tends to stick to the cylinder block and may be difficult to unscrew. Use a strap-wrench (available from Halfords and other accessory shops) or the Renault tool Mot 445 to free it.

To renew the filter –

Materials: New filter cartridge.
Tools: Strap wrench or special tool Mot 445.

1 Drain the oil (Section 9.1).
2 Unscrew the filter and discard it.
3 Clean the joint face on the cylinder block and smear the joint ring on the new filter with clean engine oil.
4 Screw the filter into position until it just touches the joint face on the cylinder block. Then screw it by a further quarter-turn, using the strap wrench, slacken it back and finally screw it in by a half to three-quarters of a turn.
5 Refill the sump, run the engine and check for oil leakage past the filter joint when the engine is hot.

9.3 Checking and adjusting the valve clearances

To keep your engine in good tune, check the valve clearances (see below) at 6000-mile intervals. If there is

Fig. 9.2 Adjusting the valve clearances. The Renault tool shown, Mot. 13, makes the job easier. A rocker adjusting screw is shown at 1 and the lock-nut at 2

noticeable tapping or clicking from the valve cover on top of the engine, however, or if the car seems to lack power or liveliness, the tappet clearances should be checked at once, without waiting for the routine service to fall due.

The clearance must also be reset whenever the cylinder-head nuts are tightened down, as this compresses the cylinder-head gasket and the resulting movement of the cylinder head reduces the valve clearances.

The adjusting screws on these engines are not slotted to take a screwdriver blade but have parallel flats machined on them. A small spanner or an adjustable may be used to turn them, or a tool can be made up by partly flattening a piece of tube so that it grips the flats. The most satisfactory method, however, is to use the Renault adjusting tool which combines a spanner to fit the lock-nut, with a socket of the correct shape to take the adjusting screw. Make sure that you get the correct wrench. There are different types to suit various engines. You will also need a set of feeler gauges.

Methods of turning the engine when adjusting the clearances are described on page 16. Renault mechanics sometimes use a remote-control for the starter switch which allows them to turn the engine over with the sparking plugs installed (but not firing) while the operation of the valves is watched. If the engine is in good condition, after using the starter in this way the crankshaft will come to rest with the exhaust valve of one of the cylinders open. Each exhaust valve can thus be opened in succession and the valve clearances can be checked as described below.

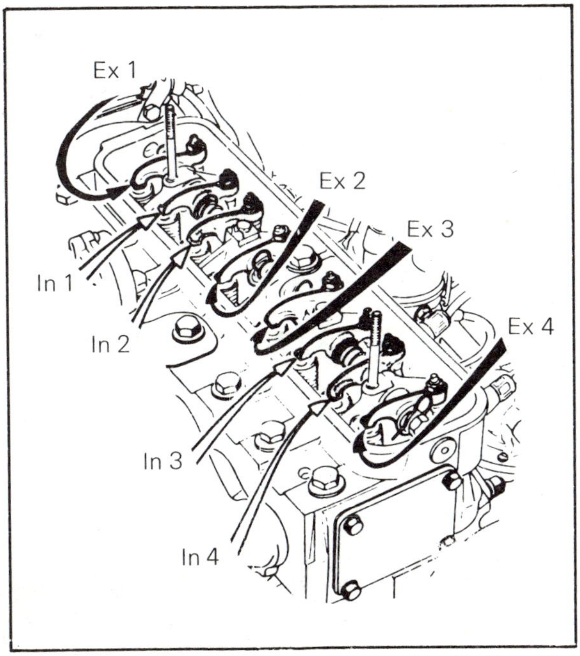

Fig. 9.3 The inlet and exhaust valve rockers can be identified from this drawing

This table should also be used when the engine is rotated by the more conventional methods described on page 16. No. 1 cylinder is that nearest the gearbox. The rocker clearances are –

Hot:	Inlet	0.18 mm (0.0075 in.)
	Exhaust	0.25 mm (0.010 in.)
Cold:	Inlet	0.15 mm (0.006 in.)
	Exhaust	0.20 mm (0.008 in.)

Exhaust valve fully open	Check/adjust clearances on following valves Inlet	Exhaust
1	3	4
2	1	3
3	4	2
4	2	1

The inlet and exhaust valves can be identified from Fig. 9.3.

The clearances should be checked *only when the engine is cold* (after standing overnight, for example) *or when it is at its normal running temperature.* Four or five miles on the road should be sufficient to ensure that the temperatures of the cylinder block, cylinder head, valves, push-rods and rocker gear have become stabilized. It is not sufficient just to run the engine for a few minutes in the garage before checking the clearances.

To check and adjust the clearances–

1 Disconnect the breather hose, pipes and cables from the valve cover, unscrew the valve cover retaining nuts and lift off the cover.

2 To check the clearances, slide a feeler gauge between the end of the rocker and the tip of the valve stem. It should be a light drag fit – not too loose nor too tight.

3 If adjustment is needed, slacken the lock-nut at the push-rod end of the rocker (preferably use a ring spanner, as the edges of the flats on the nut can easily be burred-over by an open-jawed spanner). Turn the adjusting-screw until the correct clearance is obtained and hold it in this position while tightening the lock-nut.

4 Re-check the clearance, which will probably have altered during the first attempt at tightening the lock-nut.

5 Replace the valve-rocker cover. Make sure that the gasket is correctly fitted and tighten the screws evenly. Check for an oil leak after the engine has been run.

9.4 Servicing the crankcase ventilation system

The crankcase ventilation system used on the 800-01 engines consists of a hose connected between the valve rocker cover and the carburettor air intake, above the choke flap. At 6000-mile intervals check that the hose is not clogged by sludge and renew it if it has become soft and spongy.

On the 800-05 engines, there are two hoses, one leading from the rocker cover to the carburettor intake, and a second hose which is connected to the first hose by a T-junction and leads to the inlet manifold. A 1.5 mm

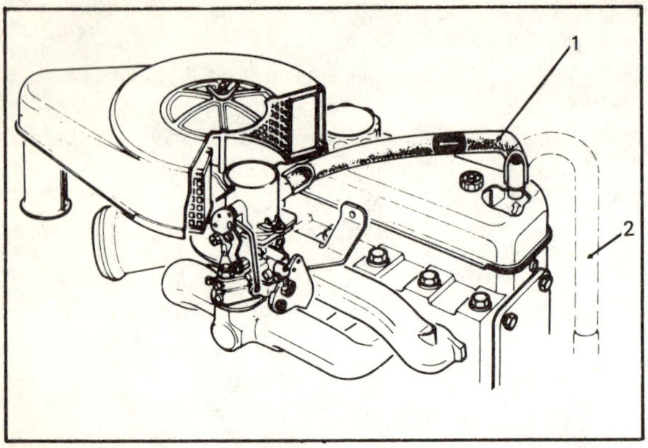

Fig. 9.4 The earlier crankcase ventilation system. 1, arrangement for normal climates. 2, position for 'extreme-cold' climates

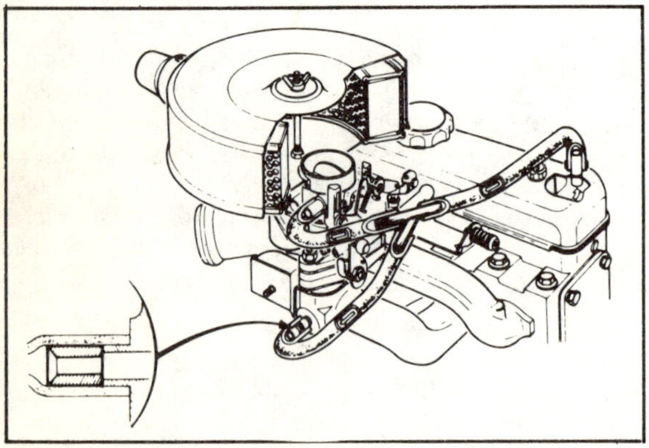

Fig. 9.5 The dual ventilation circuit used on later cars. The restrictor in the lower pipe is shown inset

(0.059 in.) calibrated jet is inserted in the end of the pipe where it is connected to the manifold. Clean this jet and don't forget to fit it when the pipe is changed, or the mixture strength will be upset.

Engine overhauls

As indicated at the beginning of this chapter, a surprisingly large amount of work can be done without removing the engine from the car. Owing to the use of light alloy for the cylinder head and other specialized features of the engine, such as the fitting of removable 'wet' cylinder barrels, however, the use of special Renault tools is advisable for some jobs.

In some cases we suggest alternative ways of doing the work but where we recommend that a special tool should be used, it would be unwise to adopt makeshift methods unless this cannot be avoided.

It is also essential to quote the chassis number and the engine type and number of your car when ordering spares. A number of modifications have been introduced over the years and in some cases only the new type of component is available as a spare. This may mean that suitably modified parts must also be used with the new unit.

It must be assumed, of course, that if you are prepared to tackle major overhauls you will have had some experience of engine dismantling, fitting and assembly, or will be able to rely on the help of a knowledgeable friend.

The time factor

It is not always easy to estimate the time required for engine overhaul jobs, since so much depends on the facilities available. The following times, however, are suggested for typical jobs: Partial engine overhaul (see Chapter 8), 2–3 days; top-overhaul and decarbonizing, allow at least one full day – preferably a week-end; removing and refitting engine, 10–11 hr.

Decarbonizing and top-overhaul

Removal of the cylinder head, cleaning off deposits of carbon and re-seating the valves is usually termed 'decarbonizing', although a more correct term, in view of the work involved, is a 'top-overhaul'.

If the job is confined solely to removing and refitting the head – to replace a faulty gasket, for example – only the appropriate sections apply.

The lists of materials and tools required which follow cover a complete top-overhaul, but can, of course, be modified to suit the actual stages carried out.

Materials: Gasket set. Water hoses. Set of valve springs. Spare exhaust valves (have at least two in reserve as a safety margin). Valve-grinding paste. Emery paper. Rags. Paraffin. Tins, jars, boxes for parts.

Tools: Set of spanners. Socket spanners. Screwdrivers. Pliers. Plastic-faced mallet. Blunt scraper for carbon. Wire brush. Valve-spring compressor. Torque wrench. Syringe or plastic tube. Straightedge. Feeler gauges. Electric drill with wire brushes – desirable but not essential. Mot 31 – not essential.

9.5 Removing the cylinder head

The following points are vitally important when removing the cylinder head, in view of the use of light-alloys in the head and cylinder block, and the installation of removable cylinder barrels.

The cylinder-head bolts must be slackened progressively in the opposite sequence to that shown in Fig. 9.6 and must be undone only when the head is cold, in order to avoid distortion of the head.

If the engine is rotated while the cylinder head is off, the friction between the piston rings and the cylinder barrels may lift the barrels and disturb their seals. This can be avoided by clamping the flanges of the barrels down, using short strips of metal, drilled to take a cylinder-head bolt and held in place by screwing the bolts into the cylinder block with suitable distance pieces between the heads of the bolts and the strips. Renault dealers use the

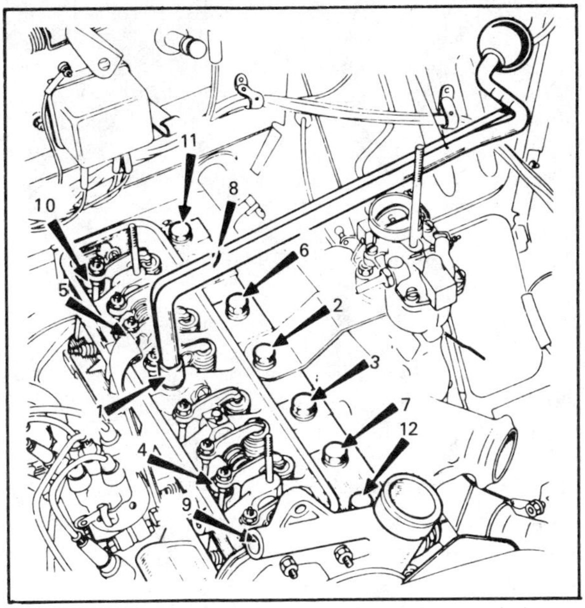

Fig. 9.6 The cylinder-head bolts should be tightened progressively in the sequence shown, to avoid distorting the head

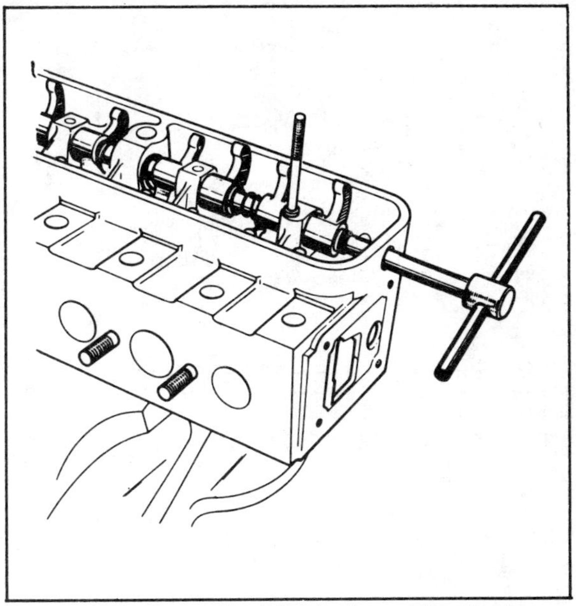
Fig. 9.7 Withdrawing a rocker shaft, using the special tool Mot. 31

more sophisticated liner clamp (Mot. 521) shown in Fig. 9.9.

Materials and Tools: see page 40.

1 Begin by disconnecting the battery, draining the cooling system (Chapter 10) and taking off the air filter.

2 Next disconnect the wires, cables and hoses from the carburettor, alternator, ignition distributor and the cylinder head.

3 Remove the drive belts as described in Chapter 10

4 Remove the ignition distributor (Chapter 12).

5 Disconnect the gearchange control bracket, and push the assembly towards the bulkhead. Also disconnect the choke cable, accelerator control, the fuel pipe from the carburettor and the exhaust clamp between the manifold and the silencer.

6 Take off the valve cover.

7 Slacken the cylinder-head bolts progressively in the order shown in Fig. 9.6 and remove them.

8 Lift the cylinder head, complete with the rocker gear, valve and springs. If it sticks, free it by rotating the engine with the sparking plugs still in place or tap it gently with a block of wood. Care must be taken not to disturb the cylinder barrels.

9 Withdraw the push-rods and place them on one side in the order in which they were removed. Each rod must be reassembled with its original tappet and rocker.

9.6 Dismantling the cylinder head

Materials and Tools: see page 40.

If you do not intend to carry out a top-overhaul – for example, if the only reason for removing the cylinder head is to renew a faulty cylinder-head gasket – the combustion chambers can be decarbonized without further dismantling, although it is better to remove the manifolds to allow the inlet and exhaust ports to be cleaned out. In any event, it is best to decarbonize the combustion chambers before removing the valves, to avoid the risk of damaging the valve seatings in the cylinder head.

During a top-overhaul, of course, it will be necessary to remove the valves for inspection and refacing of the valves and seatings, or renewal of any valves which are in too poor condition to justify refacing and refitting them. To dismantle the cylinder head –

1 Take off the inlet and exhaust manifolds if this has not been done previously. The carburettor can be left on the inlet manifold.

2 Remove the valves, as described in Section 9.8; but if the cylinder head is to be decarbonized, defer removing the valves until the combustion chambers have been cleaned (see below).

3 Remove the fan, pulley and the water pump and its plate.

4 Take off the cylinder-head end-plate.

5 It is not necessary to remove the rocker shafts and rockers unless these are worn and the rockers are a sloppy fit on the shaft. To withdraw the shafts, remove the rubber blanking plugs from the cylinder head and unscrew the end-plugs from the shafts. Take off the four spring clips and the two end springs and unscrew the two shaft retaining bolts from the pedestals. Each shaft can then be withdrawn by screwing the special tool Mot. 31 into the end of it, or by using a suitable length of threaded rod.

6 If the engine has covered a large mileage, the water

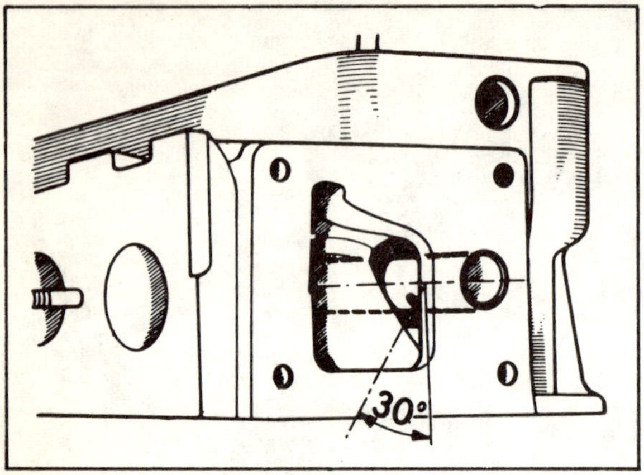

Fig. 9.8 The correct alignment of the water distribution tube in the cylinder head. The holes must point towards the exhaust valve seats, at an angle of 30° as shown

distribution tube in the cylinder head may be corroded and should be renewed. Tap it out, using a suitable length of rod or dowel. This calls for some care, as a corroded tube can be rather fragile and may collapse. The new tube must be inserted with the holes pointing downwards towards the exhaust valve seats at an angle of 30° as shown in Fig. 9.8. The end of the tube which has two holes which are close together should be at the plate end of the block. Peen the ends of the pipe outwards to retain it in place and prevent it rotating.

9.7 Decarbonizing the cylinder head

Materials and tools: see page 40.

1 Decarbonize the combustion-chamber faces before removing the valves, to avoid any risk of damaging the valve seatings. Scrape off every trace of carbon.

2 Thoroughly clean the cylinder-block and manifold mating faces of the head, taking particular care not to score them. Use Magnus Magstrip liquid to dissolve remnants of gasket.

9.8 Removing and cleaning the valves

The valve-spring caps are retained by split-cone collets and a valve-spring compressor is needed to remove them.

Fit a set of new valve springs (tired springs will undo most of the benefit that should be obtained from a top overhaul).

If you are fitting new valves or collets, make sure that the pattern of the ridges on the inside of the collets matches the grooves in the valve stem. There are several alternative arrangements of the grooves, and also the inlet and exhaust valve patterns may be different.

Materials and tools: see page 40.

1 Compress each valve spring with the spring-compressor until the spring cap is clear of the split collets. Remove these and release the spring.

2 Take off the valve-spring retainer, sleeve and spring. Draw the valve out of its guide.

3 Clean the undersides of the valve heads, the stems and also the ports in the heads which could not be reached when the valves were in position. Be careful not to score the faces of the valves and their seats in the combustion chambers. Wire-wool soap-pads quickly remove carbon.

4 Scrape the valve stems clean. Don't use emery cloth on the sections that work in the guides. Clean out the guides themselves by drawing a paraffin-soaked rag through them.

5 Check each valve for fit in its own guide. If there is any noticeable degree of sideways shake, take the head to your dealer for advice. If he confirms that the valves and guides are worn, allow him to renew the guides, to re-cut the seats in the head and to fit new valves.

9.9 Reseating the valves

If the seating faces on the exhaust valves are badly pitted, they can be trued-up by using a valve refacing tool (your garage should be able to do this for you).

Badly-pitted valve seatings in the cylinder head can be refaced with a special tool – normally this is also a job for your garage. If the pitting is only slight, however, the valves can be ground-in in the conventional manner, as described below.

The object of grinding-in the valves (or more correctly, lapping-in) is to obtain a gastight seal between each valve and its seating. The importance of making a really good job of valve-lapping cannot be over-emphasized, since not only the cylinder compressions but the service life of the valves depend on a first-class seal between the valves and their seatings.

Valve-grinding paste usually comes in a tin which contains two grades, fine and coarse. The coarse paste should be used only in an emergency, to remove pitting when proper reconditioning cannot be carried out, but light pitting may be removed with the fine paste, grinding being continued until a good matt finish has been obtained on the valve and seat.

Materials and tools: see page 40

1 Smear a little grinding-paste on the face of the valve and rotate the valve quickly and lightly on its seat with the suction-cup grinding tool, first in one direction and then in the other, by spinning the handle of the tool between the palms of the hands. From time to time, raise the valve from its seat and turn it through a quarter of a turn, before continuing the grinding. This will ensure that an even, concentric surface is obtained. A light coil spring, placed beneath the head of the valve, will make the job easier, as it will lift the valve whenever pressure on it is relaxed.

2 Check the progress of the grinding-in frequently. When correctly ground, both the valve seat in the cylinder head and the face of the valve should have an even, clean, grey matt finish with no signs of bright rings or

any evidence of pitting. Bright rings are caused by grinding with insufficient grinding paste, while 'tramlines' are usually the result of continuously grinding the valve on its seat without taking up a different position.

3 Check the effectiveness of the seal by making a series of pencil marks across the face of the valve with a soft lead pencil. Replace the valve and rotate it once through a quarter of a turn on its seat. Each pencil mark should be erased at the line of contact. If any of the lines are unbroken, either the valve or its seat is not truly circular and renewal or refacing of the valve or seat (or both) is required.

4 When grinding-in has been completed, wash the valves and seats with petrol or paraffin, making sure that all traces of grinding paste have been removed. Lubricate the valve stems with a little clean engine oil before refitting them and reassembling the new oil seals, springs and retainers. The most closely spaced coils of the valve springs must be nearest to the cylinder head.

9.10 Decarbonizing the pistons

Materials and Tools: see page 40.

1 Rotate the crankshaft until two of the pistons are at the tops of the cylinders. Clamps *must* be fitted to the cylinder barrels to prevent them being disturbed – see Section 9.5.

2 Stuff clean rags into the bores of the remaining cylinders and in the water-ways and other openings in the cylinder block.

3 Remove the carbon from the piston crowns with a suitable blunt scraper, taking care not to score the surfaces. Then burnish the crowns with a wire brush.

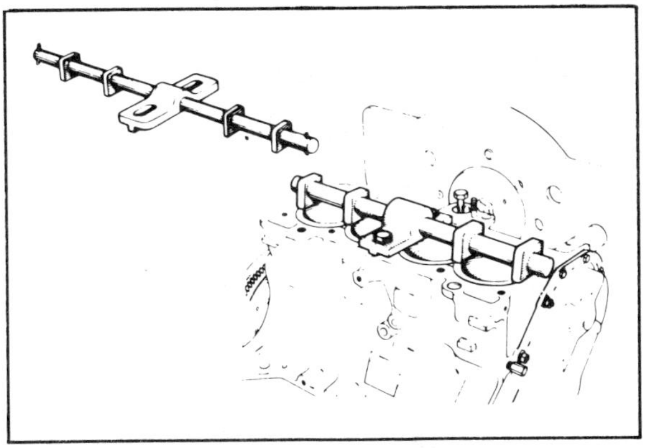

Fig. 9.9 The latest version of the Renault cylinder barrel clamp, Mot. 521

9.11 Refitting the cylinder head

Refitting the cylinder head is largely a reversal of the dismantling process, but the following points are very important –

The cylinder head and block must be scrupulously clean. Use a syringe or a length of plastic tube to blow any oil out of the cylinder-head bolt holes in the block. Oil at the bases of the holes will prevent the bolts being tightened down fully.

Check the cylinder head for signs of warping by placing a straightedge across the gasket face of the head in several different positions and measuring the gap, if any, between the head and the straightedge with a feeler gauge. The maximum permissible bow in the head is 0.05 mm (0.002 in.). If the head is distorted, a Renault dealer can probably grind it true, but the maximum amount of metal that can be removed is 0.15 mm (0.04 in.). If this will not remove the distortion a new head must be fitted.

The flanges of the cylinder barrels must protrude slightly above the block to provide the correct 'nip' between the barrels and the gasket when the head is tightened down. Renault dealers use a dial gauge mounted on a special block to check the protrusion, but a straightedge and a feeler gauge will do. Place the straightedge across each barrel in several positions and measure the gap between the underside of the rule and the top of the block. The correct protrusion is given in Section 9.13. If the protrusion is incorrect it can be adjusted by selecting the correct thickness of bottom seal as described in Section 9.13.

Materials and tools: see page 40.

1 Insert the front and rear push-rods in their original positions and turn the engine until the rods are as low as possible. Remove the liner clamps.

2 Place the gasket on the cylinder block, with the crimped edges towards the block or the word 'Top' upwards. Gasket cement should not be used.

3 Insert the remainder of the push-rods in their correct positions and lower the head on to the block, engaging the outer push-rods with their rockers and pushing the inner rockers aside if they foul the push-rods.

4 Screw in the cylinder-head retaining bolts finger-tight and then raise the rockers and position them over the push-rods, making sure that each rod seats correctly in the base of the adjusting screw.

5 Tighten the cylinder-head bolts progressively in the order shown in Fig. 9.6 to a torque of 45 lb ft (60 Nm). Then slacken each bolt a quarter of a turn and retighten it to the correct torque figure.

6 Adjust the valve rocker clearances as described in Section 9.3.

7 The remainder of reassembly is a reversal of dismantling. After 500 miles have been covered, unscrew each cylinder-head bolt a quarter of a turn and retighten the bolts in the correct sequence to the torque setting of 45 lb ft (60 Nm) if the engine is cold, or to 48 lb ft (65 Nm) if it is hot – that is, within 50 minutes after it has stopped. Re-check the valve clearances.

9.12 Removing the engine

The engine must be removed complete with the gearbox, the units being separated and refitted only with the engine out of the car.

Normally it is best to hire a Renault lifting bracket. It is also advisable to use a proper engine hoist.

If an improvised rope or wire sling must be used, make sure that this is sufficiently strong and check that it is fitted so that it cannot damage any auxiliaries.

Nylon-cord multiple-pulley hoists can be purchased from most accessory dealers and can handle the weight safely, but be sure that the beam to which the hoist is attached is strong enough. To provide a safety factor, it should be able to support the weight of at least three men at the centre. If a suitable beam is not available or if you are working in the open it will be necessary to buy or hire an engine lifting tripod or gantry or to make one from scaffold poles and clamps.

To remove the engine–

Materials: Any spares found to be necessary, including new roll pins for universal joints and new engine mounting rubbers. See also sections in Chapters 10, 13 and 14 mentioned in text.

Tools: Spanners. Sockets. Pliers. Screwdrivers. Pin-punches. Lifting bracket or sling. Jack. Axle stands. Engine lifting hoist. Gantry or tripod, if required. See also sections in Chapters 10, 13 and 14 mentioned in text.

1 Preliminary work includes disconnecting the battery, taking off the bonnet, draining the cooling system and putting protective covers over the wings.

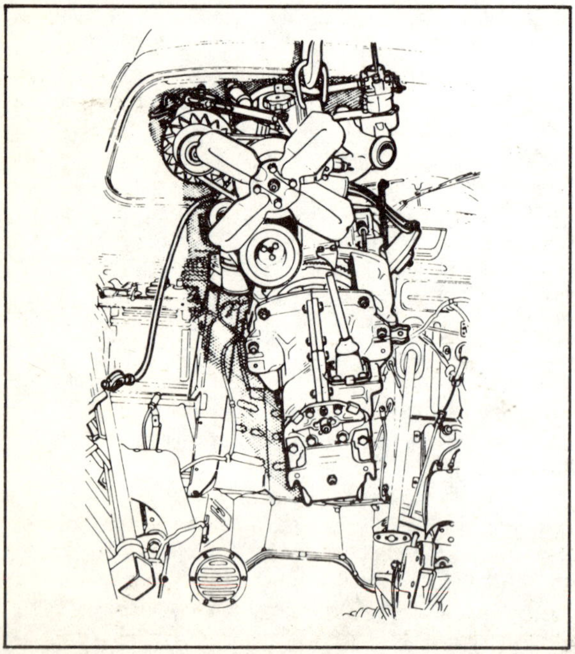

Fig. 9.10 Lifting out the combined engine and gearbox assembly

2 Remove the radiator tie-bars, unhook the gear-change lever return spring, remove the nuts which secure the gearchange rod mounting to the radiator and free the rod from the gearbox lever.

3 Disconnect the hoses between the radiator, the heater and the water pump.

4 Disconnect the steering arms at the rack and the steering shaft at the flexible coupling.

5 Remove the radiator and then take off the steering rack assembly.

6 Remove the exhaust pipe between the manifold and the silencer.

7 Remove the clutch idle lever, when fitted.

8 Take off the air cleaner.

9 Disconnect the following items: the starter motor lead, the accelerator and choke cable, the speedometer cable and the oil-pressure switch wire.

10 Disconnect the earthing strap between the body, the battery and the engine and the leads from the dynamo or alternator and the ignition coil.

11 Pull the fuel pump inlet pipe off the pump and plug the open ends of the pump union and the pipe.

12 Fit a lifting bracket to the cylinder-head bolts or place a sling around the engine.

13 Raise the front of the car and support it on axle stands. Take off the gearbox undertray and drain the gearbox.

14 Punch out the drive-shaft roll pins which retain the inner universal joints (this is not necessary with a type 354 gearbox) and fit retaining clips to the joints to prevent them coming apart – see Chapter 13.

15 Disconnect the upper suspension ball joints (see Chapter 14) and pull the drive shafts out of the gearbox.

16 Wedge the front wheels to limit their lock and to prevent the drive-shaft joints from being strained.

17 Take the weight of the engine on the hoist and remove the gearbox front mounting pad and the engine side mounting pads.

18 Lift the engine and gearbox assembly out of the car.

19 If necessary, separate the gearbox from the engine as described in Chapter 13 and remove the clutch from the flywheel.

Refitting the engine

Refitting the engine is a reversal of the removal sequence, but the following points should be noted:–

20 Lubricate the clutch shaft and sun-wheel splines with molybdenum disulphide grease.

21 Make sure that the roll-pin holes in the shafts and sun wheels are correctly lined-up and fit new roll pins. Seal the holes in the pins with a suitable sealant which can be obtained from a Renault dealer. Make sure that the correct shims are fitted beneath the steering rack – see Chapter 14.

22 The thermostat must be correctly positioned so that the bridge piece does not blank off the hole for the heater water circulation – see Chapter 10.

23 Don't forget to refill the engine and gearbox with oil and to fill the cooling system with new coolant as described in Chapter 10.

24 The clutch cable will require adjustment – see Chapter 13.

9.13 Changing the cylinder barrels, pistons and connecting-rod bearing shells

New cylinder barrels and pistons are supplied in a 'liner-piston' kit, the barrels, pistons, piston rings and gudgeon pins being in matched sets. Mark the parts in each box with the cylinder numbers 1 to 4 as soon as they have been unpacked, so that there is no risk of mixing them. The anti-rust coating should be wiped off with a solvent such as petrol just before use. Do not scrape the parts clean.

On earlier engines the cylinder barrels are fitted with copper seals, but from 20th December 1968 impregnated paper seals were used. This called for modification of the cylinder block, and the later blocks can be identified by the fact that the water drain plug is fitted on the manifold side instead of on the timing-cover side. Only the later type of block is available as a spare. The earlier type of barrels with copper seals can be fitted to the later block, but the new type of barrels with paper seals must not be installed in the earlier type of block.

The correct protrusion of the barrels above the cylinder block when copper seals are fitted should be 0.08–0.15 mm (0.003–0.006 in.). With impregnated paper seals, the liners should protrude by 0.04–0.12 mm (0.002–0.005 in.).

When fitting a liner with a copper seal, select a seal which is 0.9 mm (0.036 in.) thick. If necessary the protrusion can be altered by using a seal of a different thickness. The alternative sizes are 0.95 mm (0.038 in.), 1 mm (0.040 in.) and 1.05 mm (0.042 in.).

Impregnated paper seals are available in the following thicknesses: 0.07 mm (0.003 in.) – blue spot; 0.1 mm (0.004 in.) – red spot; 0.14 mm (0.005 in.) – green spot.

The gudgeon pins of earlier engines are a push-fit in the pistons and a sliding fit in the connecting-rod bushes. The pins are located by circlips fitted to grooves in the pistons. If the bushes in the connecting rods are worn – and this can be checked by trying a new pin in each bush – fitting new bushes is a job for a Renault dealer since they must be accurately reamed to size after they have been installed, using the special Renault tool set.

The later engines, beginning with the 1970 model (late 1969 onwards), have a different arrangement, the gudgeon pins being a press-fit in the connecting rod and turning freely in the piston. In this case removal of the pistons from the connecting rods and refitting them should be left to a Renault dealer as a special set of tools must be used in conjunction with an arbor press, and it is also necessary to heat the connecting rods to a temperature of 250°C (482°F) in an electric oven before fitting the pins.

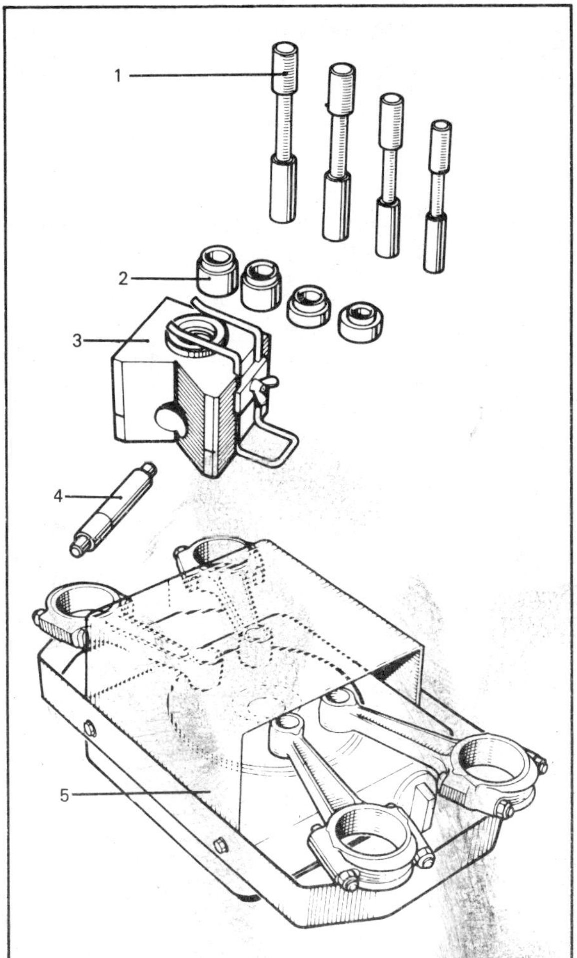

Fig. 9.11 Renault dealers use the tools and jigs shown to remove and replace the gudgeon pins on later models.
1 Assembly mandrels and guides
2 Piston thrust pads
3 Piston support base
4 Gudgeon-pin extracting mandrel
5 Electrical hot-plate

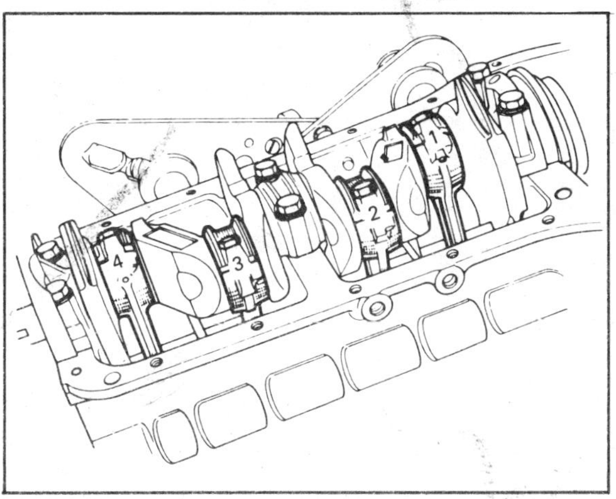

Fig. 9.12 Mark the connecting rods on the sides away from the camshaft, No. 1 being at the flywheel end of the engine

Materials: Any new parts required, including new cylinder-barrel seals of correct thickness and connecting-rod nut locking washers. Marking paint.
Tools: Spanners and sockets. Torque wrench. Hammer. Soft-faced mallet, Centre-punch. Straightedge. Feeler gauges. Cylinder-barrel clamps.

1 Drain the cooling system and the engine oil and remove the sump. The sump-retaining screws can be undone with the engine in the chassis, provided that you are equipped with slim spanners and nimble fingers (or *vice versa*!).

2 Take off the cylinder head and fit retainers to the cylinder barrels as described in Section 9.5. Wipe the big-end caps clean and if they are not numbered, number them with paint or centre-punch dots from 1 to 4, on the opposite side of the engine to the camshaft, No. 1 bearing being that nearest to the flywheel.

3 Unscrew the connecting-rod cap nuts and take off the caps and the lower bearing shells, keeping each shell with its cap unless new shells are to be fitted – which would normally be done as a matter of course during a partial overhaul.

4 Remove the cylinder barrel clamps and lift out the barrels, pistons and connecting rods as assemblies. If new parts are not being fitted, take particular care to keep all the assemblies together and in the correct order as removed from the engine.

5 If new piston and liner assemblies are being fitted to the later type of engine, let your Renault dealer fit the pistons to the connecting rods, if this has not already been done. He should check each rod for truth at the same time. With the earlier type of piston and connecting-rod assembly, the pistons must be immersed in boiling water before the gudgeon pins are pushed into position. To make sure that the pistons and rods are fitted the right way round, hold the piston with the hole in the skirt below the gudgeon pin towards you and turn the connecting rod so that the number on the big-end boss is on your left-hand side – see Fig. 9.13. Fit a circlip in the groove furthest away from you, press the pin into position and fit the second circlip. Make sure that each circlip is correctly located in its groove.

6 The piston-ring gaps must be spaced 120° apart. The gaps will be correct and the ends of the rings must not be filed.

7 Before reassembling, clean the gasket faces on the cylinder head and block. Also clean the locations for the cylinder barrels inside the block – *but do not scrape them clean with a sharp tool.*

8 Fit the correct thickness of seal, as determined earlier, to each cylinder barrel. Fit the upper halves of the shell bearings to the connecting rods and install the barrel assemblies in the crankcase. Fit the barrel clamps.

9 Lubricate the crankpins and pull the connecting rods down on to them. Fit the bearing shells in the big-end caps and install the caps, tightening the nuts to the correct torque (Chapter 17).

10 Rotate the crankshaft to make sure that the bearings are not binding.

9.14 Removing and refitting the crankshaft and main bearings

If the crankshaft is simply being removed and refitted during engine dismantling, and it is not intended to

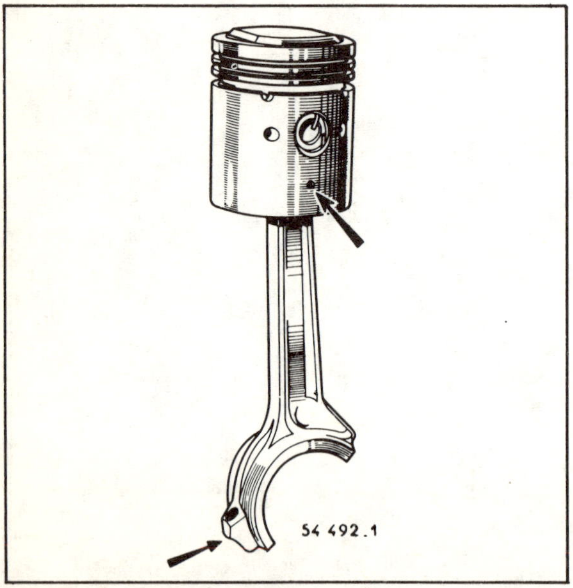

Fig. 9.13 When fitting a piston and connecting-rod assembly, the hole in the piston skirt must be towards you and the number on the connecting rod on your left-hand side

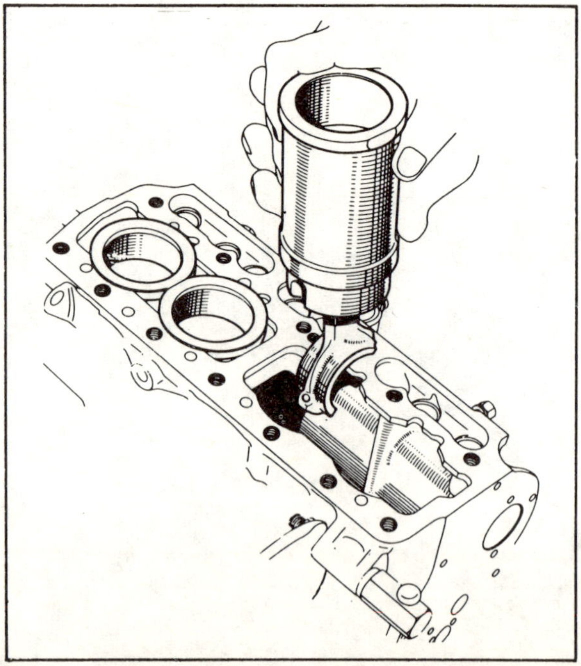

Fig. 9.14 Installing a connecting-rod, piston and cylinder-barrel assembly in the cylinder block

renew the main-bearing shells (although this would, of course, normally be done if the engine had covered more than 20 000–30 000 miles), check the crankshaft end-play before removing the bearing caps.

Insert a feeler gauge beside one of the thrust washers at the centre bearing and prise the crankshaft in each direction.

The maximum permissible movement is 0.05–0.25 mm (0.002–0.010 in.). This is controlled by thrust washers, which are available in 2, 2.05, 2.1 and 2.15 mm thicknesses. The correct end-float can be obtained by selecting the apropriate washers.

To remove and refit the crankshaft and bearings and to fit new bearing shells if necessary –

Materials: Any new parts required. Paraffin. Rags. Marking paint. Engine oil.

Tools: Spanners. Sockets. Torque wrench. Hammer. Soft-faced mallet. Centre-punch. Feeler gauges. Syringe.

1 Remove the flywheel by unscrewing the retaining bolts. *New locking plates should be used when reassembling.*

2 Number the bearing caps on the opposite side of the engine to the camshaft with paint or centre-punch dots if this has not already been done, starting at the flywheel end.

3 Undo and remove the bearing caps.

4 Having removed the retaining bolts from No. 1 cap, tap it upwards with a plastic-faced hammer.

5 Remove the oil seal from this bearing and the two side seals for the cap.

6 Lift out the crankshaft and take out the bearing shells from the crankcase. Also remove the thrust washers. If the bearings are to be re-used, it is important to keep each pair with its bearing cap so that they can be fitted in the original positions.

7 Make sure that the crankshaft oilways are clear by flushing them with paraffin from a syringe, followed by clean engine oil.

8 The bush in the end of the crankshaft, which locates the gearbox input shaft, should be renewed. It can be withdrawn by screwing a thread tap into it and pulling on the shank of the tap, or by partly filling the recess with grease, inserting a closely-fitting bar, or even a hard-wood dowel, and giving the end of the bar a sharp tap with a hammer. The hydraulic pressure will then eject the bush. When fitting the new bush, use a suitable tabular drift and be very careful to insert the bush squarely and not to burr the internal bore.

9 When reassembling, fit the upper sections of the bearing shells into the crankcase. These are the halves which have oil feed holes and grooves. The tags must locate in the cut-outs. Smear the thrust washers with grease to hold them in position and insert them. The sides which are faced with anti-friction metal must face the crankshaft webs.

10 Fit the bearing shells into the bearing cap, noting that only the centre cap has an oil hole. Lubricate the shells and fit the caps, screwing in the bolts only finger-tight at this stage.

11 All the cap bolts can now be tightened progressively to 45 lb ft (65 Nm, 6.5 kg m). When this has been done, check that the crankshaft still rotates freely and also that the end-play is correct.

9.15 The timing chain, tensioner and camshaft

The timing chain and tensioner cannot be renewed, or the camshaft withdrawn, without taking the engine out of the car and removing the cylinder head, sump and the timing cover. The distributor driving shaft will also have to be withdrawn before the camshaft can be removed.

Normally the timing chain and tensioner do not give trouble during the life of the engine between major overhauls, but if the engine is being stripped for a partial overhaul, it is a worthwhile precaution to renew the chain, the two sprockets and the tensioner.

On later models the chain tensioner automatically takes up the initial clearance and this type is interchangeable with the early tensioner described in item 4 below. Before removing the tensioner pull the shoe back and hold it in

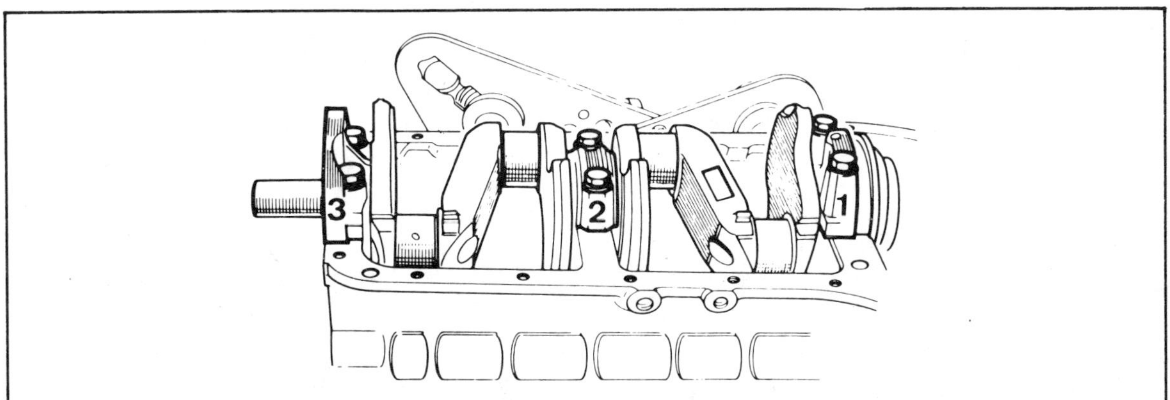

Fig. 9.15 The main bearing caps should be numbered as shown before they are removed

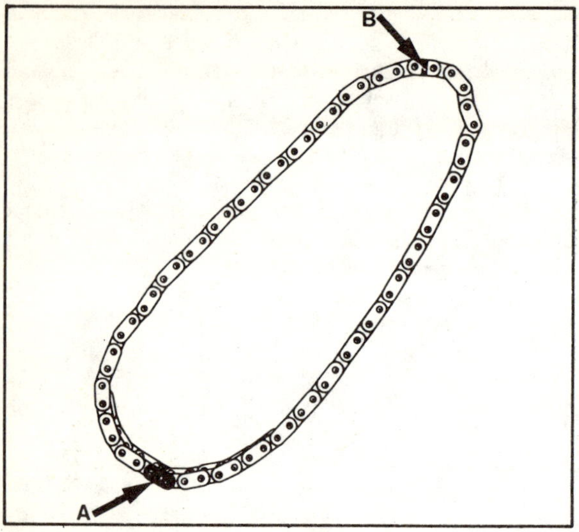

Fig. 9.16 To make it easier to time the engine, the chain has the two marks shown, as described in the text

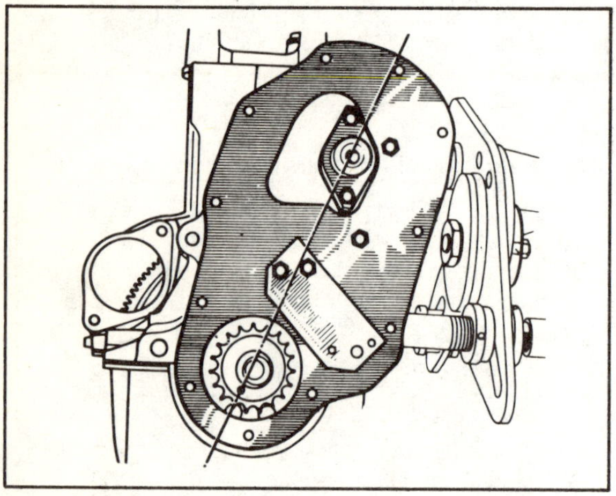

Fig. 9.17 Before refitting the crankshaft sprocket, line-up the timing dot with the centres of the camshaft and crankshaft

place by twisting a loop of wire round the shoe and the body of the tensioner. Then, to prevent involuntary take-up of the shoe, insert a keep, made from card or metal 2 mm thick between the body and the shoe. New tensioners are fitted with a plastic keep. After refitting the tensioner, pull out the keep, press the shoe in until the piston touches the bottom of the body, and then allow the shoe to move outwards towards the chain without assisting the spring action.

The end-float on the camshaft is controlled by the thickness of the thrust flange and cannot be adjusted. Check it by inserting a feeler gauge between the thrust plate and the front bearing journal. It should be between 0.05–0.25 mm (0.002–0.010 in.).

Materials: Any new parts required. Paraffin. Rags. Engine oil.

Tools: Spanners. Sockets. Torque wrench. Feeler gauges. Sprocket puller. Vice and distance pieces. Soft-faced hammer. Straightedge. 3 mm Allen key. Special tools B.Vi.28, B.Vi.48, T.Ar.65, B.Tr.02, if required (see items 6 and 8).

1 Remove the engine (Section 9.12) and the cylinder head (Section 9.5).

2 Remove the sump (the oil having been drained before engine removal).

3 Remove the distributor driving gear – see Section 9.16.

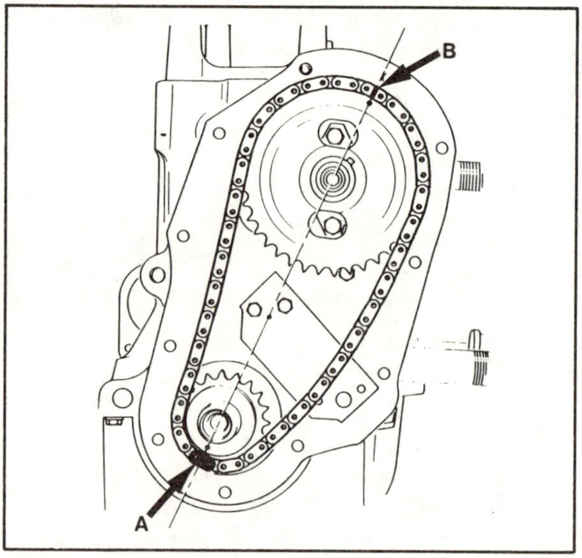

Fig. 9.18 When fitting the chain, make sure that the marked links A (yellow) and B (groove) are opposite the timing dots on the sprockets

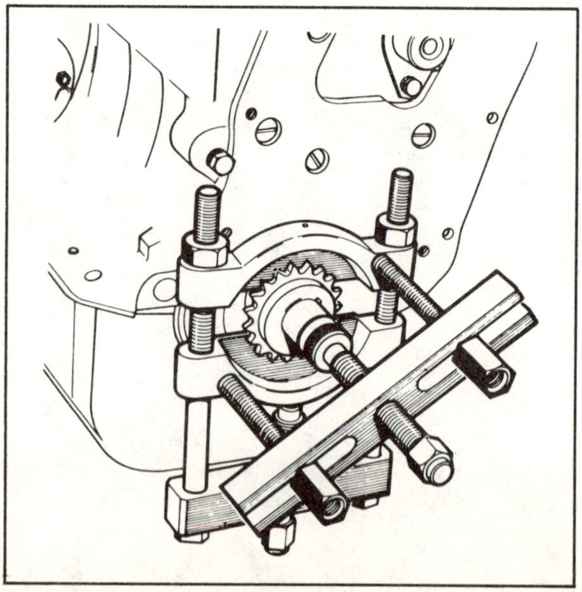

Fig. 9.19 Using the extractor T.Ar.65 and clamp bar B.Tr.02 to pull off the crankshaft sprocket

4 Remove the timing cover from the rear of the engine. With the earlier type of tensioner unscrew the bolt from the body. Insert a 3 mm hexagonal Allen key into the cylinder and turn the key clockwise until the tension of the pad on the chain has been released. Unscrew the two retaining bolts and take off the tensioner.

5 Remove the oil feed plate.

6 It is advisable to use a sprocket extractor (Special tools B.Vi.28 and B.Vi.48) to withdraw the camshaft sprocket, which is a tight fit on the end of the camshaft. If levers must be used, be very careful not to damage the sprocket or the engine plate.

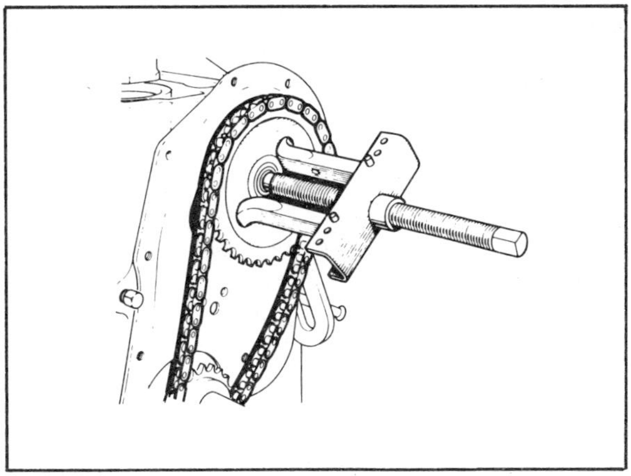

Fig. 9.20 An extractor should be used to pull off the camshaft sprocket. The Renault tools shown are the extractor B.Vi.28, fitted with jaws B.Vi.48

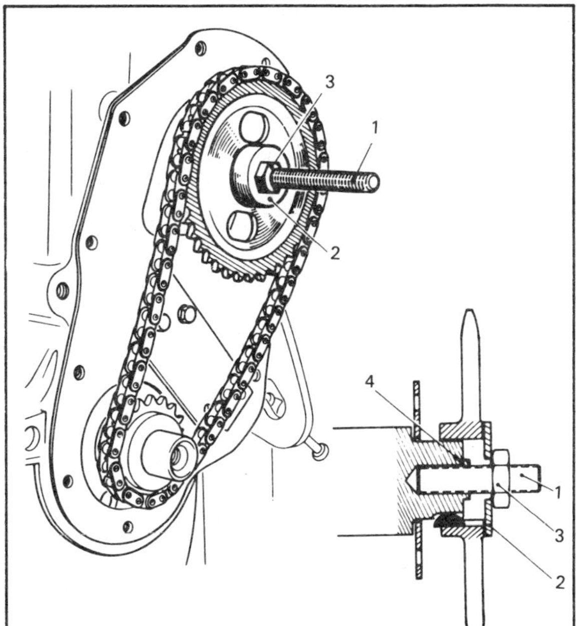

Fig. 9.21 A screwed length of rod 1, should be used with a washer 2, and a nut 3 to refit the camshaft sprocket. The hole in the washer must be large enough to clear the projection 4 on the camshaft

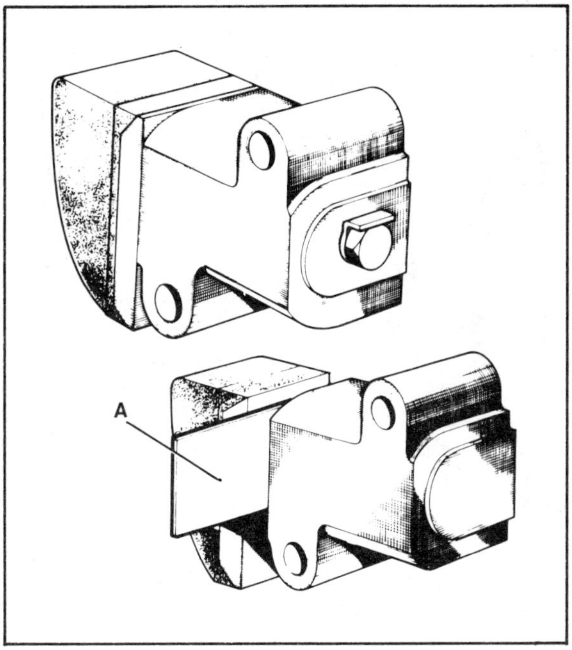

Fig. 9.22 Two types of chain tensioner. *Above,* the type which requires manual adjustment of the initial take-up. *Below,* the automatic take-up type fitted with a temporary 'keep', A

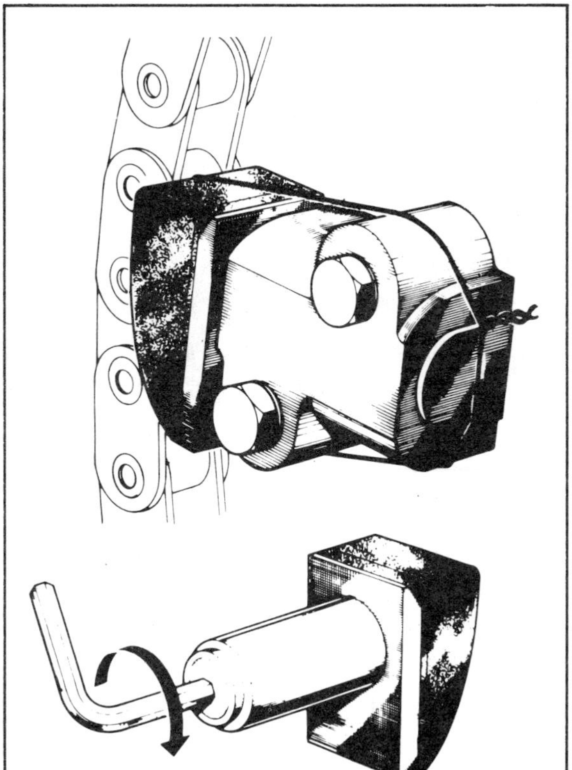

Fig. 9.23 An automatic initial take-up tensioner should be wired as shown before the chain is removed. Below is shown the method of locking the piston in the shoe

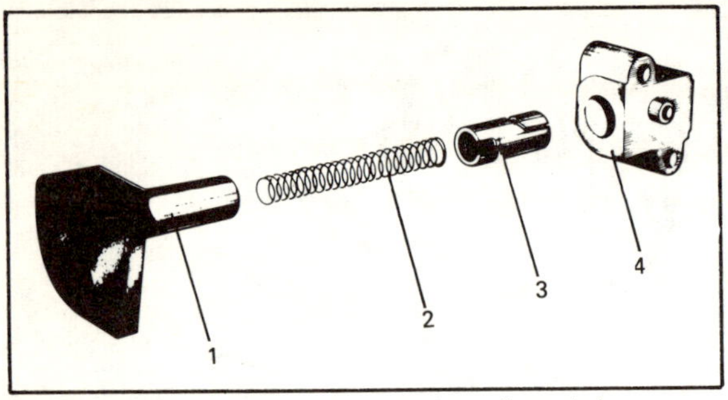

Fig. 9.24 The automatic initial take-up tensioner dismantled

7 Having removed the camshaft sprocket complete with the chain, take off the camshaft stop flange, unscrew the timing gear backplate screws and withdraw the backplate and the oil filter gauze for the tensioner. The camshaft can be pulled out if required.

8 An extractor should also be used to pull off the crankshaft pulley, the best tool to use being the Renault extractor T.Ar.65, with the clamp bar B.Tr. 02.

9 When reassembling, the official method of fitting the sprocket to the camshaft is to drill and thread a hole in the end of the camshaft so that a length of screwed stud, a nut and a washer can be used to draw the sprocket on to the shaft as shown in Fig. 9.21. The hole in the washer must be greater than the diameter of the ridge on the end of the camshaft so that the correct end-float will be obtained when the washer contacts the outer diameter of the nose of the shaft – this is also shown in Fig. 9.21. Drilling and tapping the hole in the shaft would normally be a job for your Renault dealer or a machine shop. An 8.5 mm diameter hole must be drilled to a depth of 20 mm and then tapped with a 10 mm by 150 mm thread.

10 The crankshaft sprocket can be fitted by heating it in boiling water and then tapping it into place, using a hammer and a tube or socket of a suitable diameter.

11 The timing dots on the sprockets must be aligned as shown in Fig. 9.17. To make sure of correct alignment there is a yellow link on the chain, A in Fig. 9.18, which must be fitted opposite the dot on the crankshaft sprocket and a saw-cut on the link B, which must be opposite the camshaft sprocket.

12 Having fitted the chain tensioner, insert a 3 mm Allen key in the cylinder and turn it clockwise until the tensioner pad assembly is in contact with the chain. Fit and lock the cylinder retaining bolt.

13 Fit the timing gear plate and the oil delivery plate and refit the timing cover, using a new gasket. Refit the camshaft pulley.

14 Fit the distributor driving shaft as described in Section 9.16.

9.16 Fitting the distributor driving shaft

Removal of the distributor driving shaft depends on the method used to retain the distributor itself. It may be possible to withdraw the shaft after removing the sleeve with its rubber seal without the use of special tools. When the distributor is secured by a bridge-piece which clamps against a flange on the distributor, the special tools Mot. 468 and Mot. 04–01 shown in Fig. 9.25 will be needed. The sequence of removing and refitting the sleeve is as follows–

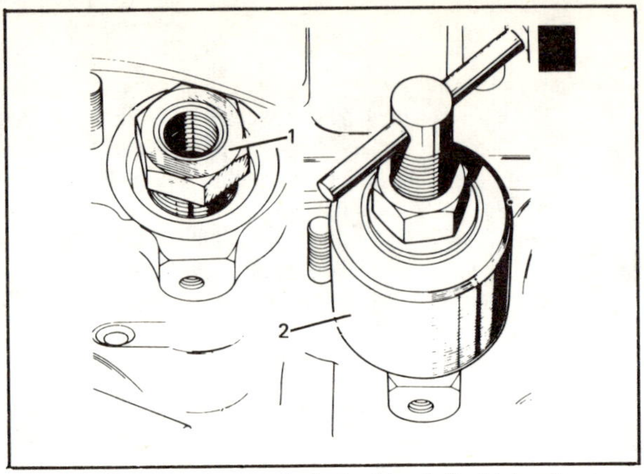

Fig. 9.25 When removing the distributor drive shaft retaining sleeve, screw the extractor from tool Mot. 468 (shown at 1) into the sleeve and use Mot. 04–01 (shown at 2) to withdraw the sleeve

1 Screw the extractor sleeve from Mot. 468 into the distributor sleeve.

2 Screw the screw from Mot. 04–01 into the extractor sleeve and draw out the sleeve by turning the screw. The distributor drive end fitting and the drive gear can then be withdrawn. The screw from Mot. 04–01 can be used to pull the drive gear out.

3 To refit the gear, first insert the drive gear and then fit the guide rod from Mot. 468 into it. Install the sleeve in the cylinder block with its chamfer towards the block and then fit the assembly mandrel from tool Mot. 468 on to the sleeve. Using a tube of suitable diameter on the mandrel and a hammer, tap the sleeve into position.

4 Remove the mandrel and the guide rod, screw the screw from Mot. 04–01 into the gear and raise and lower the gear to check that there is an end-float of 0.15–0.55 mm (0.006–0.022 in.) between the gear and the base of the sleeve.

5 With either type of assembly, fit the distributor drive end-fitting with the slot set at 60° to the centre line of the engine and with the largest offset towards the clutch.

9.17 The oil pump, pressure-relief valve and suction filter

The oil pump can be reached by raising the car and dropping the sump (Section 9.18). The pump cover, complete with the pick-up filter and the pressure-relief valve, can then be withdrawn.

Late in 1970, a modified oil pump was fitted in which the pressure-relief valve spring is retained by a screwed

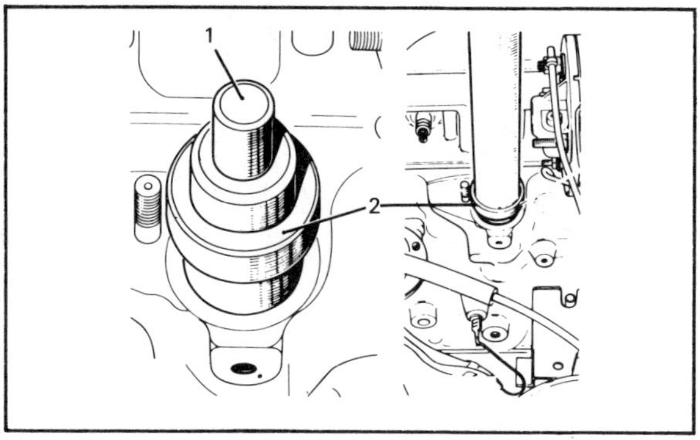

Fig. 9.26 Tools Mot. 04–01, shown at 1, and Mot. 468 being used to install the distributor drive shaft sleeve

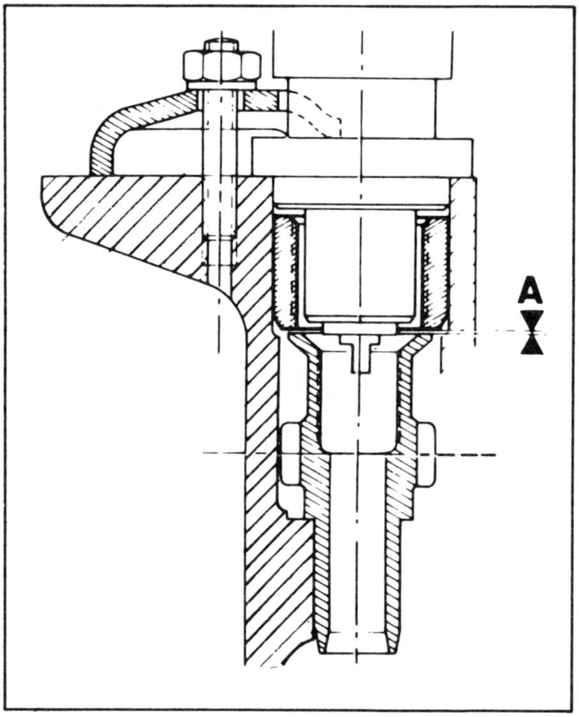

Fig. 9.27 The correct end-play between the distributor driving gear and the sleeve, shown at A, should be 0.15–0.55 mm (0.006–0.22 in.)

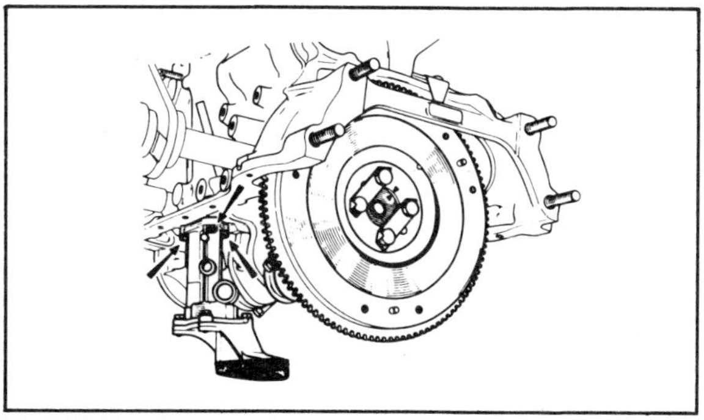

Fig. 9.28 The oil pump can be removed when the sump has been dropped. It is retained by the bolts shown

plug instead of by a blanking disc. The relief valve spring for this pump is 38.5 mm ($1\frac{17}{32}$ in.) long, instead of the 29 5 mm ($1\frac{5}{32}$ in.) spring used with a pressed-in plug. Only the modified pump body and spring are available as spares, but the longer spring may be fitted to the old pump body. If the screwed plug is not fitted with a locking washer, peen its flange over into the slot in the pump body.

After February 1972 the pump is located by a sleeve on the cylinder block and only this type is supplied as a replacement. Bolts 22 mm (about $\frac{7}{8}$ in.) long must be used with this pump.

Low oil pressure may be due to wear in the oil pump, in which case the most satisfactory course is to fit a replacement. Pressure will also be lost, however, due to general wear throughout the engine bearings, and a complete overhaul will then be needed to restore normal pressure.

Three other possible causes of low oil pressure must not be overlooked –

1 *A clogged suction filter.* This can be cleaned when the sump has been dropped.

2 *Leakage at the flange of the suction pipe where it is bolted to the pump cover.*

3 *A badly-seating pressure-relief valve.* The valve is dismantled as shown in Fig. 9.29. Clean the ball and its seating the cover. Do not stretch the spring. If you are doubtful about its condition, fit a new one.

9.18 Removing and refitting the sump

If the sump is to be removed with the engine in the car, it will first be necessary to drain the oil, raise and support the front of the car and remove the tubular cross-member from beneath the sump. The anti-roll bar bearing caps must also be taken off and the bar swung out of the way. Otherwise, the procedure for detaching and refitting the sump is quite straightforward.

Materials: Paraffin. Clean cloth. Soft bristle brush.

Tools: Jack. Axle stands. Spanners. Screwdriver. Sump-locating studs – see item 3.

1 Having carried out the preliminary dismantling described above if the engine is in the car, undo the sump retaining bolts progressively to avoid any risk of distorting the flange.

2 Clean the sludge out of the sump, using paraffin, a brush and clean cloth. Also clean the oil filter gauze with the brush but be careful not to damage the mesh. *Do not leave any threads or lint from the cloth in the sump or on the filter gauze.*

3 When refitting the sump, screw four locating studs (which can be made by cutting the heads off spare sump-retaining bolts and slotting the ends to take a screw-driver) into the cylinder block, one at each corner, fit the rear main bearing gasket, smear the ends with sealing compound and then fit the side gaskets with their ends overlapping the rear main bearing gasket.

4 The front main-bearing gasket must then be fitted with its ends resting on the side gasket, again using

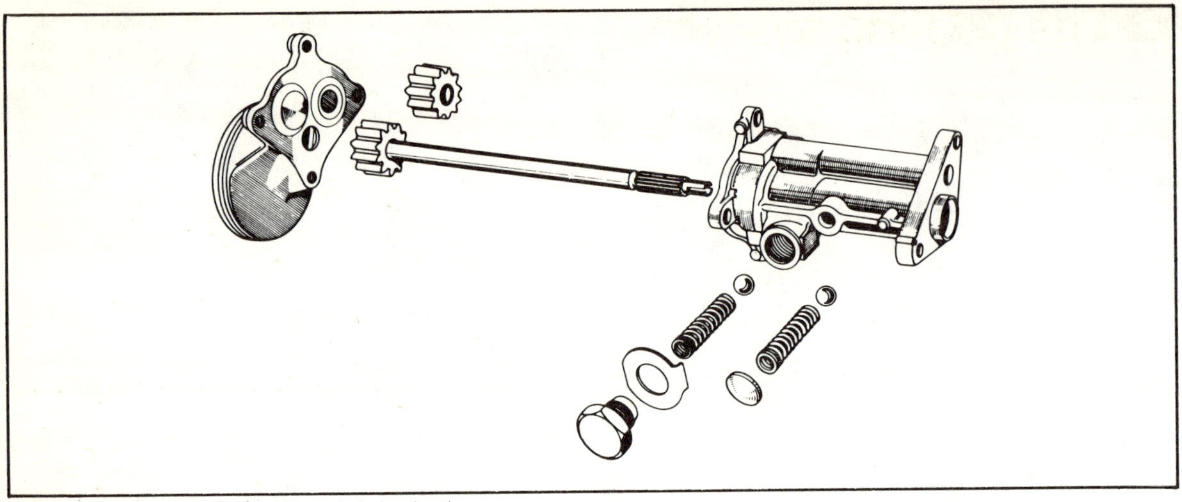

Fig. 9.29 The gear-type oil pump dismantled, showing the earlier type of relief valve, spring, ball and screwed plug on the left, and the later type of valve, which is retained by a disc, on the right

jointing compound on the overlapping sections.

5 Offer up the rear end of the sump so that its gasket location lines-up with the rear main bearing gasket and with the sump resting up against the floor panel if the engine is in the car.

6 Push up the front part of the sump so that it is parallel with the cylinder gasket face and then push it up squarely on to the locating studs.

7 Fit two of the retaining bolts, one on each side, and check by feeling with your fingers that the rear main bearing gasket is correctly positioned. Fit the remainder of the bolts finger-tight, unscrewing the locating studs and replacing them by bolts, and then tighten all the bolts evenly, being careful not to overtighten any of them, with the risk of distorting the sump flange.

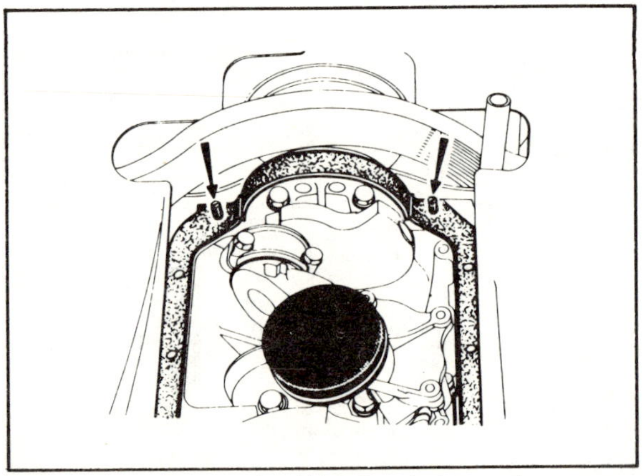

Fig. 9.30 Fitting the sump oil seal is made easier by screwing short guide studs (two of which are shown) into each end of the crankcase

10 The cooling system

A sealed, pressurized cooling system is used on all models. The coolant – a mixture of water, ethylene glycol and corrosion inhibitors – is drawn from the base of the radiator by a pump, circulated through the engine and returned to the top of the radiator. Smaller hoses feed coolant to the heater radiator when required, to the inlet manifold or the carburettor mounting flange to provide reasonably constant temperature for the carburettor and inlet passages, and also to the water-heated choke fitted to some carburettors.

The radiator has a simple filler plug and is kept full at all times. The coolant expands, of course, as it warms up and the surplus flows through an overflow pipe into an expansion bottle, fitted with a cap containing a valve which opens to relieve any excess pressure in the system.

As the engine cools down, fluid is drawn back through the overflow pipe to the radiator. At the same time the valve in the cap of the expansion bottle allows air to enter the bottle, preventing the creation of a semi-vacuum in the system.

The system normally requires no attention, other than checking the level in the expansion bottle, for about three years or until about 27 000 miles have been covered. By then, most of the corrosion inhibitor in the coolant will have become exhausted and it is necessary to drain the system, flush it out and refill it.

The time factor

Routine jobs such as topping-up, draining and flushing the system, checking for leaks, and so on, do not call for preplanning. Suggested times for other jobs are: Removing and refitting thermostat, 40 min; removing and refitting the radiator, 1 hr; fitting a new drive belt, 30 min; adjusting belt tension, 10–20 min; fitting a new water pump, 1 hr.

10.1 Topping-up the system

The coolant level in the expansion bottle (on the right-hand side of the engine compartment) should be checked when the system is cold. It should be between the two marks which are moulded on the side of the bottle.

If the cap needs to be removed when the engine is hot, place a cloth over it and unscrew it slowly. *Allow all steam or air pressure to escape before removing the cap.*

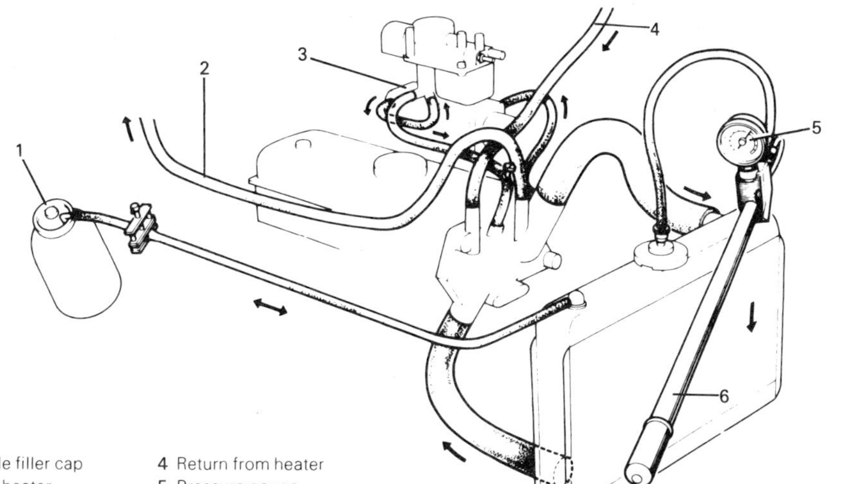

1 Expansion bottle filler cap
2 Feed to interior heater
3 Carburettor heating circuit (when fitted)
4 Return from heater
5 Pressure gauge
6 Hand pump

Fig. 10.1 The layout of the cooling system. A Renault dealer can check for leaks by using the special pump and pressure gauge shown.

If frequent topping-up is needed, check the system for leaks (see Section 10.2). Use the Renault coolant or the correct proportion of water and anti-freeze for topping-up (one-third of anti-freeze for temperate climates) to prevent the risk of weakening the anti-freezing solution (see also Section 10.3). Renault dealers can check the specific gravity of the system with a special hydrometer, to ensure that there is an adequate safety margin. If plain water has to be used in an emergency, drain the system as soon as possible afterwards and refill it with the correct coolant.

If the cap is very tight, it may be necessary to use a strap wrench to unscrew it. If you have purchased a wrench to unscrew the oil filter this will probably be quite suitable. Obviously, force must be applied carefully owing to the risk of breaking the glass bottle.

Whenever the radiator filler cap or the expansion bottle is removed or refitted, the rubber seal must be renewed. If the old seal is refitted coolant leakage will occur and the system may overheat, as indicated by the oil pressure/water-temperature warning light on the instrument panel being illuminated.

To top-up the bottle –

1 Unscrew the cap from the top of the expansion bottle, which is fitted on the right-hand side of the engine compartment.

2 Top-up the fluid to bring the level between the two marks.

3 Refit the cap to the bottle, run the engine until it reaches its normal temperature and check for leaks.

10.2 Checking for leaks

It is often difficult to trace the source of a small leak which necessitates frequent topping-up. Perished water hoses are likely culprits. Get the engine really hot and rev it up while carefully examining each hose. It is a good plan to renew the hoses and the expansion bottle valve every three years.

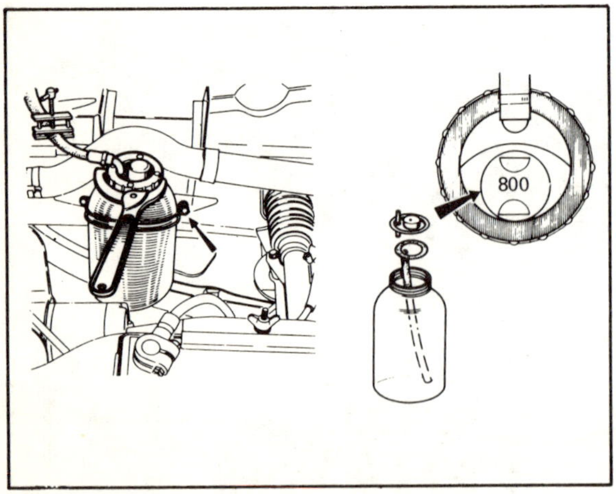

Fig. 10.2 *Left:* before removing the cap from the expansion bottle when the engine is hot, clamp the hose as shown. The arrow indicates the spring on the retainer for the bottle, which should not be fully compressed. *Right:* the filler cap and expansion valve

If you are really baffled, a Renault dealer will be able to check the system by using a combined pump and pressure gauge which is connected in place of the radiator filler cap as shown in Fig. 10.1.

Sometimes internal seepage occurs past the cylinder-head gasket. Tighten the cylinder-head nuts progressively, *using a torque wrench, to the torque quoted in Chapter 17.* If necessary, ask a garage to do this for you.

A preparation known as Bars Leaks, obtainable from garages and accessory shops, will usually cure internal seepages and external leaks very effectively. It is an inexpensive precaution to add it to the cooling water whenever the system is flushed-out and refilled.

10.3 Anti-freeze solution

When the car leaves the factory the anti-freeze mixture for use in temperate countries will provide protection against frost down to −35°C (−31°F). Vehicles exported to countries which experience very cold winters are protected down to −45°C (−49°F).

It is important to use a properly-inhibited anti-freeze to prevent any risk of corroding the aluminium cylinder head, or the aluminium radiator matrix which may be fitted to a later model. A Renault dealer can supply the correct type of inhibited glycol, but it would be better to use the ready-mixed Renault coolant, which is available in 2 litre (3½ pint) or 10 litre (2 gal) tins.

10.4 Draining and refilling the system

The system should be drained, flushed-out and refilled after about 27 000 miles or 3 years in service.

When filling the system it is particularly important to prevent any air-locks and the sequence described below should be followed. A bleed screw is provided, either in the carburettor hot-water feed pipe or on the right-hand side of the engine bulkhead beside the heater feed pipe.

The clamp shown in Fig. 10.2 is a Renault special tool, Mot. 453, but a similar clamp can be made from strips of steel, drilled at the ends to take screws and nuts. Alternatively, a G-clamp or a self-locking wrench can be used, provided that suitable packing is inserted to prevent the pipe being damaged.

Materials: Renault coolant or anti-freeze mixture.

Tools: Spanners. Hose clamp.

1 Set the interior heater control to 'Hot', remove the radiator filler plug and open the bleed screw referred to above. Remove the drain plugs from the base of the radiator and the side of the cylinder block. Loosen or remove the expansion bottle cap.

2 When the system has drained, flush it out as described in Section 10.5

3 Refit the drain plug and refill the system, following the sequence given below to prevent air-locks.

4 Fill the expansion bottle with new coolant until the

level reaches the upper level mark. Refit the filler cap.

5 Open the bleed screw described above (if it is not already open).

6 Refill the system through the radiator filler opening, pouring the coolant in very slowly.

7 Start the engine and continue to add coolant until it begins to flow from the bleed screw. Close the screw. Allow the engine to run until it reaches its normal running temperature and the thermostat has opened. This will be indicated by the upper radiator hose becoming noticeably warmer.

8 Switch off the engine, top-up the system and fit the radiator filler cap.

9 After the engine has cooled down, check that the level in the expansion bottle is correct and if necessary top it up.

10.5 Flushing the system

To flush the system, drain off the coolant as described in Section 10.4 when the engine is cold, insert a hose in the radiator filler and allow water to run through the system until clear water is flowing from the drain holes.

If the engine is hot when drained, *begin by using warm water* to avoid any risk of cracking or distorting the cylinder head or block.

After a fairly high mileage has been covered, normal flushing may not dislodge the sediment in the radiator, which must then be reverse-flushed by removing it, inverting it and connecting a hose to the outlet pipe so that a good flow of water under pressure can be forced through the matrix in the reverse direction to the normal flow. *Do not use a scale-removing compound before flushing.* It may corrode the aluminium components.

10.6 Renewing the expansion bottle valve

The valve at the top of the expansion bottle should not normally require servicing but if coolant should accidentally enter it at any time, it must be renewed. It is intended to pass only air.

If water is being lost and the hoses seem to be sound, have the valve checked by a Renault dealer. To do this he will connect a special test rig, consisting of a pressure gauge mounted on a hand pump, to an adaptor which screws into the radiator filler cap opening. The pressure in the system is pumped up to 0.9 bar (about 13 lb/sq in.) and then allowed to drop until it stabilizes at a reading on the gauge which should correspond with the pressure stamped on the valve, with a tolerance of 0.1 bar (about 2 lb per sq. in.) each way.

This pressure is expressed in millibars. If the valve is set to open at 800 millibars, for example, this is equivalent to 0.8 bar on the gauge.

As the expansion tank valve plays an important part in ensuring that the cooling system operates at its most efficient temperature, it is a good plan to change the valve as a precaution after two years in use, as described below –

Materials: New valve and gasket.
Tools: Strap-wrench, if cap is tight. Hose clamps – see Section 10.4

1 Clamp the hose leading from the radiator to the valve.

2 Unscrew the valve cap, remove the valve and fit the replacement, with a new gasket *between the valve and the bottle.*

3 Screw the cap down firmly and remove the hose clamp.

4 Fill the bottle up to the upper level mark.

5 If the bottle has been removed, when refitting it tighten the clamping bolt that retains one end of the clamp until the spring coils touch and then unscrew it by one turn.

10.7 Checking the thermostat

As explained earlier, the thermostat regulates the cooling-water temperature. It therefore has a vital effect on the engine efficiency and the fuel consumption. Thermostats, of course, are not infallible and if overheating occurs, or if the engine is slow to warm-up, it is logical to check this item; but remember that overheating can be caused by a number of other faults (see the chart in Chapter 5).

Many authorities recommend that the thermostat should be changed every two years, as corrosion, deposits of sludge or hard scale, or a distorted valve, can all cause sluggish action.

The thermostat is inserted in the outlet pipe of the pump housing. To remove and check it –

Materials: New thermostat, if required.
Tools: Screwdriver. Pliers. Pan of hot water. Thermometer (not essential).

Fig. 10.3 The thermostat must be fitted the correct way round, so that the water aperture 1 is not blocked. The bridge piece 2 must be between the ridge and the boss on the pump body as shown in Fig. 10.4

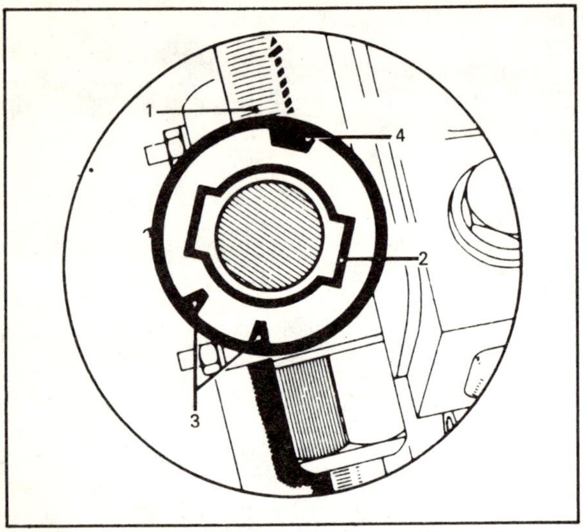

Fig. 10.4 Correct fitting of the thermostat – see Fig. 10.3. 1, water aperture. 2, bridge piece. 3, ridges. 4, boss. The ridges and boss are not fitted on later systems

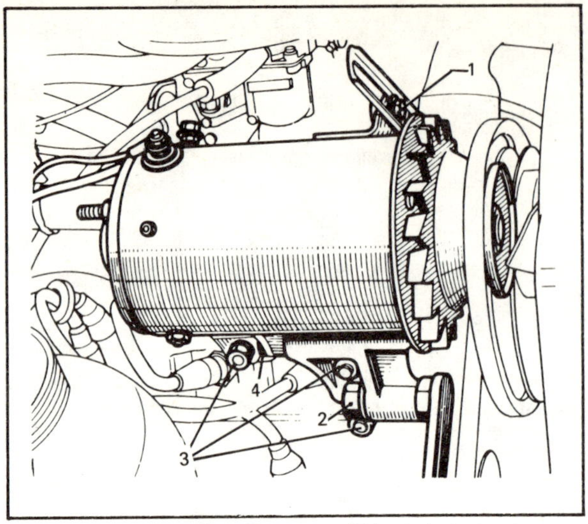

Fig. 10.5 To tension the fan and generator driving belt, slacken the bolt 1, and swing the generator outwards or inwards. To adjust the water pump belt, slacken the bolt 2 and move the tensioner as described in the text. Bolts 3 and 4 retain the tensioner assembly

1 Before disconnecting the hose and removing the thermostat, drain sufficient coolant to reduce the level to below the water pump.

2 When the thermostat is cold or warm, the valve should be closed. If it is open, discard the thermostat and fit a new one. If the valve is closed, suspend the thermostat in a pan of water which is nearly at boiling point. The valve should then open fully. If a suitable thermometer is available, the water can be heated while watching the operation of the thermostat. It should begin to open, and should be fully open, at the temperatures given in Chapter 17. Provided that a used thermostat is operating approximately within the range quoted it can be refitted.

3 When installing the thermostat, make sure that it is fitted so that the water aperture 1 in Fig. 10.3, is not blocked. On earlier engines the bridge piece 2, must be placed between the ridges 3, and the boss 4. On later engines these ridges and the boss were discontinued.

10.8 Adjusting tension of fan, water pump and generator driving belts

The correct tension of the driving belts is important. If a belt is too slack, it will slip, overheat, become glazed and will have a short life. Too tight a belt, on the other hand, will also have a short life and will place a heavy load on the bearings of the unit which the belt drives.

Because of the importance of the correct tension, Renault dealers use a special tool to measure it, consisting of a bar which has at its centre a sliding plunger calibrated in millimetres. When checking at home, depress each belt at the centre between the pulleys, using firm thumb pressure. Each belt should deflect by about ¼ in. at the centre of its longest run.

Tools: Spanners.

1 The belt that drives the generator can be adjusted in the conventional manner by slackening the bolt in the slotted strut above the alternator and the two pivot bolts, and swinging the generator towards or away from the the engine. If a lever is used to move the generator, apply it only at the pulley end.

2 To adjust the belt that drives the water pump, slacken the clamping bolt for the tensioner (beneath the generator) and swing the tensioner inwards or outwards. On 1969 and later models the nut has a left-hand thread.

3 When a diaphragm-spring clutch is fitted, the engine must be turned until two of the clutch cover securing bolts are spaced one on each side of the camshaft pulley, before the water pump driving belt can be removed.

10.9 Removing and refitting the water pump

If the water pump develops a leak or loses its efficiency (usually due to corrosion of the impeller and housing) a replacement pump should be fitted.

To remove and refit the pump –

Materials: New pump and new hoses, if required. New gasket.

Tools: Spanners or sockets. Pliers. Soft-faced hammer.

1 Disconnect the battery and drain the cooling system. Slacken the water pump and generator belts, remove the belts and tilt the generator back.

2 Remove the nuts which secure the gearchange control rod support and the radiator tie-rod.

3 Disconnect the hoses between the radiator and the water pump and the water pump and the heater.

4 Slacken the mounting bolts at the base of the radiator and tilt the radiator forward.

5 The water pump securing bolt can now be removed and the pump taken off by tapping it with a plastic-faced hammer or a block of wood.

6 When refitting the pump, clean the gasket faces and use a new gasket, which should be fitted without gasket cement.

10.10 Removing and refitting the radiator

A leak-stopping compound may be successful in curing a minor leakage from the radiator, but persisting leakage or damage to the radiator calls for repair by a radiator specialist – especially when an aluminium matrix is fitted. As an alternative to having the existing radiator repaired, it may be cheaper to fit a reconditioned component.

To remove and refit the radiator –

Materials: New radiator hoses. Mounting rubbers. Coolant (if the old coolant is not to be re-used). New roll pin for gear-control lever if four-speed gearbox is fitted.

Tools: Spanners or sockets. Hose clamps – see Section 10.4. Hammer. Punch for roll pin if four-speed gearbox is fitted.

1 Clamp the hoses close to the radiator and drain the radiator, or drain the complete system if fresh coolant is to be used. Disconnect the pipe leading to the expansion bottle.

2 Remove the nuts securing the gearchange control support and the radiator tie-bar and also the nut retaining the radiator side tie-bar.

3 When a four-speed synchromesh gearbox is fitted punch out the gear-control lever roll pin.

4 Remove the bottom bolts which retain the radiator and the steering rack assembly. Lift out the radiator.

5 When refitting the radiator, use a new roll pin for the gear-control lever if a four-speed gearbox is fitted. Refill the system as described in Section 10.4.

11 The carburettor and petrol pump

As will be seen from the specifications in Chapter 17, Renault 4 models may be fitted with Solex or Zenith carburettors. There are a number of differences between the various models. When ordering spare parts such as jets or gaskets, it is important to quote the type and specification numbers which are stamped on a tag fitted under one of the float-chamber cover screws.

The whole of the information given on the tag must be quoted in order to ensure that the correct replacements are supplied.

It does sometimes happen, however, that the tag from a Solex or Zenith carburettor is lost during dismantling and in such a case your dealer should be able to tell you the correct carburettor specification if you give him the vehicle type number and chassis number, and the engine type, model and number, taken from the data plates in the engine compartment.

The usual adjustments are provided on all carburettors for the idling speed and mixture strength. Other adjustments (depending on the model), which are normally needed only when the carburettor is being assembled, such as the float setting, fast-idle speed, initial throttle opening, acceleration pump stroke and the de-fuming control valve, can be adjusted, but special gauges and setting tools must be used.

These adjustments, therefore, should never be disturbed in service. The work is definitely a job for a Renault dealer. It must also be remembered that these adjustments – and the jet settings – are critical in maintaining the acceptable legal standard of exhaust emissions.

The time factor

It is difficult to allot definite times to many carburettor jobs, especially when adjustment and tuning are involved. If you are a perfectionist, for example, it is quite possible to spend a morning or an afternoon on carburettor servicing and road-testing. Some suggested times are: Remove and refit the carburettor, 30 min; service the carburettor, 1 hr; carburettor idling adjustments, 45–60 min; clean or change the air cleaner element, 30 min; clean the fuel pump filter, 15 min; remove and refit the fuel pump, 30–40 min.

Carburettor idling adjustments

All engines are very sensitive to correct adjustment of the idling speed and mixture strength. If an engine will not tick-over properly, or stalls in traffic or when the throttle is suddenly closed, the most likely cause is incorrect setting of the idling speed and mixture control screws.

You cannot expect to obtain good idling, of course, if the air cleaner is dirty or if there are ignition or mechanical faults, but provided that an engine is otherwise in good tune, setting the idling adjustments is a straightforward job.

First make sure, however, that the crankcase ventilation

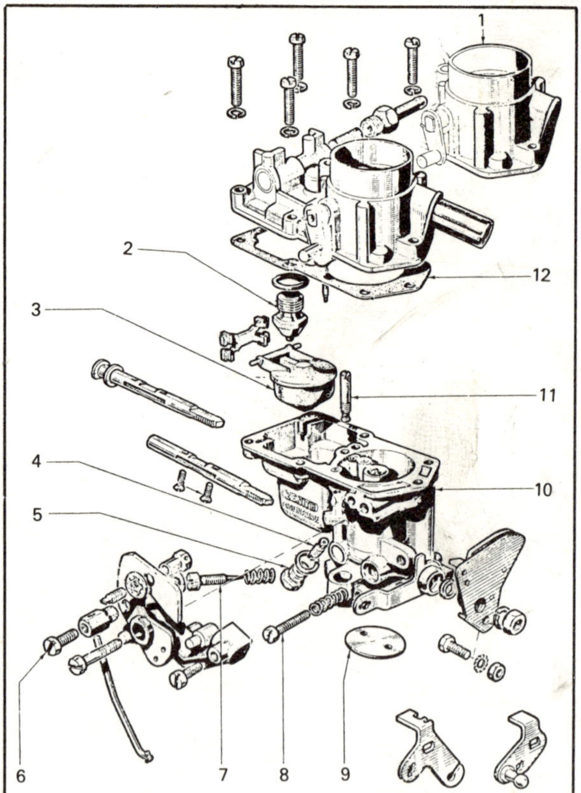

1 Top cover
2 Float needle valve
3 Float
4 Main jet
5 Main jet plug
6 Fast-idle rod locking screw
7 Volume-control screw
8 Idling speed adjusting screw
9 Throttle plate
10 Carburettor body
11 Idling jet
12 Gasket

Fig. 11.1 The Zenith 28 IF carburettor fully dismantled

system is not clogged and that the oil-filler cap is firmly in place on the valve cover; otherwise the idling mixture strength will be upset and it will not be possible to obtain good slow-running. Servicing the system is mentioned on page 50.

On all carburettors except the Solex EISA-4 types the idling speed is adjusted by a throttle-stop screw and the mixture strength by a mixture adjusting screw. On the Solex carburettor mentioned the idling speed is controlled by a screw which regulates the airflow within the carburettor.

A single mixture adjusting screw controls the mixture strength in all carburettors.

A flexible-stem screwdriver, obtainable from Renault dealers (part No. Mot. 561) makes it easier to reach the adjusting screws, but if this is not available the adjustments can be carried out with the air filter removed.

11.1 To adjust all types except the Solex EISA-4

1 With the engine at normal running temperature, turn the throttle-stop screw so that the engine will run fast enough to prevent stalling.

2 Screw the mixture adjusting screw in or out until the engine runs evenly. The throttle screw should be re-adjusted if the engine is running too fast, followed by further adjustment of the mixture screw. Repeat the operation until satisfactory idling is obtained. If the mixture is too rich, the engine will run with a rhythmic beat and the exhaust may show dark smoke. If it is too weak, the engine is likely to stall or spit-back when the throttle is suddenly opened and the exhaust will sound irregular and 'splashy'.

3 Screw in the fuel screw in order to weaken the mixture slightly, resulting in a drop in speed of about 20–25 rpm, in order to obtain a 'clean' exhaust.

Special notes

Don't try to obtain too slow a tick-over. The idling speed should be about 600–700 rpm. If the carburettor is adjusted to idle very slowly when the engine is hot, stalling may be experienced when it is cold. Check by depressing the clutch pedal. The idling speed should not drop excessively and the engine should not become 'lumpy'.

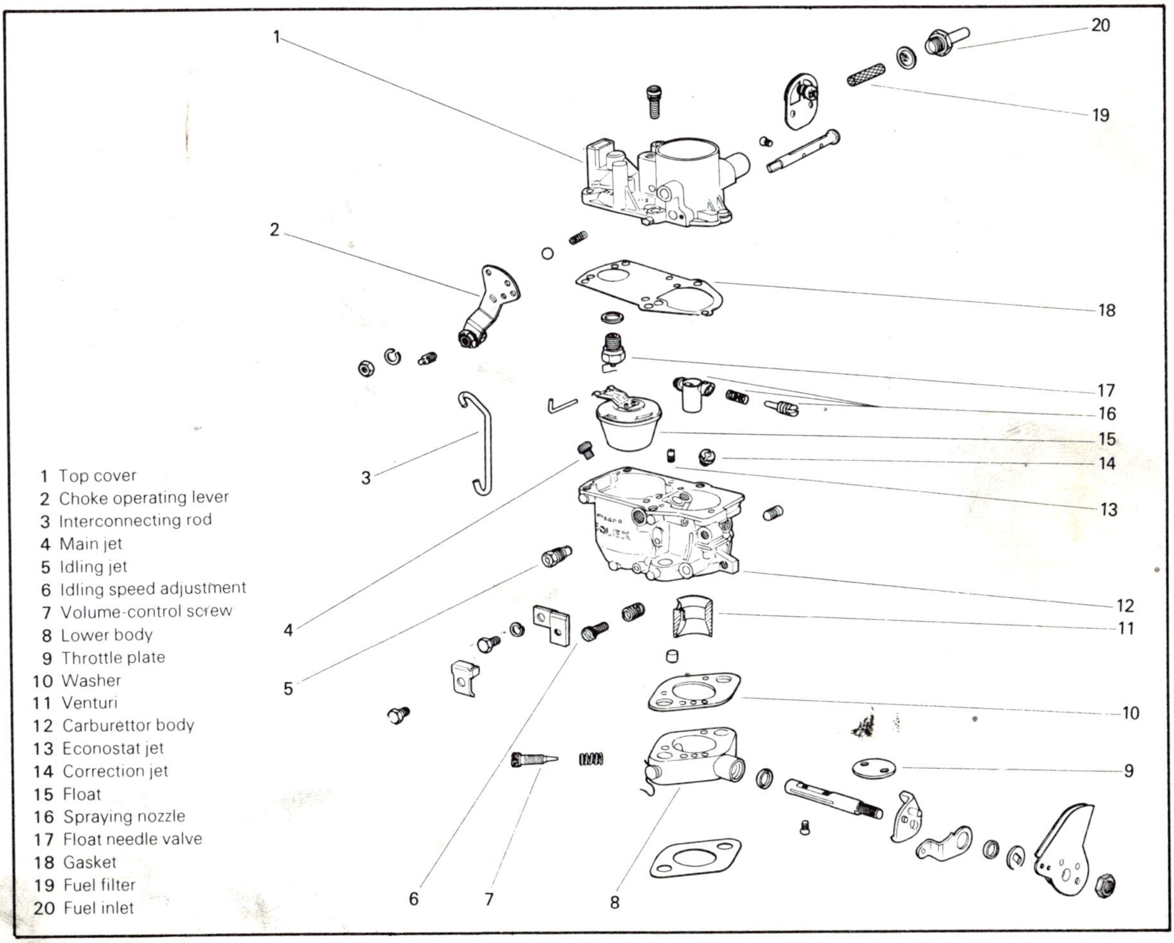

Fig. 11.2 The Solex 26 DIS-5 carburettor

11.2 To adjust the Solex EISA-4 carburettor

The principle of obtaining smooth, stable idling is exactly the same as with the other carburettors but the engine speed is regulated by the air screw. This and the mixture control screw are shown in Fig. 11.3. The other three adjusting screws, *which are preset at the factory, must not be altered in any circumstances.*

1 Adjusting the air screw to give an idling speed of about 750 rpm plus or minus 25 rpm.

2 Turn the mixture screw in either direction until the highest posssible idling speed is obtained and then re-adjust the speed with the air screw.

3 Repeat the adjustments once or twice to make sure that the mixture screw is giving the highest idling speed and then readjust the air screw to restore the correct idling speed.

4 When the settings have been stabilized in this way, finally screw in the mixture screw so that the engine speed drops slightly (by about 25 rpm of a rev counter is available) to reduce the exhaust pollution to an acceptable figure.

11.3 Cleaning the float chamber and jets

It should not be necessary to carry out a routine check of the carburettor, including cleaning the float chamber, jets and jet passages, at very frequent intervals, but it is worth doing this during the 12 000-mile service in order to forestall possible trouble. A certain amount of very fine sediment finds its way past the filters and this, together with globules of water, will accumulate in the float-chamber bowl, causing misfiring, poor idling or difficult starting, depending on which jets become clogged.

For routine servicing it is not necessary to remove the carburettor from the engine but before dismantling it, thoroughly clean the outside, so that there is no risk of transferring dirt and grit into the vulnerable interior passage.

Materials: Any new parts required. New gaskets and sealing washers.
Tools: Screwdriver. Pointed-nose pliers. Small spanners.

1 Remove the air cleaner.

2 Disconnect the choke link rod (fast-idle) when

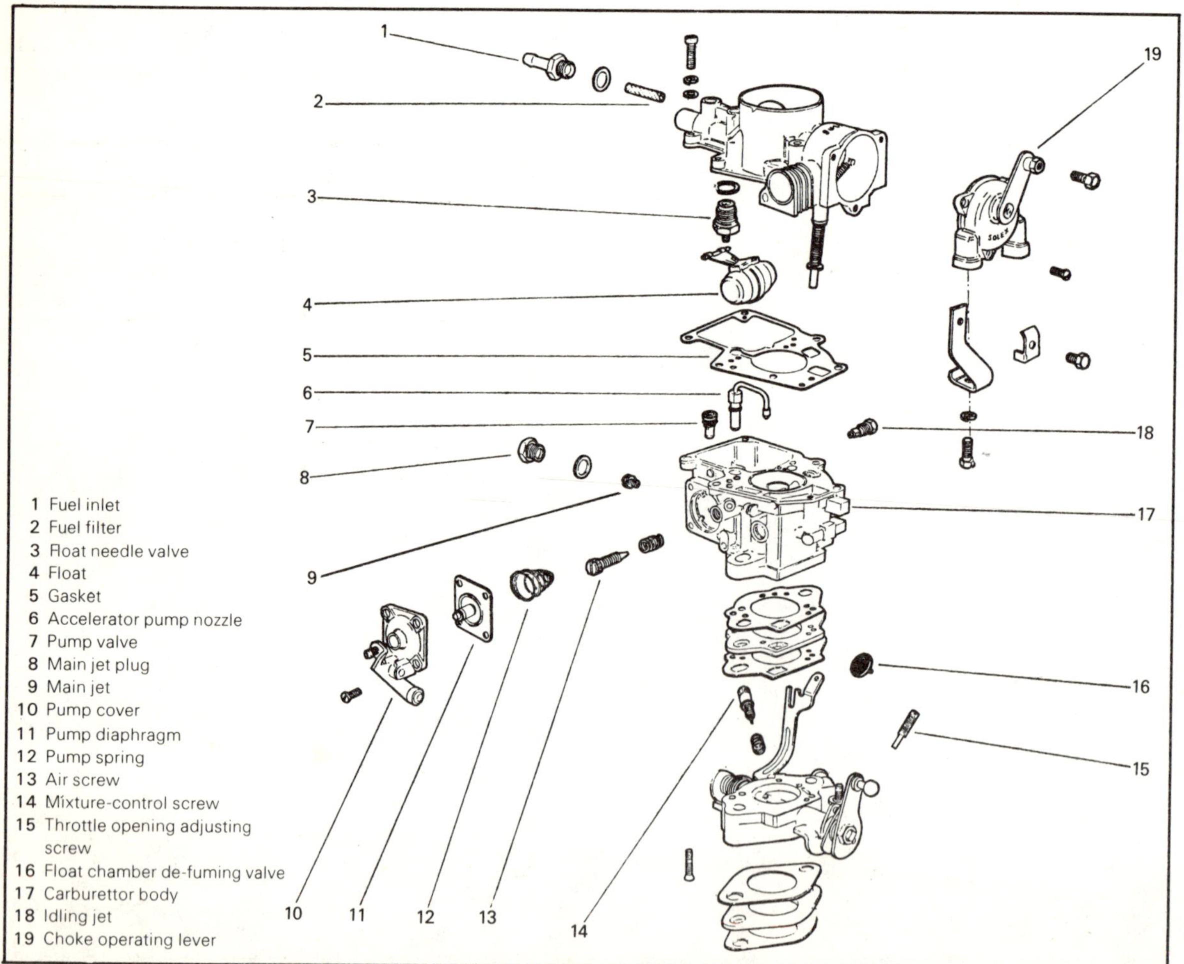

Fig. 11.3 The Solex EISA-4 carburettor

necessary *but be careful not to alter any adjustments.* When the upper end of the rod is clamped by a screw, mark the rod so that it can be refitted in the same position.

3 Remove the upper part of the carburettor body, taking care that the gasket is not torn. If there is any doubt about its condition, fit a new gasket.

4 Remove the float and the needle valve. Check for leakage of petrol into the float. Unscrew the needle valve body from the carburettor and swill it in petrol. Make sure that the tip of the valve is not ridged and that the valve slides freely in the body. If there is any doubt about the valve, fit a new assembly.

5 If a filter is fitted in the carburettor fuel inlet it is retained by the inlet union. Swill the filter in petrol and make sure that the mesh is not damaged.

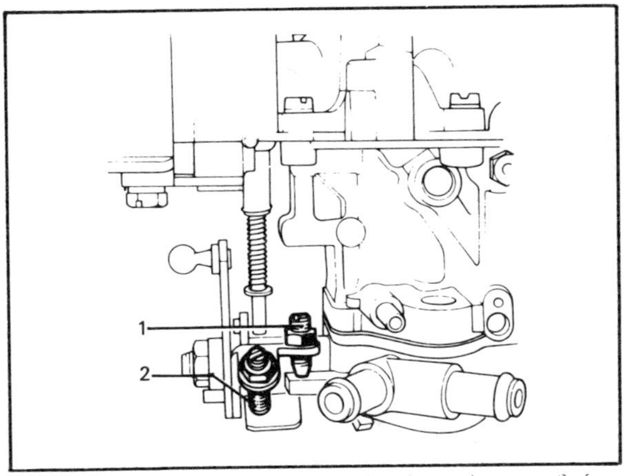

Fig. 11.4 The stop-screw 1, and the initial throttle opening screw 2 of a Solex EISA-4 carburettor must not be disturbed

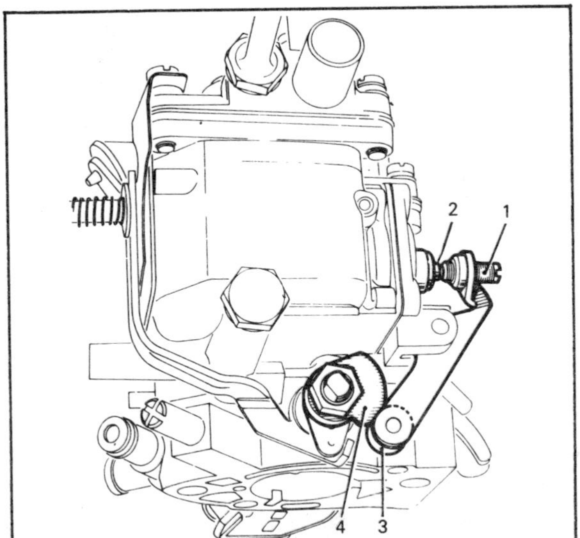

Fig. 11.5 The accelerator pump linkage on a Solex EISA-4 carburettor. The adjusting screw 1, which acts on the pump plunger 2, must not be altered. The cam 4 operates the pump lever through the roller 3

6 Wash out the float chamber with petrol, being careful to remove any sediment.

7 Remove the jets. These are clearly shown in the illustrations.

8 Wash the jets in petrol, blow through them in the reverse direction to the normal petrol flow to make sure that the drillings are clear and flush-out the jet passages with petrol. *Do not probe the jets with wire* – this will damage the carefully calibrated drillings and upset engine performance.

Special notes

Do not dismantle the carburettor further than just described. The linkage that controls the accelerator pump stroke and the fast-idling speed when the choke is in use, must be accurately adjusted. As was emphasized earlier, this is definitely a job for a Renault dealer or a carburettor specialist. If the adjustments have not been tampered with, they cannot alter of their own accord.

When hot-water hoses are connected to the carburettor flange, clamp the hoses as close as possible to the carburettor before disconnecting them, if the carburettor is to be removed for servicing. This will avoid the necessity for bleeding and topping-up the system as described in Chapter 10 when the carburettor has been refitted. It will still be necessary, however, to check that there is no air lock in the choke housing or in the return hose.

The carburettor air filter

If the filter element is allowed to become clogged, performance will suffer and fuel consumption will be increased,

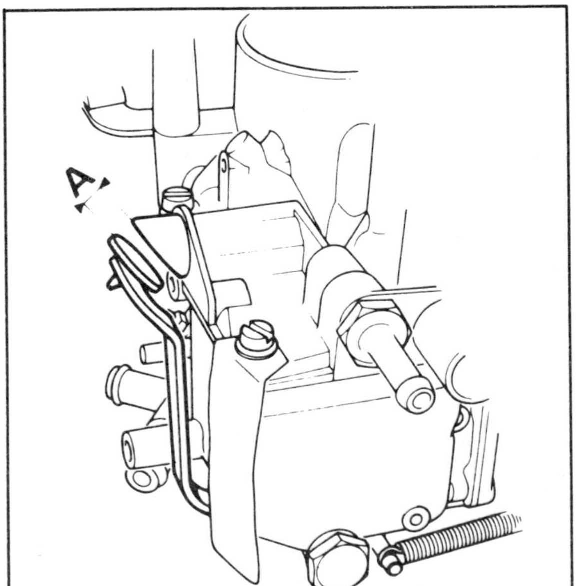

Fig. 11.6 Another adjustment on the Solex EISA-4 which should not be altered unnecessarily. The de-fuming valve opening A is pre-set and should be 3–4 mm (1/8 – 5/32 in.)

owing to the restriction on the air entering the carburettor. The filter should be serviced at 12 000-mile intervals or more frequently in very dusty conditions.

Set the air entry pipe towards the front, close to the exhaust pipe during the winter months (air temperature below 10°C (50°F)) and towards the rear in warmer weather. This improves the engine flexibility and the fuel consumption in cold weather and helps to prevent the carburettor icing-up. On some engines an adjustable flap allows warm air to be drawn from near the exhaust manifold in cold weather. The lever should be in the 'Winter' position marked on the filter cover when the air temperature is below 10°C (50°F) and should be moved towards the 'Summer' position during the summer months.

11.4 Changing the air filter element

Materials: New paper-element filter.

1 Remove the cover from the cleaner and lift out the pleated-paper element.

2 Clean the inside of the housing thoroughly.

3 Do not attempt to clean the element – fit a new one.

The accelerator cable

A spring-compensated fork is fitted to the pedal-end of the cable, as shown in Fig. 11.7.

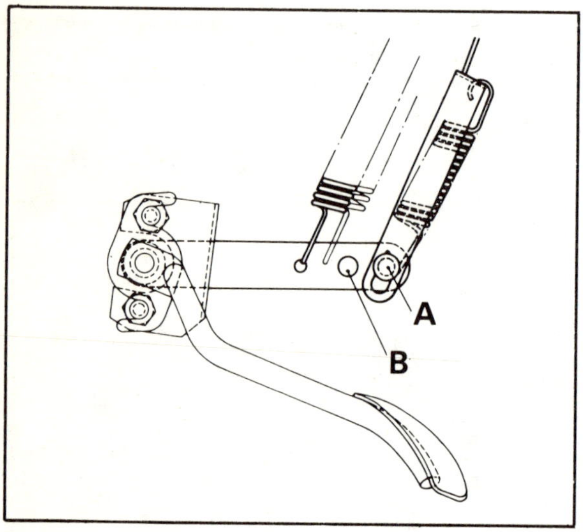

Fig. 11.7 The throttle cable connection at the accelerator end of the cable. Hole A should be used when the carburettor throttle has 82° of movement and hole B when the throttle moves through 52½°

The outer hole A, must be used when a Solex or Zenith carburettor is fitted in which the carburettor throttle plate rotates through nearly a right-angle (82°, to be exact), and in the inner hole B, with a Zenith carburettor in which the throttle turns through a smaller arc (52½°), so make a note of which hole is used before disconnecting the cable.

When fitting a new cable, adjust it as follows–

1 Make sure that the idling speed is correctly adjusted, that the choke control is pushed fully home, and that the cam is resting on the idling speed adjusting screw.

2 With the accelerator pedal raised, tension the cable moderately by tightening the cable adjustment.

3 Press the pedal down and check that when it is 5 mm (about 1/5 in.) from the floor, the carburettor throttle butterfly is fully open. Then fully depress the pedal and check that the additional travel is taken up by the compensator so that the carburettor throttle is not strained.

The petrol pump

Provided that the filter is cleaned at regular intervals as described below, the mechanically-operated petrol pump should seldom give trouble.

If the pump does not deliver petrol to the carburettor, make sure there is fuel in the tank (the petrol gauge may be faulty) and check that the unions in the pipe connecting the tank to the pump are tight. Also see that the pump filter is clean, that the gasket is in good condition, and that the clamping screw is firmly tightened. An air leak at the gasket is the most frequent cause of pump failure.

If, after extended service, an early type of pump begins to give trouble, it is not advisable to attempt to repair it without special equipment. The most satisfactory course is to take advantage of the service-exchange scheme operated by Renault dealers, under which a reconditioned pump can be fitted at quite a modest cost. The later type of pump cannot be repaired.

A Renault dealer will be able to test the pressure developed by the pump and the rate of fuel flow, with the aid of a special test kit; and this is most important, as too low a pressure can cause fuel starvation at high speeds, and possibly serious damage to the valves and pistons, while too high a pressure is likely to result in excessive petrol consumption and carburettor flooding.

11.5 Cleaning the petrol pump filter

Tools: Spanner. Old toothbrush or paintbrush. Clean cloth.

1 Disconnect the tank-to-pump fuel feed pipe at the union on the pump and clamp or plug the end of the pipe to prevent fuel draining from the tank.

2 Unscrew the setscrew that retains the filter cover and remove the cover.

3 Remove the filter and clean it with petrol, using an old toothbrush or a paintbrush and taking care not to damage the mesh. Mop out any sediment which has accumulated in the base of the filter chamber.

4 Make sure that the gasket beneath the filter cover is in good condition. An air leak here can put the pump out of action.

5 Check the tightness of the bolts that retain the pump on the crankcase and the condition of the fuel hoses and clips.

12 The ignition system

Given conscientious maintenance, there is no reason why the ignition system should prove troublesome – yet it shares with the carburettor the doubtful distinction of being responsible for a large percentage of roadside breakdowns, starting problems, loss of power and heavy fuel consumption.

Most of these faults can usually be blamed on inefficient servicing and when an emission-control carburettor is fitted, incorrect ignition timing can also cause persistent trouble with engine flat-spots and stalling. Where strict emission regulations are in force the wrong settings may put the car outside the legal limits for exhaust-gas pollution.

When we recommend that some of the checks and adjustments on later cars should be done by a Renault dealer, therefore, we have all these considerations very much in mind. Fortunately, the average owner should be able to carry out most of the work described in this chapter.

The time factor

None of the jobs described in the following sections is very time-consuming. For example: Cleaning and gapping the sparking plugs, 30 min; cleaning and lubricating the distributor, 25 min ;removing the distributor contacts, refitting and adjusting the gap, 40–50 min; removing and refitting the distributor, 30 min; checking and adjusting the ignition timing, 20 min.

12.1 Cleaning and adjusting the sparking plugs

The correct type of plug is given in Chapter 17. Plugs which have similar characteristics are available from other sparking-plug manufacturers, *but it is essential to make sure that the correct 'heat' grade is used.* Fit new plugs after 10 000 miles in service – it will pay dividends in better performance and improved fuel consumption.

The use of a garage plug-cleaner is the only really effective method of removing carbon and other deposits from the internal surfaces and insulators of the plugs.

When removing and refitting the plugs be careful not to cross-thread them. Repairing damaged threads in an aluminium cylinder head can be expensive, although a Renault dealer or an engineering shop should be able to salvage the head by fitting a special thread insert.

To avoid the risk of accidental 'shorts', disconnect the battery before starting work.

Bearing these points in mind, remove and clean the plugs as follows –

Tools: Sparking-plug spanner (a universally-jointed type helps when some of the plugs are awkward to reach). Wire brush. Gap gauge and file.

1 Pull off the connectors – don't pull on the wires themselves – and unscrew the plugs. Keep the spanner square to avoid cracking the external insulators. Neglected plugs can be very tight.

2 Clean the points with a wire brush. If the internal insulators are dirty, or the plugs have been in service for more than 6000 miles (10 000 km) have them cleaned by a garage.

3 Open the gap by bending the *side* electrode only and file the sparking surfaces square to each other with clean, sharp edges. This will reduce the voltage needed to produce a good spark.

4 Set the gap between the points to 0.025 in. (0.6 mm), using an inexpensive gauge and setting tool such as the Champion plug-servicing tool sold by accessory shops, which also includes an electrode file. Bend the *side* electrode only.

5 Clean the threaded portion of each plug with a stiff brush and smear a trace of graphite grease on the threads.

6 Blow or wipe any dust or grit out of the plug recesses in the cylinder head. Make sure that the sealing washers are in good condition and seated properly on the plugs, and screw the plugs home by turning the plug spanner *without using the tommy-bar.*

Use the tommy bar only for the final half-turn to ensure a gas-tight joint. Over-tightening is unnecessary and is likely to lead to trouble. If the plugs cannot be screwed in easily by hand, ask your garage to clean-up the threads in the cylinder head with a plug-thread tap.

12.2 The ignition coil and high-tension leads

The coil requires little or no attention, apart from keeping it clean – particularly the moulded cap – and making sure that the connections are clean and tight. An internal fault in the coil will show up on an electronic test set. Otherwise, the only practicable test is to substitute, temporarily, a coil that is known to be in good condition.

Test the high-tension leads between the coil and the distributor and between the distributor cap and the sparking plugs for surface cracks by doubling the cables between the fingers. Renew them if necessary. The modern resistance type of lead should be changed, as a precaution, after two years. Never try to fit new terminals to the leads. A complete pre-assembled set must be used.

12.3 The ignition capacitor

An inefficient capacitor or condenser will cause rapid burning of the contact-breaker points and a weak spark or – if it should short-circuit internally – failure of the plugs to fire at all. The capacitor is attached to the side of the distributor.

Test by substituting a new capacitor for the doubtful one, but first check for a break or short-circuit in the flexible lead that connects it to the contact-breaker terminal post – a cause of misfiring or complete cutting-out of the ignition that is often overlooked. As an insurance against future trouble, fit a new capacitor whenever the contact-breaker points are renewed. It is not an expensive item.

12.4 Lubricating the ignition distributor

Over-lubrication should be avoided. If grease or oil is thrown on to the contact points, it will be carbonized and cause misfiring.

Materials: Engine oil. Grease.

1 Remove the distributor cap and pull the rotor off the end of the shaft. Remove the circular plate (when fitted) from a Ducellier distributor, exposing the contact-breaker mechanism.

2 On a Ducellier distributor apply two drops of engine oil to the lubricating pad in the top of the distributor shaft and smear just a trace of grease on the lobes of the cam. On an SEV-Marchal type, grease the cam lubricator.

3 Drip a few drops of oil through the hole in the contact-breaker baseplate, to lubricate the centrifugal advance mechanism.

4 Replace the plate on a Ducellier distributor. Push the rotor on to the end of the shaft, making sure that the driving lug engages with the slot in the shaft and that the rotor is pushed down as far as possible.

12.5 Cleaning the distributor cap and rotor

1 Lightly scrape the contact strip on the rotor and the terminals inside the cap to expose bright metal. *Do not file them or rub them down with emery paper.*

2 Check the carbon contact inside the distributor cap. Do not over-stretch the spring.

3 Examine the rotor for signs of 'tracking' in the form of dark tracks on the surface of the plastic. If this has occurred, or if the tip of the terminal is badly burnt, fit a new rotor.

4 Wipe the interior of the cap with a cloth moistened with methylated spirits (denatured alcohol) to remove dust or oily deposits, which will provide a leakage path for the high-tension current. A cracked cap or condensed moisture on the inside or outside of the cap is a common cause of difficult starting and misfiring. An occasional spray with a water-repelling aerosol will cure and prevent condensation troubles.

12.6 Testing the distributor cap and rotor

1 Detach two alternate sparking-plug leads, and the distributor-end of of the coil high-tension lead, from the cap. Insert the end of the coil lead into each of the empty sockets in turn. Leave the remaining leads in place and connected to sparking plugs.

2 Switch on the ignition, make sure that the contact-breaker points are closed, and with the tip of a screwdriver flick the points apart. If there has been any tracking, a spark will jump across the interior of the distributor cap.

The rotor can be checked for breakdown of the insulation as follows, without removing it from the cam spindle –

1 Remove the coil high-tension lead from the distributor cap.

2 Hold the end almost in contact with the edge of the

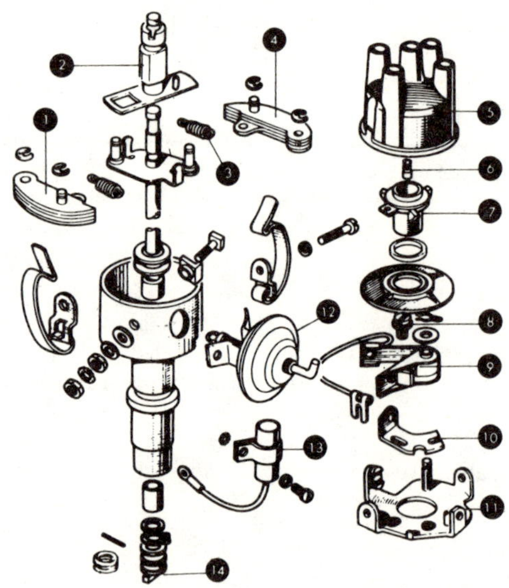

1 Centrifugal timing weight
2 Cam
3 Spring for centrifugal weight
4 Timing weight
5 Distributor cap
6 Carbon contact
7 Rotor
8 Screw retaining fixed contact plate
9 Rocker arm carrying moving contact
10 Plate carrying fixed contact
11 Contact baseplate
12 Vacuum-operated timing control
13 Capacitor (condenser)
14 Driving dog

Fig. 12.1 A typical ignition distributor fully dismantled

rotor blade and flick the contact-breaker points open as before. If the rotor is faulty a spark will jump the air gap between the high-tension lead and the rotor blade Occasionally, internal leakage develops from the underside of the electrode of the rotor, through the plastic to the interior surface, allowing the high-tension current to jump to the cam spindle and so to earth. This can be a very elusive fault to spot but will be revealed by the above test. Fit a new rotor whenever you fit new sparking plugs and you should have no trouble.

12.7 Checking the automatic timing controls

The timing of the spark varies under running conditions. It must occur earlier as the engine speed increases but must be retarded, to prevent detonation or 'pinking', when the engine is under load.

A centrifugal control which responds to engine speed, takes the form of two small weights below the contact-breaker baseplate in the distributor. Provided that it receives regular lubrication, the centrifugal timing control seldom gives trouble.

If a spring should break, it is essential to renew both springs, making sure that they are of the correct part number for the engine. Their strength determines the shape of the advance curve, giving the correct amount of advance for any speed. As recommended in Section 12.11, renewal of the springs and checking the advance curve must be left to a Renault dealer.

A vacuum-operated control is fitted to some distributors in addition to the centrifugal control (but not to UK versions). The circular housing seen in Fig. 12.1 contains a diaphragm and is connected by a pipe to a point in the carburettor, so that the diaphragm is influenced by the fluctuating partial vacuum in the induction system when the engine is running.

The action of the vacuum control either adds to, or opposes, the action of the centrifugal control, ensuring the most effective timing under all conditions of load and speed.

To check the vacuum control –

1 Make sure that the suction chamber does not contain any condensed fuel. Test the action of the diaphragm by applying suction to the union. If the diaphragm appears to be faulty, fit a new unit.

2 Check the rubber connections at each end of the vacuum pipe and renew them if they have split or are a loose fit on the pipe. Even a slight air leak will affect the action of the control.

12.8 Checking, removing and refitting the contact-breaker points

It is not necessary to remove the distributor from the engine in order to check the points.

Materials: Replacement contact-breaker set. Clean cloth. Petrol. Engine oil. Grease.
Tools: Screwdriver. Pliers.

To inspect or renew the points –

1 Remove the distributor cap by springing the clips aside and pull off the rotor arm. Gentle leverage may be used if the rotor is tight. Remove the circular plate, when fitted.

2 Lever the pivoted contact away from the fixed one. The points should have a clean, frosted appearance.

3 If the contacts are blackened, dirty or pitted, renew them. Slacken the nut on the terminal on the side of the distributor to free the fixed end of the contact-breaker spring (which is slotted to allow it to be disengaged easily), pull off the spring clip that retains the contact-breaker arm and remove the arm.

4 Remove the screw that retains the fixed contact plate and take out the plate.

5 Before fitting a new contact set, clean the contact points with petrol. Lubricate the cam with a light smear of grease.

6 Adjust the contact-breaker gap as described in Section 12.9 and check the ignition timing as described in Section 12.12.

12.9 Adjusting the contact-breaker gap

The contact-breaker gap should not be measured with a feeler gauge unless the contact faces have been trued-up to remove the pip and crater, or a new set of contacts has been installed.

When new contacts have been fitted, check the gap after they have run for about 500 miles, to allow for the initial bedding-down of the heel of the rocker arm.
Tools: Screwdriver. Feeler gauge.

To adjust the points –

1 With the distributor cap and rotor arm removed – and also the circular plate, when fitted – turn the engine until the contact-breaker points are fully open, with the fibre heel of the rocker resting on one of the crests of the cam.

2 Slacken the screw that retains the fixed contact

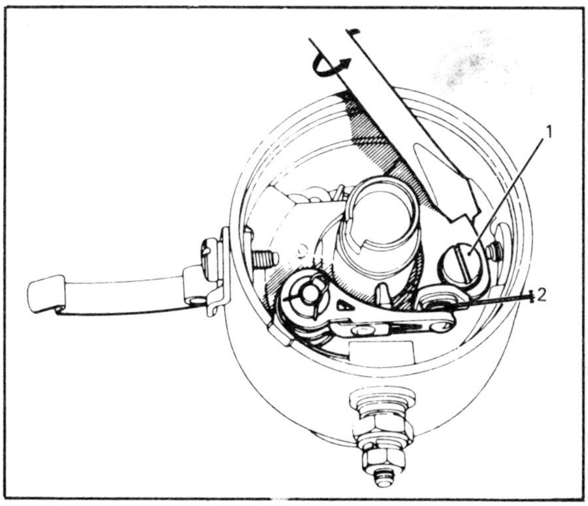

Fig. 12.2 Adjusting the contact-breaker points. Slacken the screw 1 and use a screwdriver to move the contact plate to give the correct gap at 2

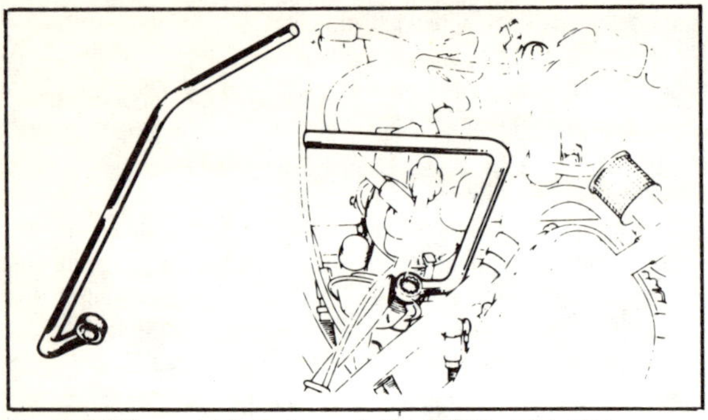

Fig. 12.3 This special Renault wrench (Ele. 556) is useful when slackening and tightening the distributor clamping bolt

plate and move the plate, either by using the adjusting tab or by inserting the tip of a screwdriver in the notch at one end of the plate and twisting it. Set the gap so that a 0.016 in. (0.4 mm) feeler gauge is a light drag fit between the points.

3 After the securing screw has been tightened, re-check the gap and then measure the gap with the rocker on each of the other three crests of the cam in turn. If there is any marked difference in the gaps, the cam or the spindle bearing, or both, are worn. If the bearing is worn a new distributor body will be required and it would be better to fit a new distributor – see Section 12.11.

4 Check the ignition timing as described in Section 12.12. Any alteration of the contact-breaker gap will alter the timing.

12.10 Removing and refitting the distributor

Tools: Spanners.

1 Remove the distributor cap.

2 Disconnect the vacuum advance pipe from the distributor.

3 Disconnect the low-tension lead from the terminal on the side of the distributor.

4 Remove the nut securing the clamp plate or the setscrew and lock-nut from the shaft housing below the distributor (depending on which method is used to retain it), and remove the distributor.

5 When refitting the distributor refer to Section 12.12.

12.11 Dismantling and reassembling the distributor

Whenever a distributor is stripped and rebuilt, it must be checked to make sure that the vacuum-operated automatic advance control, when fitted and also the centrifugal control, are operating correctly. This is particularly important in the case of emission-controlled engines.

With a Ducellier distributor, if the adjustment of the toothed segment to which the vacuum timing control (when fitted) is attached is disturbed, the timing of the engine under running conditions will be upset and the segment will have to be readjusted by a Renault dealer, using special test equipment.

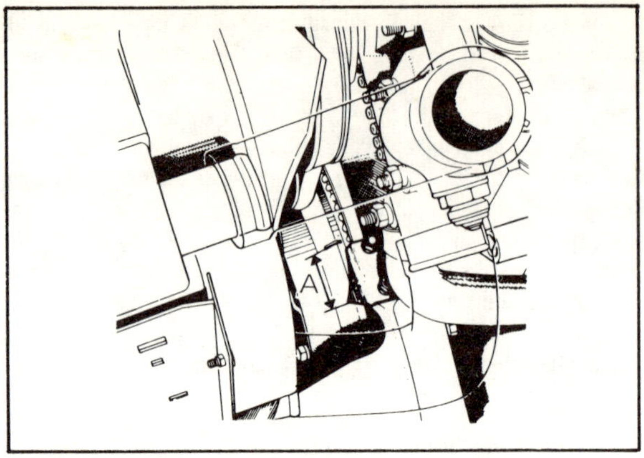

Fig. 12.4 The ignition timing pointer and the mark on the flywheel, A. The timing is set either at the top-dead-centre mark as shown in Fig. 12.5 or a specified distance ahead of this mark, as shown in Fig. 12.6

The action of the various controls can be checked only by using a distributor test-bench, which means either that the checks will have to be done by a dealer or by an auto-electrician. It may be more economical, therefore, to fit a service-exchange distributor, and this must be done if the shaft and bushes are worn.

12.12 Checking and adjusting the ignition timing

We have already emphasized the importance of correct ignition timing, especially when an emission-control carburettor is fitted.

The distributor shaft is driven by an offset dog at its lower end which engages with the diving dog at the top of a shaft in the cylinder block, driven by a skew gear from the camshaft. The basic timing cannot be lost, therefore, unless the engine has been dismantled or the shaft in the cylinder block has been removed for some other reason.

To refit the distributor, slide it into position, turn the rotor until the drive is felt to engage, and push it fully home.

Fit the clamp or the locking bolt and tighten the nut or the bolt just sufficiently to allow the distributor to be rotated by hand in order to adjust the timing.

The correct timing is then obtained by rotating the distributor body through a few degrees in either direction. The timing marks are clearly shown in Fig. 12.4 and the correct settings for the various engines are listed in Chapter 17.

Methods of turning the engine are described on page 16. An easy way to set the timing 10 mm before the tdc mark (see Fig. 12.6) on the flywheel is to stick a strip of paper 10 mm long to the rim of the flywheel with one end against the tdc mark and to turn the engine until the other end of the paper is beneath the timing pointer.

To set the static timing (i.e. when the engine is not running) –

Tools: Spanners, including sparking-plug spanner. Test

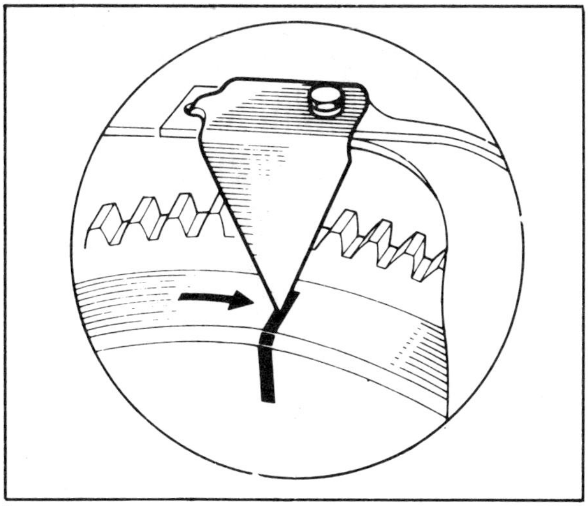

Fig. 12.5 The correct ignition setting for 1972-3 models is at top-dead-centre as shown

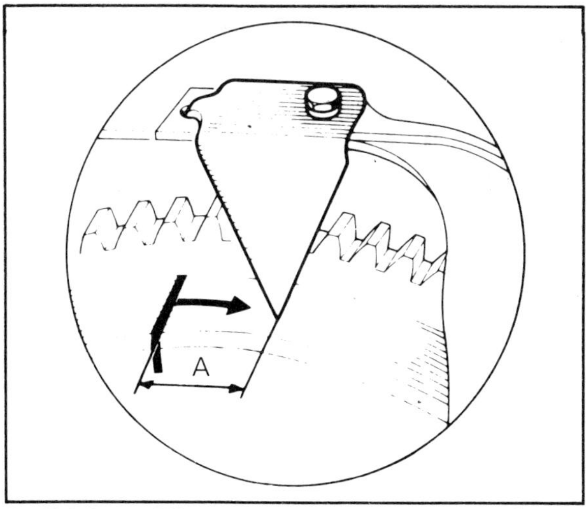

Fig. 12.6 For pre-1972 and post-1973 engines the timing is set to the distance A before top-dead-centre. This should be 10 mm ± 1 mm

lamp and leads (optional). Torch or inspection lamp if required.

1 Remove the sparking plugs and the valve cover and turn the engine until the piston in No. 1 cylinder is at the top of the compression stroke, when both valves will be closed. Line-up the timing marks correctly.

2 Remove the distributor cap and make sure that the centrifugal advance weights are not binding by turning the rotor clockwise and releasing it. Check that the contact-breaker baseplate is free to rotate slightly.

3 Slacken the distributor clamping setscrew or nut if this has not been done previously. The nut is not too accessible on some models and Renault dealers have a cranked spanner, Ele556, which is very useful when making timing adjustments.

4 Set the timing by rotating the distributor body clockwise until the contact points are just closed and then slowly turn it anti-clockwise until they just separate. If the ignition is switched on, a small spark can be seen and heard to jump across the points as they separate.

5 A more accurate method of checking the opening of the points is to connect a side-lamp bulb, mounted in a suitable holder, between the low-tension terminal on the side of the distributor body and a clean unpainted metal part of the engine. When the points are closed, with the ignition switched on, the lamp will not be alight. At the instant that they open, it will light-up. When checking the opening point, keep a light finger pressure on the rotor in an anti-clockwise direction to take up backlash in the drive. Tighten the clamping bolt and recheck the timing.

6 If it is necessary to turn the distributor through a considerable angle from the initial position in which it was fitted, the gears are not meshing correctly, being one or more teeth out. Withdraw the distributor shaft and refit it correctly as described in Chapter 9, Section 9.16. When the right timing has been obtained, tighten the clamping nut or screw to prevent the distributor body from rotating and then recheck the timing.

12.13 Timing with a stroboscopic lamp

Renault recommend that the timing should be set with the engine idling, using a stroboscopic timing lamp which is connected to No. 1 sparking plug. When the light is directed on to the timing marks, the flywheel appears to be stationary. The distributor is then adjusted to bring the marke into alignment.

A good timing light of the type used in service stations to speed-up the job of checking and adjusting the timing is a fairly expensive item and the cheaper ones that are sold by accessory shops have their limitations. Careful setting of the static timing as just described, followed by a road test as outlined in the next section, should be equally effective in ensuring peak engine performance and fuel economy.

12.14 Checking the timing on the road

The static or stroboscopic setting should be regarded only as the starting point for a series of road tests during which the timing can be precisely adjusted by rotating the distributor a fraction of a turn at a time to suit the condition of the engine and the fuel that will normally be used.

Tools: Spanner. Stop-watch.

1 Make a series of tests on a level road. Note carefully, by stop-watch readings, the time taken to accelerate from 20 mph to 40 mph in top gear, with the throttle fully open in each case and over the same stretch of road. The best ignition setting is that which results in the shortest time to accelerate over the speed range. This will also give the most economical fuel consumption.

2 When altering the timing by the roadside, move the distributor by only a fraction of a turn. Be particularly careful not to over-advance the ignition.

13 The transmission
Clutch, gearbox, drive shafts

All the Renault 4 models have front-wheel drive, the combined transmission and final-drive unit being mounted in front of the engine. Synchromesh gearboxes are fitted.

The drive is taken from the engine forward through a cable-operated clutch to the synchromesh gears, and then back to the final drive and differential pinions into which the front-wheel drive shafts are splined. Each shaft has a universal joint at its inner and outer end.

For the benefit of the novice it should perhaps be explained that overhaul of the transmission components, or at least the major assemblies, calls for the use of special tools and gauges and it is for this reason that it is the practice, in many garages nowadays, to fit service-exchange assemblies, rather than to carry out major repairs to worn or defective units.

A complete overhaul of a synchromesh gearbox, for example, is beyond the scope of the average owner. Special service tools will be needed to do the job properly, and it will probably be necessary to renew the majority of the parts in a worn gearbox – which is something that you will only find out, of course, after you have stripped the box!

As we suggest in Chapter 8, there may be little difference between the total cost of the spares needed and the price of an exchange gearbox, with everything in favour of the professionally-rebuilt unit.

The time factor

Where a routine maintenance job such as topping-up the oil in the transmission is concerned, the time factor must obviously depend on whether or not the work can be done quickly and conveniently with the car over a pit or raised on a garage lift or whether one has to wriggle under the side of the car and do the job the hard way!

As regards more ambitious work that is likely to be tackled at home, the following are some estimated times:

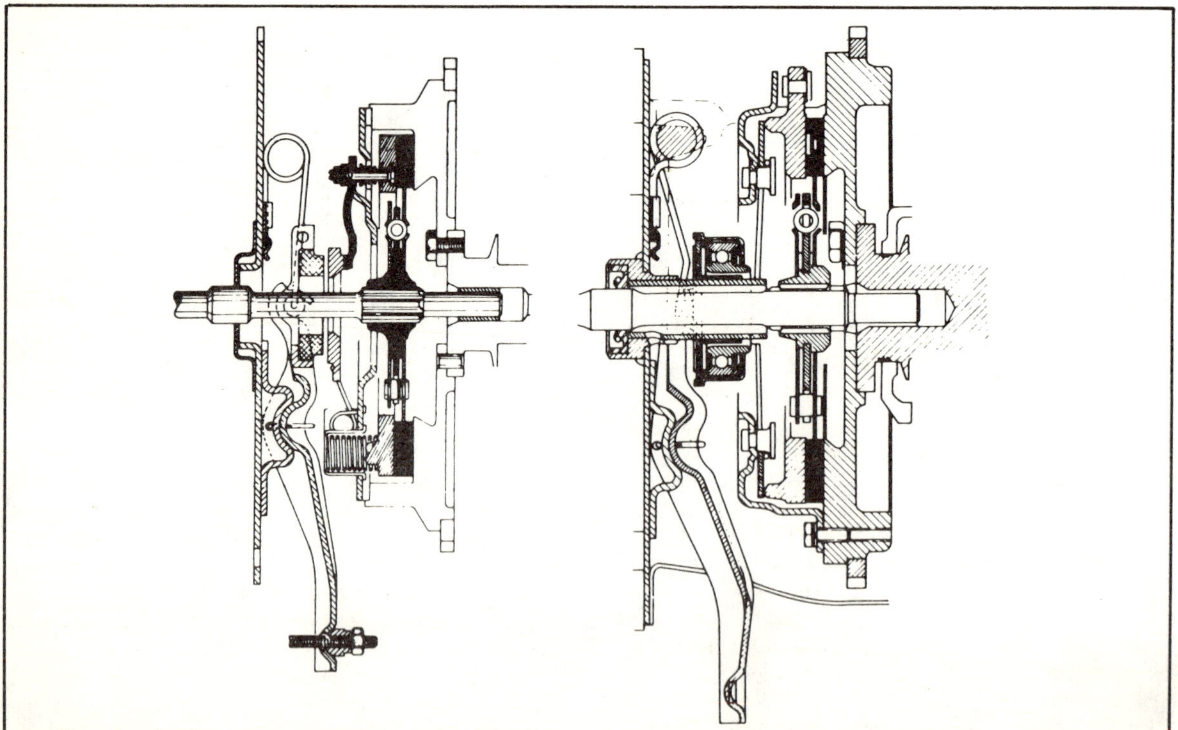

Fig. 13.1 Early and later clutch assemblies. *Left*, the PKH 4.8 coil-spring clutch. *Right*, the 160 DBIR diaphragm-spring clutch fitted to 1969 and later models

clutch adjustment, 20 min; fitting a new clutch driven plate and/or clutch cover assembly (including removing and refitting the gearbox), 8 hr; removing and refitting a gearbox, 7 hr; removing and refitting one drive shaft, 2 hr.

The clutch

The clutch is a good example of the repair-by-replacement policy described earlier. Neither the clutch cover assembly nor the driven plate can be dismantled and both must be renewed as complete assemblies.

The clutch release mechanism is operated by a cable. Normally, the only maintenance needed is to check that there is a free movement of 10–20 mm (about 3/8–3/4 in.) at the clutch pedal, before the weight of the clutch spring is felt. This will gradually decrease as the clutch friction-lining wears, and occasional adjustment will therefore be needed, as described below.

13.1 Adjusting the clutch-operating cable

On earlier cars the clutch cable is connected at its forward end to a relay lever beside the gearbox, which is attached at its base to a rod which runs back to the clutch withdrawal lever. On later models the clutch-operating cable loops back and is connected directly to the withdrawal lever. In either case adjustment is carried out at the lever as shown in Fig. 13.2.

To check and if necessary adjust the free movement at the withdrawal lever –
Tools: Spanners.

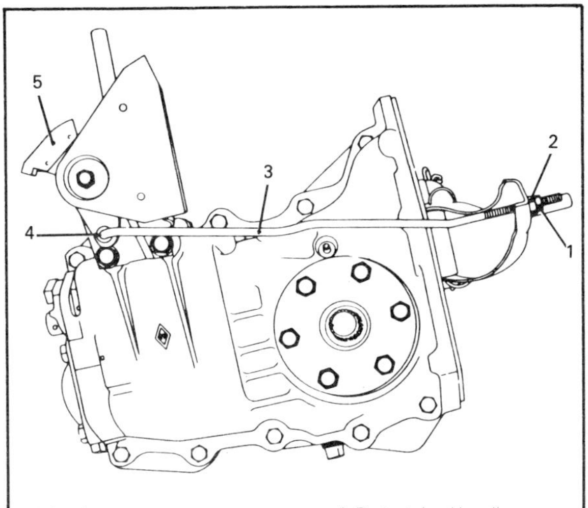

1 Lock-nut
2 Adjusting nut
3 Clutch rod
4 Rod retained by clip
5 Relay lever

Fig. 13.2 The clutch-operating rod mechanism used on earlier cars. On later models the clutch cable is directly connected to the clutch fork, with a similar adjustment.

1 Press the withdrawal lever forward until the weight of the clutch spring is felt and pull the cable or rod rearwards. There should be a clearance of 2½–4 mm (3/32–5/32 in.) between the adjusting nut and the lever.

2 If necessary slacken the outer lock-nut and turn the adjusting nut to obtain its correct clearance.

13.2 Clutch overhaul

Three types of clutch have been fitted. The first two have coil springs retained in pockets in the clutch cover. The very early type, PKH4, has a graphite thrust release bearing, while the later PKH4.8 clutch has a needle-roller and ball-bearing thrust race.

The later clutch, type 160 DB1R, has a diaphragm spring and a ball-bearing thrust race. This clutch is fitted to 1969 and later cars and care must be taken when ordering spares to make sure that the correct assembly is obtained. The type number is stamped on the clutch cover.

A point to bear in mind with early clutches is that the assembly is dynamically balanced by fitting plain washers under the spring washers on some of the bolts which secure the cover assembly to the flywheel. When dismantling, therefore, the clutch cover and the flywheel should be marked if the old assembly is to be fitted, and the positions of the balancing washers should be noted.

When a new cover assembly is being fitted, however, the balance washers must not be refitted. The bolts under which they were installed must be replaced by similar bolts to those used without balance washers.

Also, if a new coil-spring clutch cover assembly is being fitted do not forget to remove the spacers which are fitted under the toggle levers to make installation easier. These will fall out when the pressure plate is depressed.

Although it is sometimes sufficient to renew a worn driven plate alone (if this has failed after a fairly low mileage, for example), in practice it is a worthwhile insurance against future trouble to renew both the plate and the cover assembly at the same time. It is also advisable to renew the clutch release bearing.

To remove and refit the clutch assembly –

Materials: New parts as required. Paraffin. Rags. Marking paint or scriber. Loctite normal compound.
Tools: Spanners. Pliers. Screwdriver. Alignment tool (see item 6).

1 Remove the gearbox as described in Section 13.7.

2 If the clutch cover assembly is to be refitted, mark the flange of the cover and the flywheel to ensure reassembly in the same relative positions and make a note of the position of any balancing washers that may be fitted, as mentioned above.

3 Unscrew the cover retaining screws progressively in a diagonal sequence to release the tension of the spring without distorting the cover flange. Remove the cover and driven plate.

4 Clean the driven plate and the clutch assembly, brushing or blowing out any clutch dust from the latter

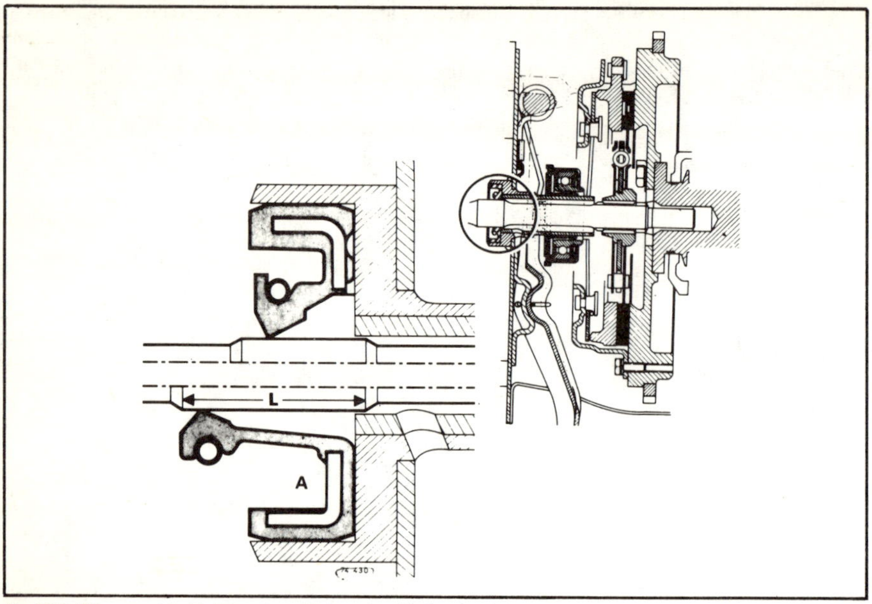

Fig. 13.3 When a guided ball-bearing withdrawal pad is fitted to the clutch shaft a later type of oil seal, A, is fitted. The length L is then 21 mm (53/64 in.) instead of 17.5 mm (1 1/16 in.)

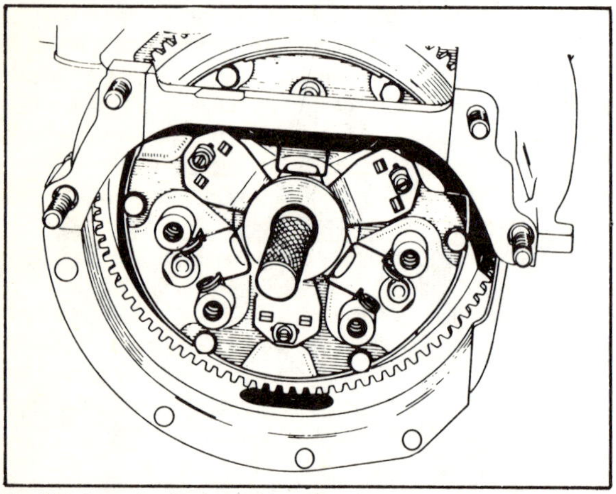

Fig. 13.4 Centering the clutch-driven plate during assembly by using a mandrel which fits the crankshaft spigot bearing and the clutch hub

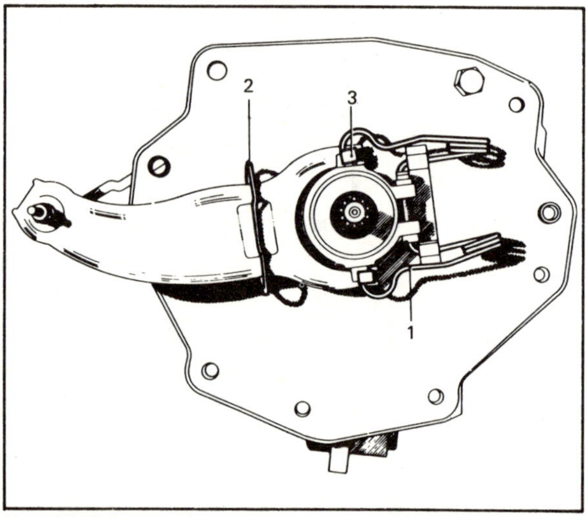

Fig. 13.5 The earlier type of clutch release fork and thrust bearing, used with the PKH 4.8 clutch.
1, pedal return. 2, fork pivot spring. 3, tabs on fork

(*don't inhale the dust*). Do not swill the cover in a paraffin bath, as this will remove the essential lubricant from the cover assembly.

5 Check the diaphragm spring in the cover assembly for any signs of wear or fractures and the driven plate for worn linings and loose or broken compression springs and worn hub splines. If oil has reached the driven plate, the rear main crankshaft bearing may be worn or the oil seal may be faulty. These items are normally dealt with during an engine overhaul. Oil can also leak past a worn gearbox first-motion shaft seal. Fitting a new seal is described in Section 13.4. If the spigot bearing in the end of the crankshaft (into which the first-motion shaft of the gearbox fits) is worn, it should be renewed as described in Chapter 9, Section 9.14. If the flywheel is worn, it can be removed by unscrewing the retaining bolts. If the flywheel is not too badly scored it can be refaced by a Renault dealer. When refitting it (see Section 9.14 in Chapter 9) new locking plates must be used and these must cover the locating dowel holes.

6 When refitting the clutch, it is essential to centralize the hub of the driven plate. An improvised aligning tool can be made up from a length of wooden dowel, built up to the correct diameters to fit the spigot bearing in the flywheel and the bore of the clutch hub by wrapping it with insulating tape or masking tape.

7 With the aligning tool in place, and with the deeper or the tapered side of the splined hub of the driven plate facing the gearbox, refit the clutch cover assembly. Before tightening the retaining screws progressively in a diagonal sequence, make sure that everything is properly lined-up, including the alignment marks and any balancing washers if the old cover is being refitted.

8 Refit the gearbox as described in Section 13.7.

13.3 Fitting a new clutch withdrawal bearing

The method of removing the withdrawal bearing depends on the type of clutch – see Figs. 13.5 and 13.6.

To remove an earlier type of bearing (Fig. 13.5) –

Materials and tools: as for 'Gearbox removal' (Section 13.7).

1 Remove the gearbox as described in Section 13.7.

2 Disengage the pedal return spring, 1 in Fig. 13.5, from the withdrawal pad trunnions and free the pivot spring 2, from its support.

3 Lift one of the tabs 3, on the fork and withdraw and remove the withdrawal bearing.

4 When reassembling, grease the withdrawal bearing trunnion with molybdenum disulphide grease.

To remove the later type of bearing –

1 Remove the gearbox.

2 Unlock the spring from the thrust bearing and remove the bearing.

3 When reassembling, lubricate the bearing sleeve and the fork fingers with molybdenum disulphide grease.

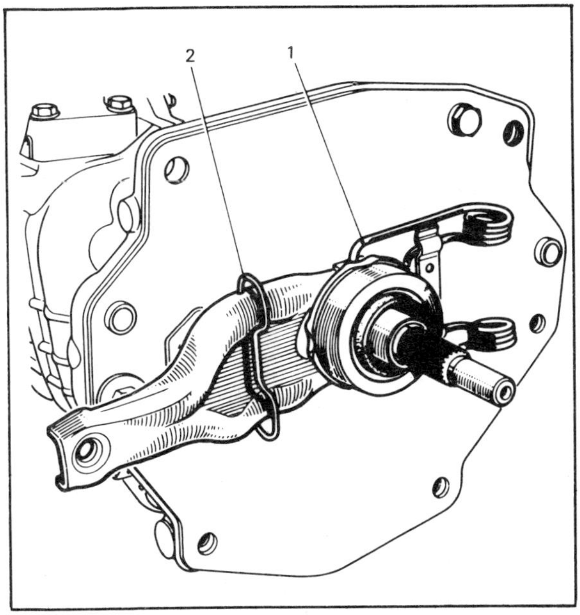

Fig. 13.6 The later clutch release assembly, used with a 160 DBIR clutch.
1, return spring. 2, spring clip

13.4 Renewing the gearbox first-motion shaft oil seal

We have treated this as a clutch job because the seal should be renewed during a clutch overhaul.

When a PKH4 or PKH4.8 clutch is fitted, the oil seal is inserted in the clutch side of the gearbox rear closing closing plate. With the 160DB1R clutch, the seal is on the inner side of the closing plate and there is an earlier and a later type of seal, shown in Fig. 13.3.

These seals are not interchangeable, since the seal bearing surface on the clutch shaft used with the later type of seal is longer than with the earlier arrangement.

Materials: New seal. Adhesive tape.
Tools: As for Section 13.2.

1 Remove the gearbox and take off the rear closing plate if the seal is fitted internally.

2 Prise out the old seal and fit the replacement, with the lips facing inwards towards the gearbox, being careful to keep it square and not to damage the seal housing or the lips of the seal.

3 Cover the splines on the end of the clutch shaft with a piece of tape before refitting the gearbox closing plate to avoid damaging the lips of the seal.

The synchromesh gearbox

A synchromesh gearbox needs no attention, other than checking the oil-level during routine servicing, topping-up if necessary with EP80 gear oil and draining and refilling during the 6000–9000-mile service. Any oil leaks will be obvious while this is being done. If they are serious, ask your dealer for advice.

When trouble develops in the gearbox, considerable experience is needed to diagnose it with any degree of certainty. Excessive noise, or a tendency to jump out of gear, is usually caused by the cumulative effect of wear at a number of points, over a large mileage. Piece-meal replacements are seldom effective for very long; usually the most economical course is to fit a reconditioned gearbox.

Three different types of gearbox have been fitted to the models covered by this book: the type 328, which has three synchronized forward speeds; the 334, fitted to 1968 models (from September 1967) which has four synchronized forward speeds; and the 354 gearbox, also a four-speed synchronized type, fitted to 1974 models (from August 1973).

It will be obvious, therefore, that the correct replacement components must be obtained when ordering a reconditioned gearbox, since the related parts, such as the clutch and drive shafts, were also modified to suit the later gearboxes.

13.6 Checking the oil level in the gearbox

The level is checked by removing the combined filler and level plug from the left-hand side of the gearbox.

The plug has a 10 mm square head and the best tool to

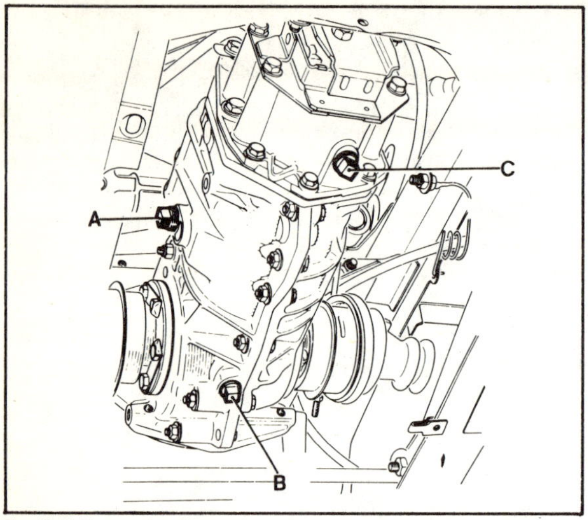

Fig. 13.7 The gearbox filler and level plug is shown at A and the drain plugs at B and C. In some cases the plug C is not fitted

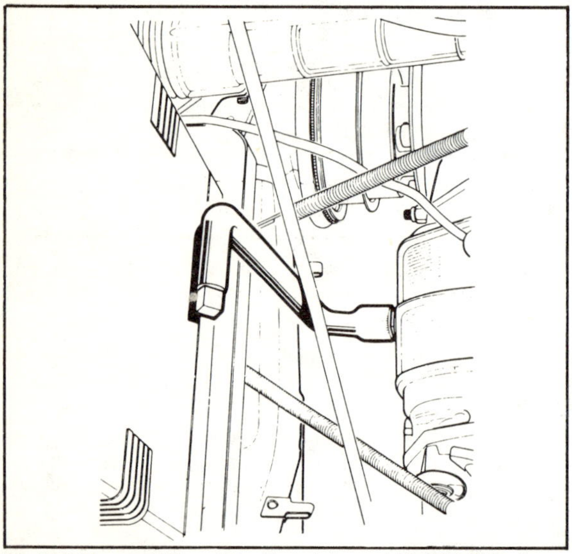

Fig. 13.8 The special Renault double-ended wrench B.Vi 380-01 fits the gearbox level and drain plugs and also the engine sump plug

use is the Renault double-ended spanner B.Vi 380–1, which also fits the engine drain plug.

1 Clean the area around the plug and unscrew the plug.

2 If oil does not flow from the plug hole, inject a little EP80 gear oil from a squeeze-bottle with a flexible spout. Wait for the overflow to stop before replacing the plug.

13.6 Draining and refilling the gearbox

Either a single drain plug or two plugs may be fitted, as shown in Fig. 13.7. The Renault double-ended wrench mentioned in Section 13.5 can be used to unscrew them.

To inject oil into the filler hole it will be necessary to use a squeeze-bottle fitted with a flexible spout, or something similar. It is easier to fill the gearbox if reverse gear is selected. It is best to change the oil after a reasonably long run, when the engine is thoroughly warmed and the oil will flow freely.

Materials: EP80 gear oil.
Tools: 10 mm spanner or adjustable spanner. Container for waste oil.

1 With the car on a level surface, clean around the plugs and remove them, positioning a suitable container beneath the drain plug.

2 When oil ceases to drip from the drain plug opening, replace the plug and inject the correct quantity of EP80 oil – see Chapter 17 – through the level plug hole.

3 Check that oil is not overflowing from the hole. If the level is slightly too high, wait until the flow stops before replacing the plug.

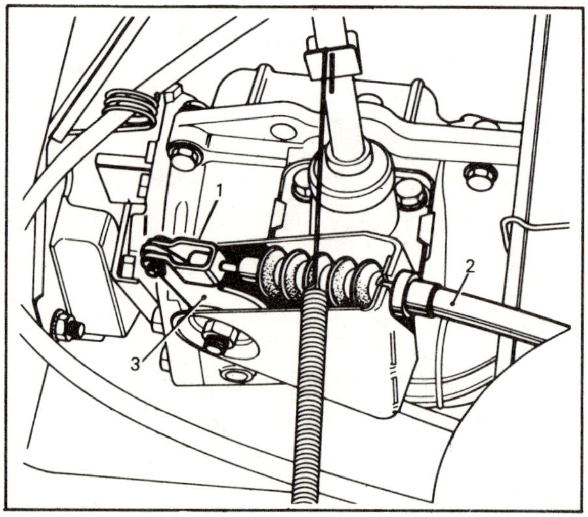

Fig. 13.9 The later type of clutch cable relay lever 1, fork. 2, clutch cable. 3, relay lever

Fig. 13.10 The earlier type of lever takes the form of a quadrant, A.

13.7 Removing and refitting the gearbox

The gearbox can be removed without disturbing the engine, the preliminary dismantling being the same as that described in Section 9.12 of Chapter 9 – except, of course, for the items relating only to the engine – so read through that section before beginning work.

1 When the preliminary dismantling has been completed, remove the tubular cross-member from between the side members, if necessary, and the gearbox front mounting pad.

2 Allow the engine and gearbox to tilt towards the front, being careful to prevent the fan blades touching the radiator if this has not been removed. Remove the bolts that secure the gearbox to the engine oil sump and the nuts securing it to the cylinder block.

3 Lift the gearbox clear. Do not allow the weight to be carried by the clutch shaft, as this will damage the clutch and may bend the shaft.

4 When refitting the gearbox, the sequence is a reversal of removal. Make sure that the roll pin holes in the drive shafts and the sun wheels are properly lined-up when a 328 or 334 gearbox is fitted, or that the drive shaft end fittings are fully home in the sun wheels of a type 354 gearbox – see Section 13.8 for details. Don't forget to refill the transmission with oil and to adjust the free play at the clutch withdrawal lever.

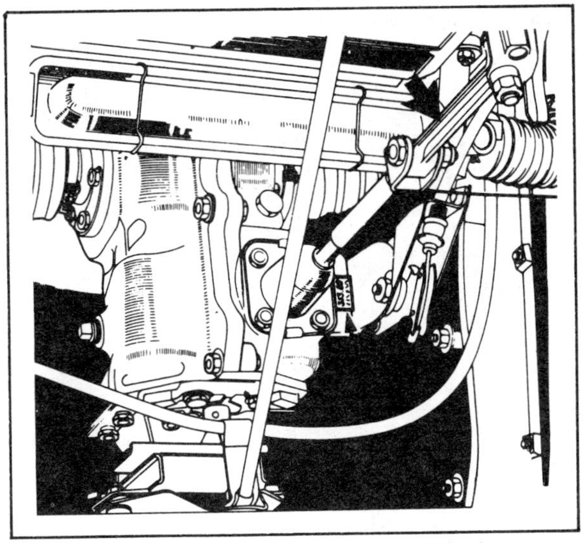

Fig. 13.11 On early cars the gearchange rod is connected to the gear lever by the link shown by the arrow

Fig. 13.13 The speedometer cable can be disconnected after slackening the setscrew shown by the arrow and pulling the cable out of the gearbox

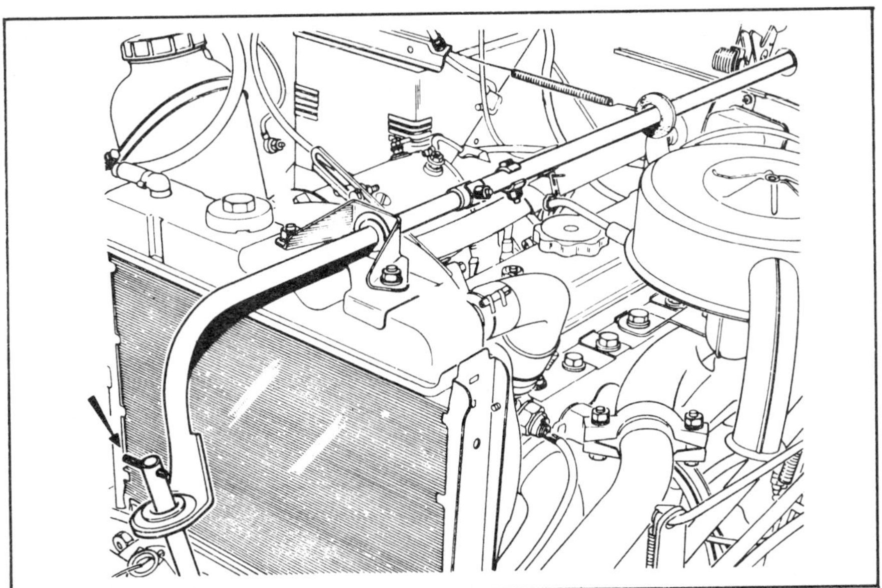

Fig. 13.12 The later gearchange rod and lever assembly. The arrow indicates the roll pin fitted to the gear lever

The drive shafts

Three different types of front-wheel drive shaft and universal joint assemblies have been fitted to the models covered by this book, and these can be identified from Fig. 13.14.

The 1969 cars have longer drive shafts to suit a front axle with a 13° castor angle. These must not be fitted to the earlier axle which has the 7° castor angle, since the suspension arms and stub-axle carriers are different.

On the other hand, it is permissible to fit a 'solid' type drive shaft with a Spider coupling on one side, irrespective of the type of shaft fitted on the other side. Your Renault dealer will be able to advise you regarding other aspects of interchangeability.

A BED type outer coupling cannot be repaired; if it is worn a complete exchange drive shaft must be fitted. A six-ball outer coupling and a Spider or Bendix Weiss four-ball inner coupling can be serviced, but we suggest that since this work calls for experience and the use of special tools, it would be better to let your Renault dealer check the shafts and recondition them if this proves to be feasible. A useful saving in labour charges can still be made, of course, by removing and refitting the drive shaft yourself. To be realistic, of course, the question of servicing the couplings is only likely to crop up when they begin to show unmistakable signs of wear, as revealed by clicking or knocking when the car is driven slowly around a corner on full lock.

The later types of joints seem to give little trouble in this respect. The earlier joints sometimes require renewal after about 20 000–25 000 miles – their life largely depends on how the car is driven, fierce acceleration and a lot of use in traffic and on winding roads shortening their lives.

13.8 Removing and refitting a drive shaft

This is a straightforward job, but when the shaft is fitted with a Bendix-Weiss four-ball joint at its inner end a retaining clip must be fitted to the joint before dismantling, to prevent it pulling apart when the shaft is withdrawn.

If a type 354 gearbox is fitted and the only reason for

Coupling at wheel end	Coupling at gearbox end	Appearance	Front axle (castor angle)
Cast "BED" (Made by Glaenzer)	Spider GI	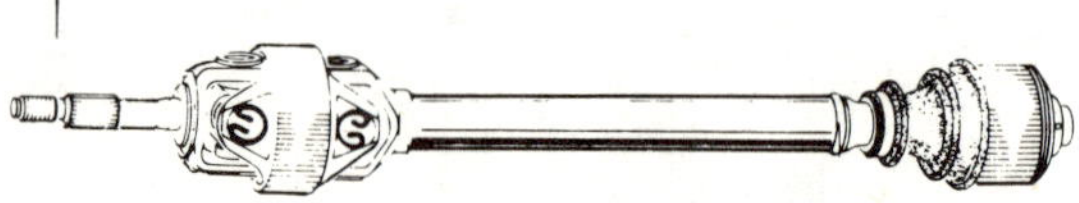	13°
Cast "BED"	4-ball	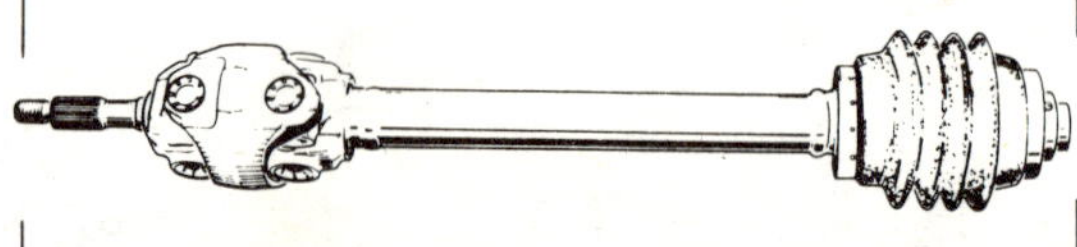	13°
Cast "BED"	Spider GI	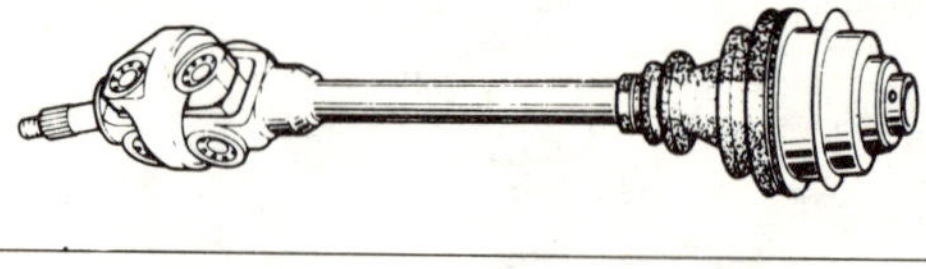	7°
Cast "BED"	Spider GI	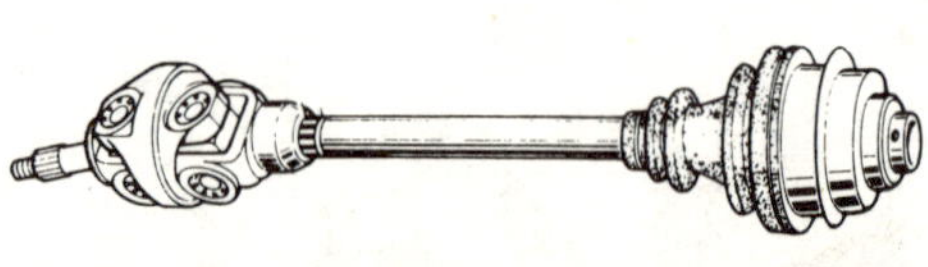	13°
6-ball	4-ball	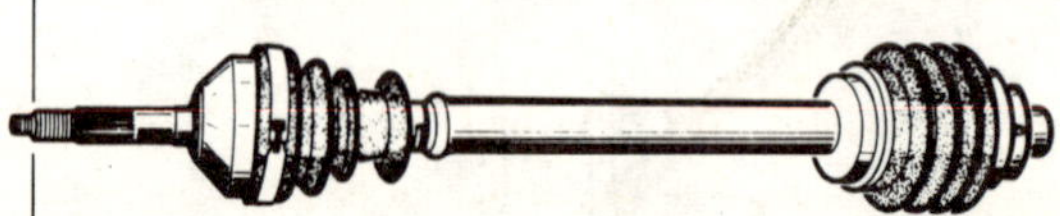	13°

Fig. 13.14 The different types of drive shafts and couplings which have been fitted to early and later models. The latest example is shown at the bottom

disconnecting the inner ends of the drive shafts is to remove the gearbox, it is sufficient to tap out the brake hose retaining clips to prevent strain (it is not necessary to disconnect the hoses) and to compress the inner couplings with the special Renault tool T.Ar.560, shown in Fig. 13.19, to free the end fittings from the sun wheels.

If this tool is not available, however, the sequence described below for the earlier gearboxes and drive shafts can be followed, apart from the references to the roll pins, which are not used with later gearboxes, the inner universal joints having extended noses which fit into the sun wheels.

When refitting these later drive shafts, make sure that the end fittings are fully home in the sun wheels after releasing the compressor tool.

Materials: Any new parts required. Molybdenum disulphide grease. Renault sealer for roll pins. Brake fluid.
Tools: The type of clip shown in Fig. 13.16 is fitted to new joints and it may be possible to obtain one from your local Renault dealer. Otherwise, make up a similar clip from a couple of lengths of wire and two worm-drive clips. Unless a type 354 gearbox is fitted, you will also need a good quality ball-pin extractor to dismantle the upper suspension ball joint and the steering arm joint, and a pin punch to fit the roll pins which locate the inner end of the shaft. Also special tools T.Av.235 and T.Av.409.

1 Jack-up the front of the car and support it really securely under the side-member. Apply the handbrake firmly. Remove the wheel.

2 Slacken the axle nut. This is very tight. If an assistant is available, get him to apply the brakes as firmly as possible while you slacken the nut, using a well-fitting socket and a strong handle. If you are working alone, lodge a length of strong steel bar or angle iron between two of the wheel nuts, with the end resting on the ground or a suitable support. Do not lodge it between the unprotected wheel studs, as this will damage the threads. Renault dealers use a special tool, Rou 436–01 shown in Fig. 14.6 and if you can hire this, so much the better.

3 Disconnect the upper suspension ball joint and the steering ball joint by removing the retaining nut and using a suitable extractor to detach the tapered pins.

4 Except when a type 354 gearbox is fitted, punch out the roll pin from the coupling at the gear-box end of the drive shaft and pull the stub axle carrier outwards to disengage the coupling from the gearbox.

5 Preferably use the special tool T.Av. 235 to push the drive shaft out of the stub-axle carrier. If you tap it out, use a soft metal drift and be careful not to damage the threads on the shaft.

6 When refitting the drive shaft, smear the splines at the gearbox end with molybdenum disulphide grease.

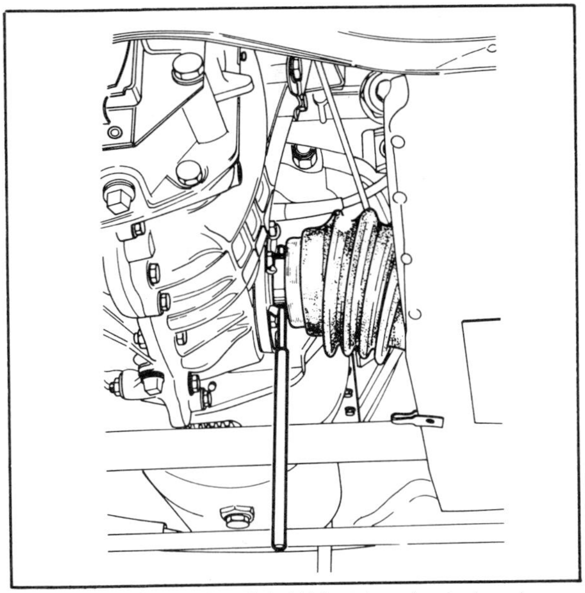

Fig. 13.15 Punching out the roll pin which retains an inner universal joint

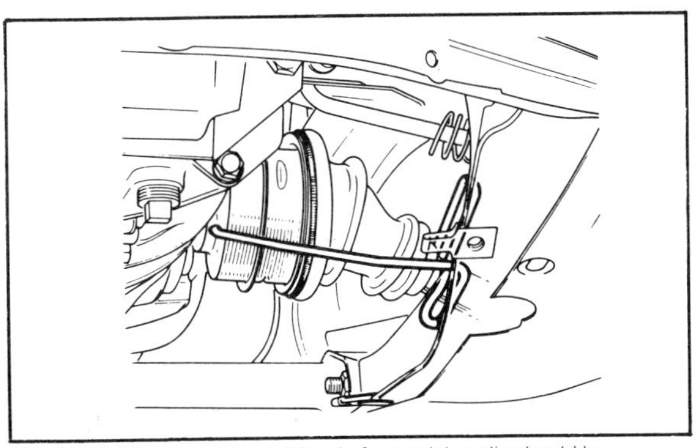

Fig. 13.16 When removing a drive shaft a retaining clip should be fitted to the inner joint to prevent it coming apart. These clips are provided with new shafts

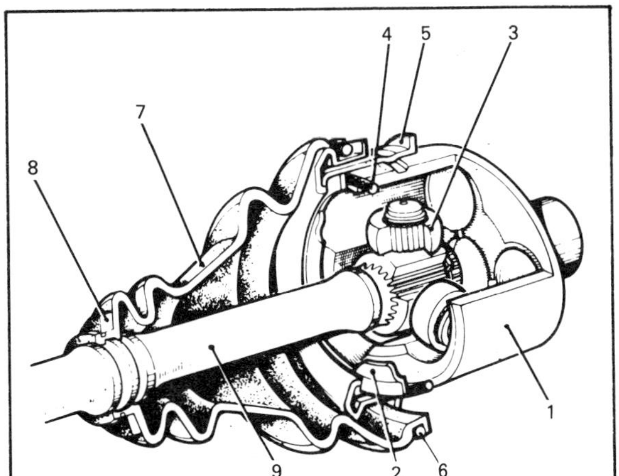

1 Yoke
2 Anti-separation plate
3 Spider
4 Grease seal
5 Sheet-metal cover
6 Retaining spring
7 Rubber bellows
8 Retaining clip
9 Drive shaft

Fig. 13.17 A typical Spider coupling. Other types of Spider joints differ only in detail.

Push the first roll pin into its hole and then fit the second pin inside the first, with the slots opposite to each other. Seal the ends of the pins with the special Renault sealer.

7 When assembling the hub to the drive shaft, it is essential to pull it into place by using the special tool T.Av. 409. Any attempt to drive the hub on with a drift will probably damage the shafts, the couplings and the differential unit.

8 Tighten the axle nut to a torque of 90 lb ft (120 Nm). If your torque wrench does not read as high as this (or you do not have a torque wrench) tighten the nut as hard as possible and then take the car to your Renault dealer to have it torqued to the correct figure.

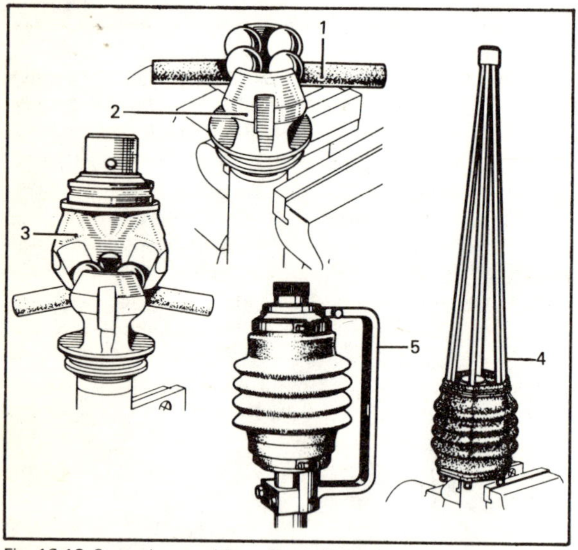

Fig. 13.18 Stages in assembling a Bendix-Weiss four-ball inner coupling. 1, rubber tube used to support the balls in the lower yoke 2 so that the upper yoke 3 can be pushed over the balls. The 'lobster-pot' 4 and gauge 5 are used when fitting the bellows to the joint in a Renault workshop

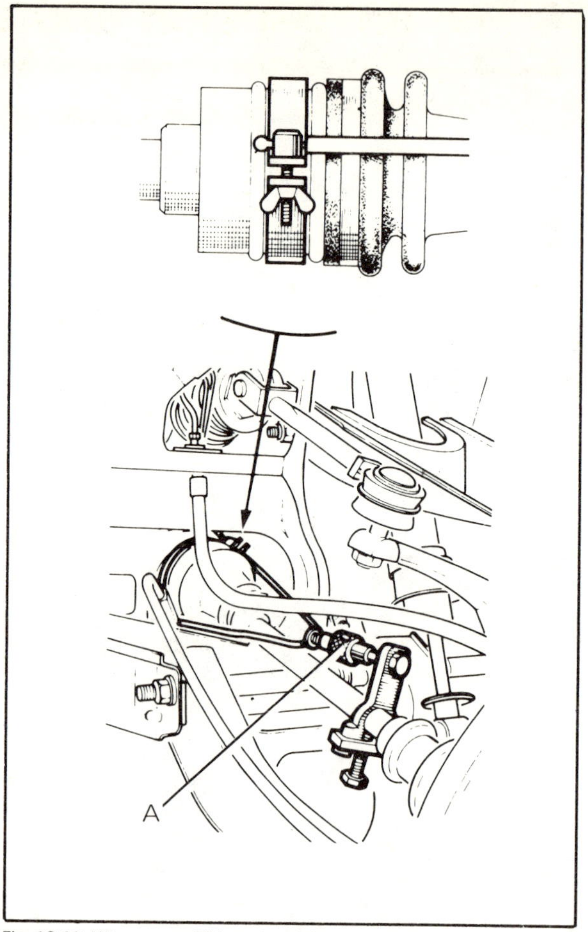

Fig. 13.19 When a type 354 gearbox is fitted, the drive shaft couplings at the gearbox end must be compressed by using the Renault tool T.Ar.560 shown at A, so that the end fittings will clear the sun wheels in the transmission

14 The suspension and steering

Satisfactory steering and good tyre life depend on the condition of the suspension and steering gear, and also on the maintenance of the correct steering 'geometry', which can be upset by a minor kerb collision.

This geometry – the castor, camber and swivel-pin angles of the front wheels – is determined by shims during the assembly of the suspension. Checks must be left to a Renault dealer, and should preferably be carried out at 6000–9000-mile intervals (especially if the rate of wear of the front tyres seems suspiciously high).

The alignment of the front wheels can be altered by adjusting the steering rack end fittings – but here again it is best to have the checks made by a dealer.

Wheel-wobble and quite severe vibration at about 40-50 mph and 60–80 mph – sometimes at lower speeds – can be caused by unbalanced wheels and tyres.

It is advisable to have this checked by a properly equipped garage every 6000 miles, preferably with the aid of a dynamic balancer which allows the degree of unbalance to be checked electronically when the wheel is spun without removing it from the front hub, but the front wheels must *not* be spun by the conventional type of electronic balancer, as this will damage the differential gears. Yet again your Renault dealer will know how to do the job properly.

The rear wheels should be balanced at the same time. They can not only cause vibration, but may cause a rear-end steering effect if they are badly out of balance. An electric-motor wheel rotator can be used on the rear wheels without causing trouble.

The suspension

The front suspension takes the form of upper and lower wishbones, connected to the stub-axle carriers at their outer ends by ball joints. The lower wishbone on each side is splined to the forward end of a torsion bar which is anchored in an adjustable housing at its rear end. This allows the tension on the bar to be adjusted to give the correct ground clearance under the car.

Adjustable torsion bars are also used at the rear but these are arranged transversely across the car and are enclosed in tubes to which the trailing arms which carry the wheels are attached. Because the bars are arranged one in front of the other, the wheelbase on the right-hand side is slightly less than on the left-hand side.

Suspension overhauls

At this stage we should put on record that we feel that any major dismantling or repairs to the suspension should be left to a Renault dealer. Special tools are needed

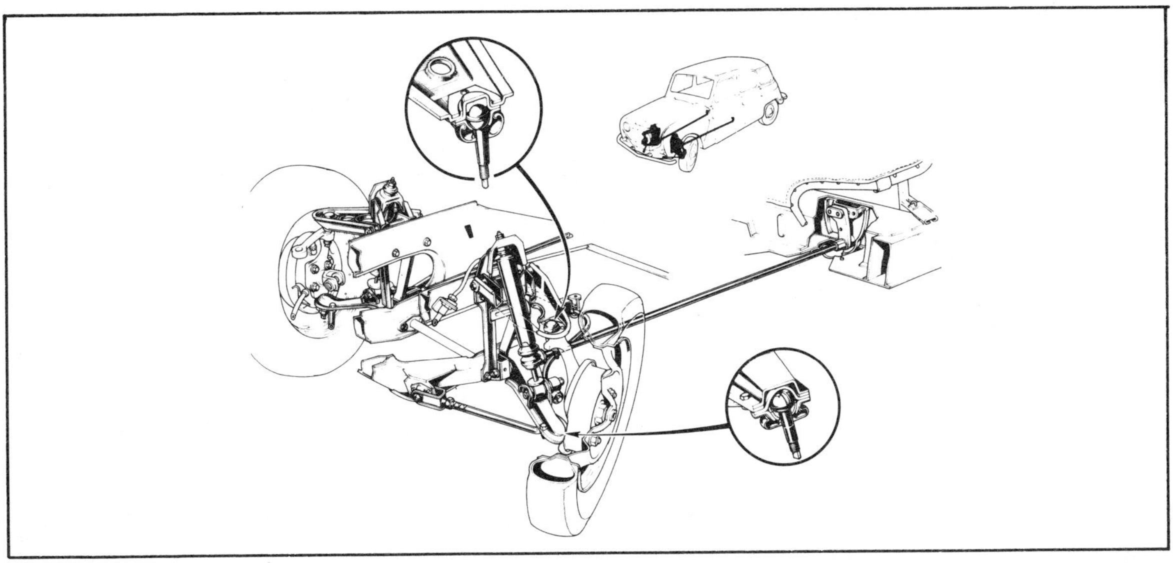

Fig. 14.1 The components of the front suspension linkage and torsion bars

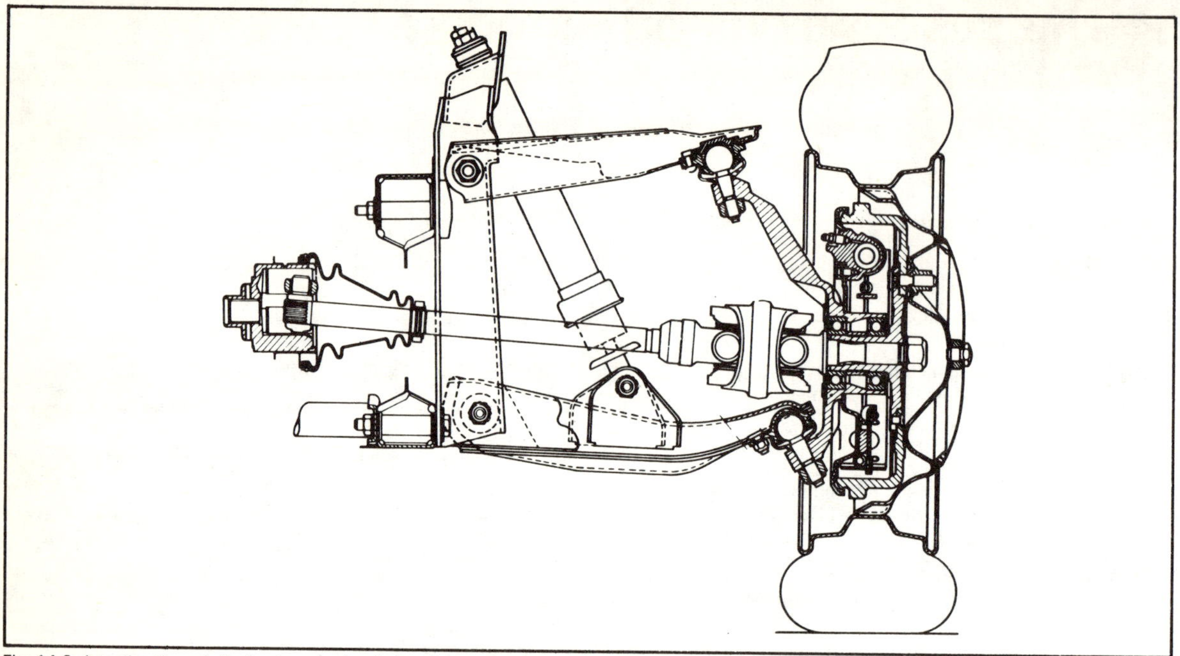

Fig. 14.2 A section through the front suspension, hub and drive shaft assembly

for most of the work and these are unlikely to be available to the ordinary owner. Gauges and jigs are also required for jobs such as checking the rear suspension arms and tracking them correctly. Failure to set-up the arms properly will result in rear-wheel steering effects and rapid tyre wear.

It is also necessary to adjust the torsion bars accurately – not only to give the correct riding height, but also to ensure the correct suspension characteristics.

For example, the torsion bars on the driver's side of the car must have slightly greater tension than those on the other side. This is checked by placing each wheel in turn on a special gauge, consisting of a plate resting on four calibrated springs, with a pointer which reads against a scale to record the load transmitted to the wheel by the torsion bar. To keep the vehicle level when making this check the other three wheels are supported on ramps which are of the same height as the test instrument.

Bearing in mind the facilities likely to be available to an owner working at home, therefore, we will confine ourselves in this chapter to the jobs which can be done without the need for specialized equipment.

Fortunately, renewal of the parts which are most likely to need routine replacement, such as the suspension and steering ball joints and the wheel bearings, come into this category, although we consider that a complete overhaul of the front-wheel hub carriers ought to be left to a dealer.

As we explain in Section 14.3, this is mainly owing to the fact that a press should be used when dismantling and reassembling. A useful saving in labour charges can still be made, of course, by removing and refitting the assembly at home.

The time factor

Suggested times for the more important suspension jobs are: Renewing an upper suspension ball joint, 1 hr; renewing a lower ball joint, 2 hr; removing and refitting the

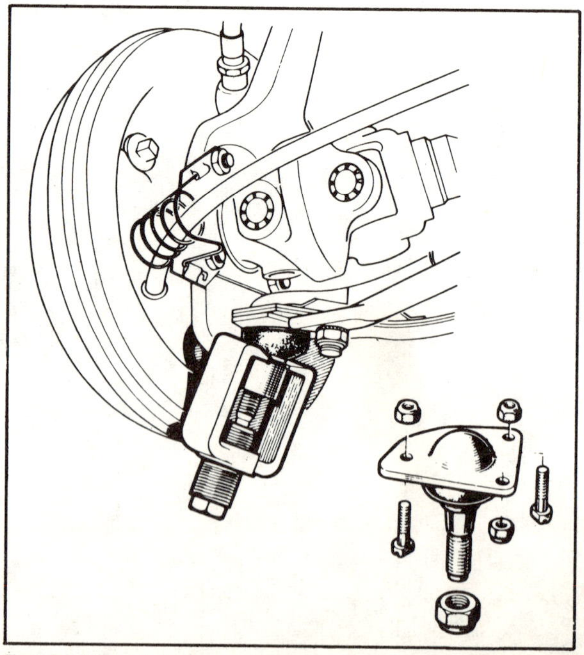

Fig. 14.3 Using a ball-pin separator to disconnect a lower ball joint from the suspension arm. A new joint is retained by bolts, as shown

stub-axle carrier assembly, 2 hr; checking and adjusting the rear-wheel bearings (one side), 45 min; removing and refitting the dampers (front or rear pair), 1½ hr.

The suspension ball joints

Wear in the upper and lower suspension ball joints will affect the steering and may be sufficient to cause the car to fail a DoE test. The rubber boots on the joints should be inspected regularly and if a boot is damaged or split, it should be renewed as described below. If the damage has existed for some time, however, entry of water and grit into the joint will probably have rendered it unserviceable and it should be changed.

14.1 Renewing an upper ball joint or rubber boot

Materials: New joint or boot. Special grease, obtainable from a Renault dealer.

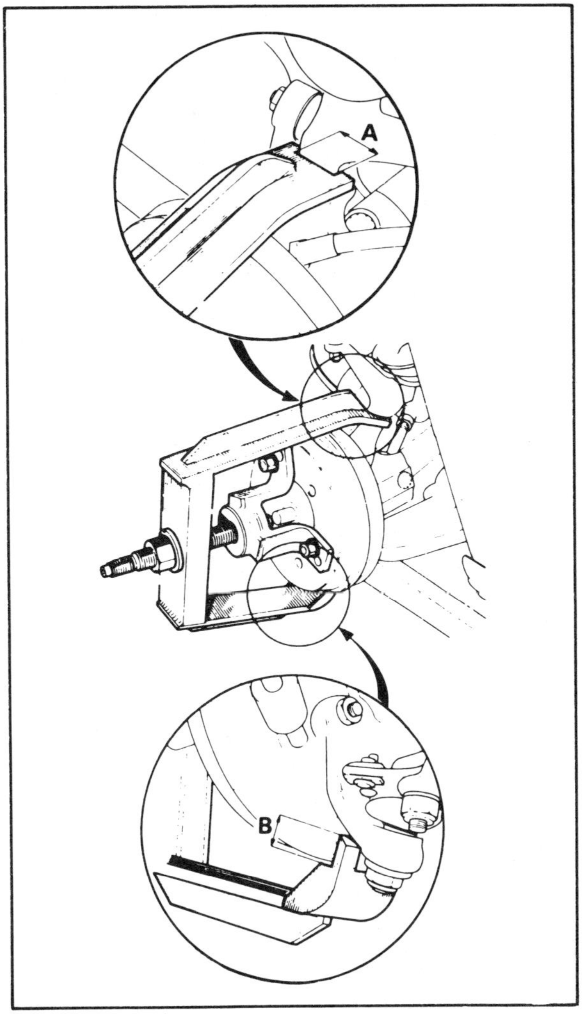

Fig. 14.4 Removing a front hub. The hub-puller Rou. 379 must be modified by filing or grinding the arms as indicated if the castor angle of the front axle is 7° instead of 13°. The distance A should be 33 mm (1 15/16 in.) and B should be 20 mm (25/32 in.)

Tools: Jack. Axle stand. Spanners. Ball-pin extractor. Punch. Electric drill. Torque wrench.

1 Jack-up the side of the car and support it on an axle stand. Remove the wheel.

2 Unscrew the nut that retains the ball pin and use a ball-pin extractor to disconnect the suspension arm from the joint.

3 If the joint is serviceable and only the rubber boot is to be renewed, remove the old boot, wipe the joint clean and half-fill the new boot with grease. Fit the plastic sleeve to the boot, slide the assembly into position and install the retaining ring, using a loop of string to pull the end into position.

4 If the joint is to be renewed, drill the heads of the two rivets and punch them out before removing the retaining bolt.

5 Fit the new joint, using the bolts supplied. If a support plate is supplied in the kit, fit this inside the suspension arm on the opposite side to the joint. Fit the new bolts, with their heads downwards, and tighten their nuts to 26 lb ft (35 Nm).

14.2 Changing a lower ball joint or boot

If it is possible to borrow or hire the special tools Rou 378 and T.Av. 235, the ball joint can be changed by pulling off the stub axle carrier, after removing the axle nut (Section 13.8). Otherwise, use the following method –

Materials and Tools: As for Sections 13.8 and 14.1.

1 Jack-up and support the front of the car.

2 Disconnect the upper ball joint and the steering arm ball joint, using a ball-pin extractor.

3 Remove the drive shaft (Section 13.8).

4 Disconnect the lower ball joint.

5 Renew the rubber boot as described for the upper ball joint or drill the rivet heads, punch out the rivets and

Fig. 14.5 Using the tool T.Av.409 to refit a front hub

fit the new joint with the bolt heads on the dust-cover side of the joint.

6 When reassembling tighten the ball-joint nut to 37 lb ft (50 Nm).

14.3 Removing and refitting the stub-axle carrier assembly

The front hub and hub carrier assembly can be removed as a unit by disconnecting the inner end of the drive shaft and disconnecting the upper and lower suspension ball joints and the steering ball joint as described in other sections of this chapter and in Chapter 13.

It is recommended that dismantling of the stub axle carrier and hub should be left to a Renault dealer, since the proper bearing extractor and a press, with suitable distance pieces, should be used to remove and refit the bearings without the risk of damaging them.

When refitting the assembly to the car the special tool T.Av409 should be used to draw the end of the drive shaft into the hub, as explained in Section 13.8.

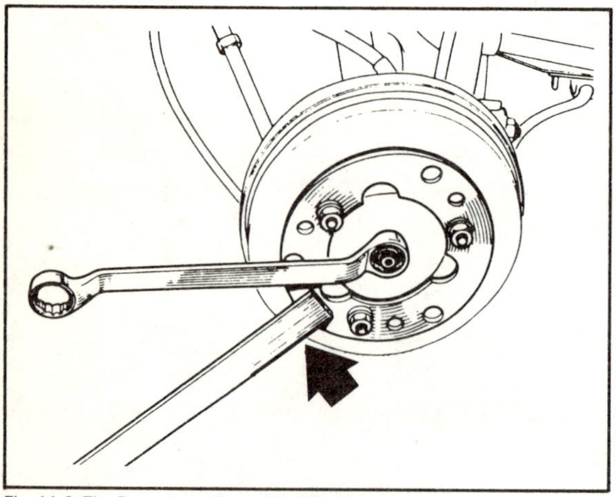

Fig. 14.6 The Renault tool Rou. 436-01 is useful (but not essential) to prevent a hub rotating while the hub nut is being slackened or tightened

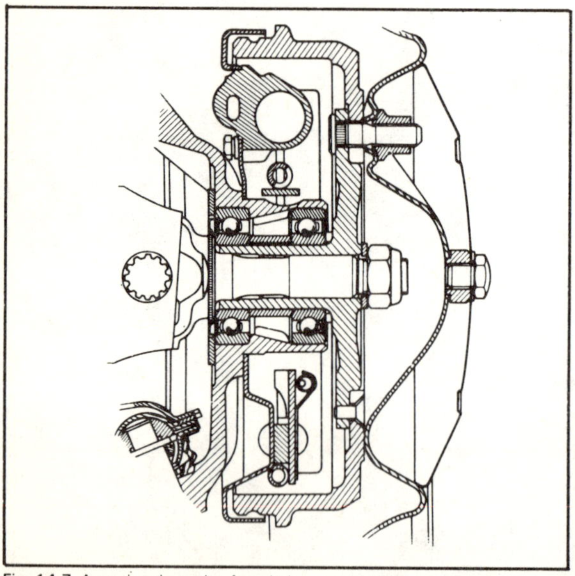

Fig. 14.7 A section through a front hub assembly, which runs on inner and outer ball races

14.4 Removing, refitting and adjusting the rear-wheel bearings

The rear-wheel bearings are of the taper-roller type and when correctly adjusted should have an end-float of 0.01–0.05 mm (0.001–0.002 in). This represents a just-perceptible movement when the wheel is pulled and pushed – not rocked – on its hub.

To remove and refit the bearings –

Materials: New bearings, if required. New oil seal. Paraffin. Cloth. High-melting-point grease. Split-pin.
Tools: As for Section 15.7, plus special Renault bearing puller, feeler gauges, wrench.

1 Remove the rear brake drum and hub assembly (Chapter 15), extracting the outer bearing and thrust washer as the drum is withdrawn.

2 Prise out the oil seal and press or drift the inner bearing track ring from the hub, if the bearing is to be removed.

3 A suitable bearing puller will be needed to remove

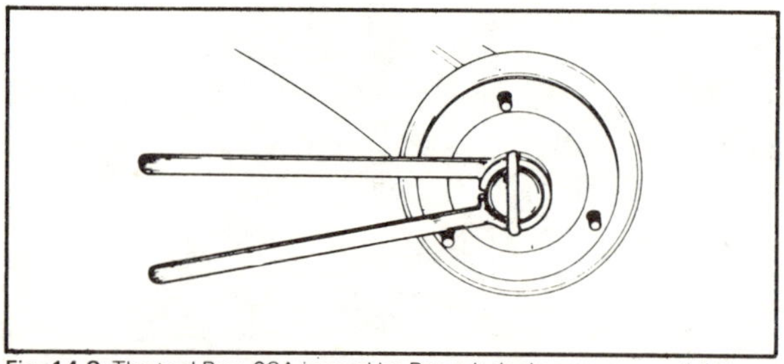

Fig. 14.8 The tool Rou. 08A is used by Renault dealers to remove tight grease cups, but the cup can be carefully tapped out

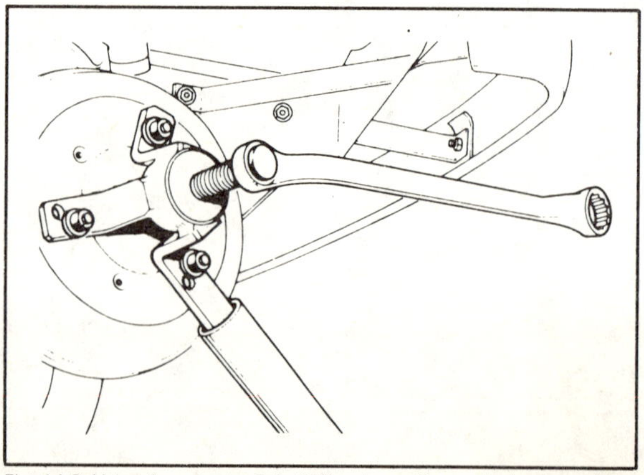

Fig. 14.9 Using the extractor T.Av.235 to draw off a rear brake drum and hub assembly

the taper-roller bearing from the stub axle, but this can be left in place if the assemblies are serviceable. Renault dealers use a special tool for the job (which depends on the diameter of the stub axle) and if you are doubtful about the condition of the bearings it will be better to allow your dealer to renew them.

4 Otherwise, clean the bearings carefully, pack them with grease, smear grease around the inside of the hub (but do not fill the recess) and fit a new oil seal.

5 Reassemble the hub and adjust the bearing end-float by tightening the axle nut to 22 lb ft (30 Nm), while rotating the drum. Unscrew the nut a quarter of a turn and check the end-float by inserting a feeler gauge between the rear face of the nut and the thrust washer.

6 When the clearance is correct, fit the nut-retaining sleeve so that one of its slots is aligned with the split-pin hole and fit a new split-pin.

7 Put about $^{1}/_{4}$oz.(10g) of high-melting-point grease into the grease cap before refitting it.

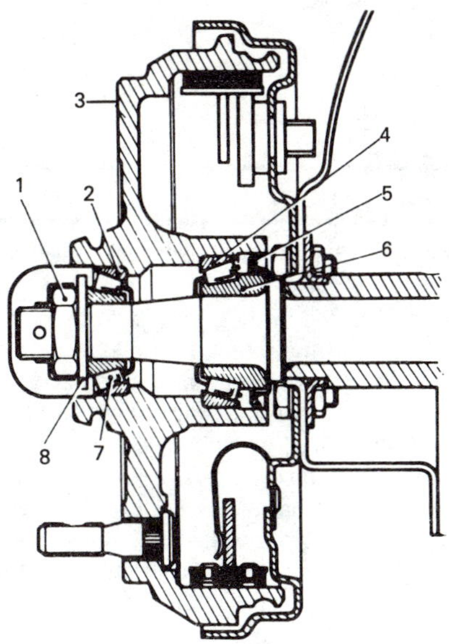

1 Hub nut
2 Outer bearing track
3 Drum and hub
4 Inner bearing track
5 Oil seal
6 Inner bearing
7 Outer bearing
8 Thrust washer

Fig. 14.10 A section through a rear hub and brake drum assembly

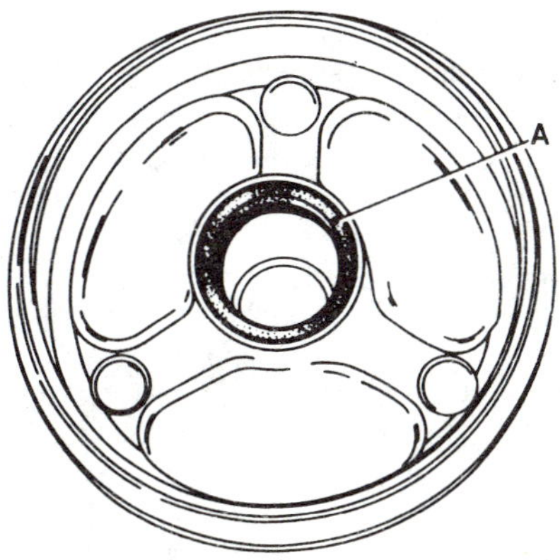

Fig. 14.11 The rear hub oil seal A should be renewed whenever the hub bearings are serviced

14.5 Removing and refitting the dampers (shock-absorbers)

Materials: New dampers, if required.
Tools: Spanners. Jack. Blocks to support wheels.

1 A number of different types of damper have been fitted to the various models, and a note must be made of the way in which the rubber and metal washers are installed before removing a damper.

2 The damper-retaining nuts and bolts must be undone only with the weight of the vehicle on the suspension – never with a road wheel hanging free. If the car must be raised, support the wheels on blocks.

3 When de Carbon rear shock absorbers are fitted,

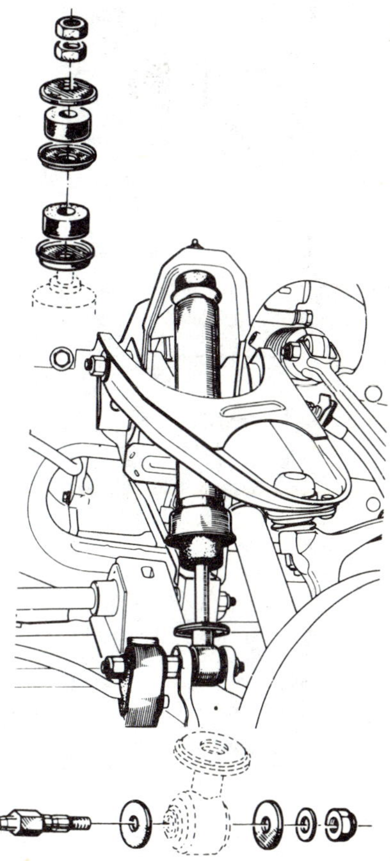

Fig. 14.12 The front shock absorber mountings. See also Fig. 14.13

they must be held in the compressed position with the aid of a wire retaining sling, as shown in Fig. 14.15, before they are removed. If the Renault sling Sus. 283 is not available, a loop of wire and a short length of rod can be used as shown in Fig. 14.15. New shock absorbers are supplied with a sling installed and this must be removed after they have been fitted.

4 It is advisable to fit new dampers after about 30 000 miles. Worn dampers can seriously reduce the quality of the 'ride' and can also affect the controllability and roadholding.

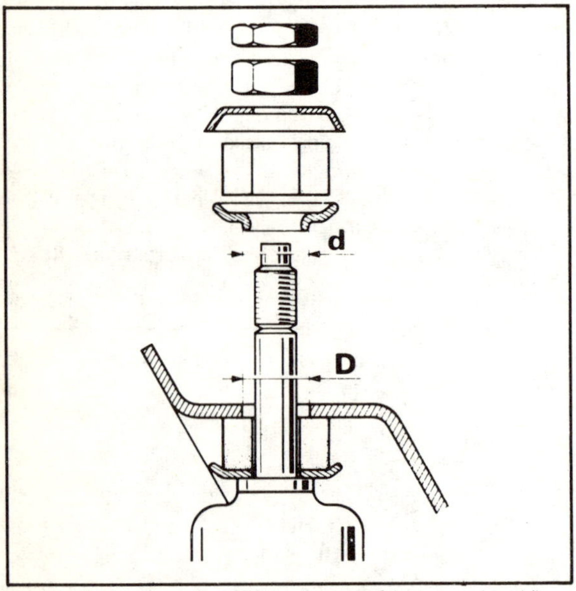

Fig. 14.13 After November 1970 the diameter of the cup washers (d) was increased, calling for a larger diameter D for the hole in the mounting bracket. This must be opened out from 15.7 mm to 16.5 mm if the later assembly is fitted to an earlier model

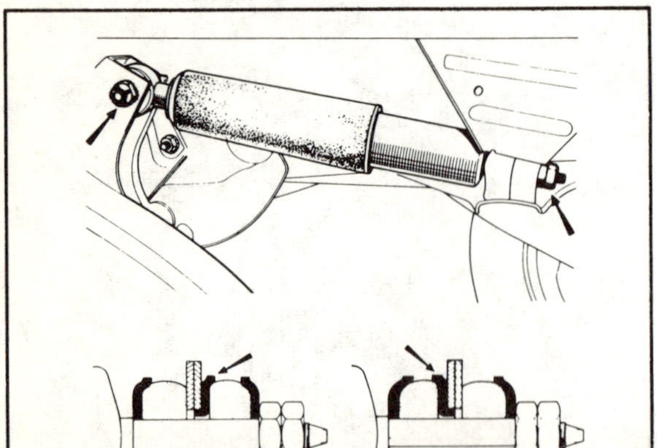

Fig. 14.14 A rear shock absorber. The mounting on the left is used only for 'Poor Road' or 'Special Version' vehicles, the mounting on the right being the normal arrangement

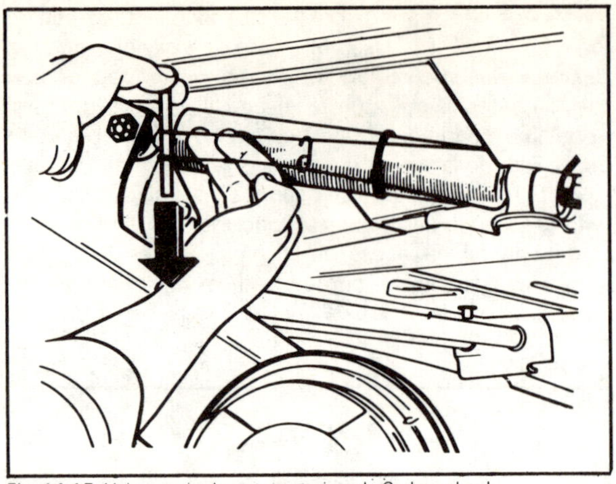

Fig. 14.15 Using a wire loop to restrain a de Carbon shock absorber as described in the text

The steering gear

The rack-and-pinion steering gear is bolted to a cross-member in the engine compartment. When the steering wheel is turned the movement is transmitted by the steering column to the pinion of the steering unit, which moves the rack from side to side. Each end of the rack is coupled to the steering arms, which in turn are connected to the stub-axle carriers by ball joints.

Prior to the 1969 models, the rack-and-pinion steering gear contained an inner return spring which assisted the castor effect of the front wheels to return the wheels to the straight-ahead position. The assembly fitted to 1969 and later models – which have an increased castor angle – does not incorporate a return spring. These models have shims fitted between the rack assembly and the chassis support to enable the front suspension geometry to be correctly set.

Whenever the later type of rack is removed and refitted the shims should be marked so that they can be refitted in their original positions.

Early in 1972 the steering rack assembly was further modified, which called for an increase of 2 mm ($\frac{5}{64}$ in.) in the length of the steering shaft. Only the modified assembly is available as a spare and if this is fitted it is necessary to make sure that the steering column lock engages correctly. If it does not do so, two 8 mm diameter flat washers, 2 mm thick, must be fitted between the coupling flange and the steering shaft.

However, remember that if a new rack assembly is fitted the shims will also need to be adjusted as mentioned above, and this is a job for a Renault dealer.

The rack and the rubber boots on the ball joints should be inspected during the 6000–9000-mile service to make sure that they have not been damaged. Pull the corrugations apart and look for cracks and splits. Apart from allowing lubricant to escape, a damaged boot or bellows will also allow water and grit to enter the joint or the rack, quickly rendering it unserviceable.

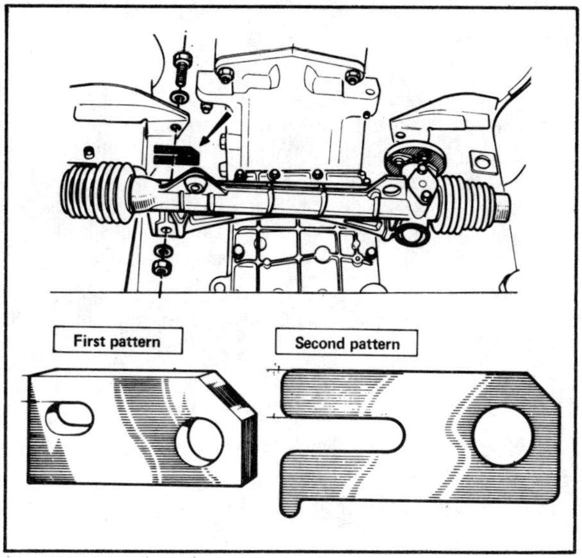

Fig. 14.16 The steering gear, showing the shims fitted between the gear and its mounting

Steering gear repairs

Before discussing steering gear repairs, one or two general points must be mentioned. The most important is that many steering troubles can be attributed quite simply to incorrect wheel alignment, the wrong tyre pressures, unbalanced front wheels and tyres or weak dampers. As indicated at the beginning of this chapter, steering alignment checks and wheel balancing must be left to a Renault dealer. It is useless to attempt to do these jobs without the aid of specialized equipment.

An adjustment is provided to take up wear in some types of steering gear. To adjust the rack damper plunger bearing preload, the thickness of the adjusting washers beneath the cover plate must be varied. It is necessary to remove the gear from the car to do this (see Section 14.7) and the work should normally be left to a Renault dealer, as special tools must be used.

When the rack-and-pinion assembly is badly worn, the safest plan is to fit a reconditioned assembly.

The time factor

Approximate times for the jobs covered in the sections which follow are: Renewing a steering arm ball joint, 30 min; removing and refitting the steering gear assembly, 1 hr.

14.6 Renewing a steering arm and ball joint

The steering arm ball joints cannot be renewed alone, although new bellows can be fitted if this is all that is required. Otherwise, new steering arm and joint assemblies must be fitted.

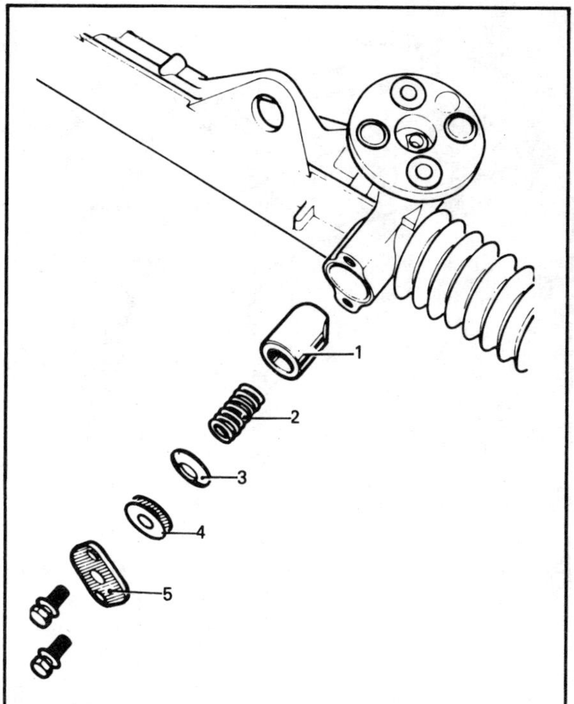

1 Cover
2 Spring washer
3 Spring
4 Adjusting shims
5 Plunger

Fig. 14.17 Adjustment of the thrust plunger for the steering rack should be done by a Renault dealer – see Fig. 14.18

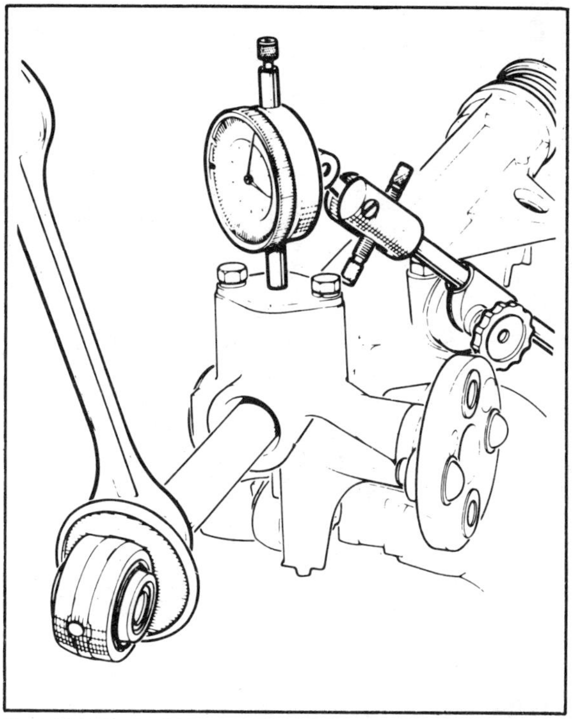

Fig. 14.18 The special tools used by a Renault dealer when adjusting the steering rack

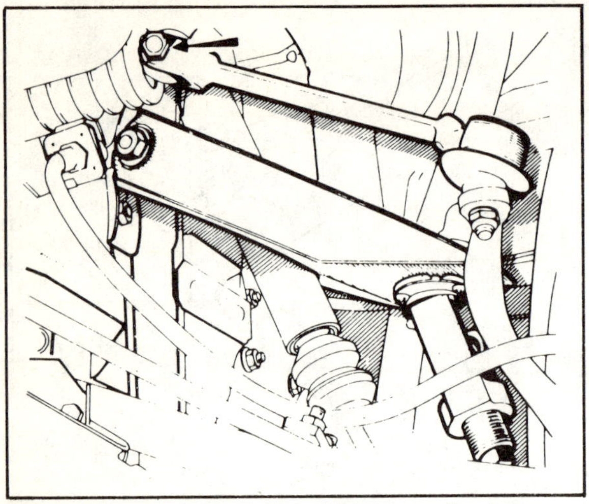

Fig. 14.19 Each steering arm is retained at its inner end by a bolt, indicated by the arrow

The steering arms are identical on pre-1969 models, but from then on the right-hand and left-hand arms are different. The right-hand arm has a single boss at its centre to identify it and the left-hand arm has two bosses.
Materials: New joint. Paraffin. Clean rags.
Tools: Ball-pin extractor. Set of spanners. Torque wrench. Wire brush. Jack. Axle stands.

1 Raise and support the front of the car.

2 Remove the retaining nut and break the taper joint between the ball pin and the steering arm, using a ball-pin extractor.

3 After fitting the new joint tighten the nut to 26 lb ft (35 Nm).

14.7 Removing and refitting the steering gear

Materials: Any spares required.
Tools: Spanners.

1 Unhook the handbrake return spring. Disconnect the steering arms from the rack and fittings.

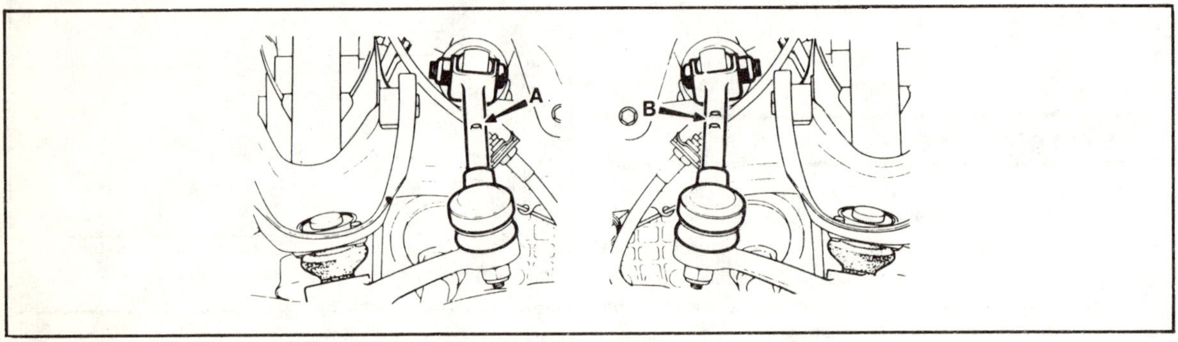

Fig. 14.20 The right-hand steering arm has a single boss A, and the left-hand arm two bosses, as at B

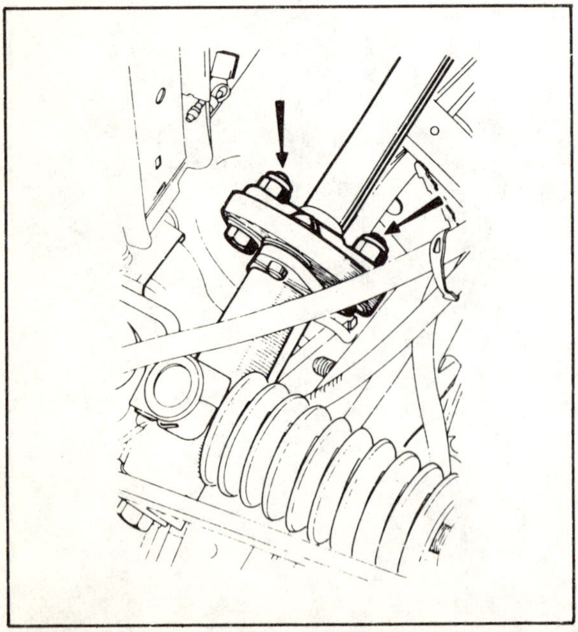

Fig. 14.21 The arrows indicate the bolts which retain the steering shaft coupling

2 Remove the flexible coupling bolts from the steering column side of the coupling.

3 Unscrew the nuts retaining the radiator tie-rods to allow sufficient movement of the radiator to permit the steering gear to be removed.

4 Undo the two steering rack assembly securing bolts and lift the assembly out. Mark the positions of the shims, when these are fitted.

5 When refitting the gear, smear the steering arm pins with grease and after tightening them, make sure that they are horizontal to ensure that the steering ball joints operate through the correct range. If necessary slacken the lock-nut on the rack end-fitting and adjust the position of the eye.

6 If a new steering gearbox is being fitted, height-adjusting shims of different thicknesses will have to be used between the steering gear and the cross-member. As this calls for the use of special wheel-aligning equipment, the job must be done by a Renault dealer.

7 In order to centre the steering rack, before replacing the rack or, for example, refitting a steering wheel, set the rack so that the dimension A in Fig. 14.23 is 71.5 mm ($2^{13}/_{16}$ in.).

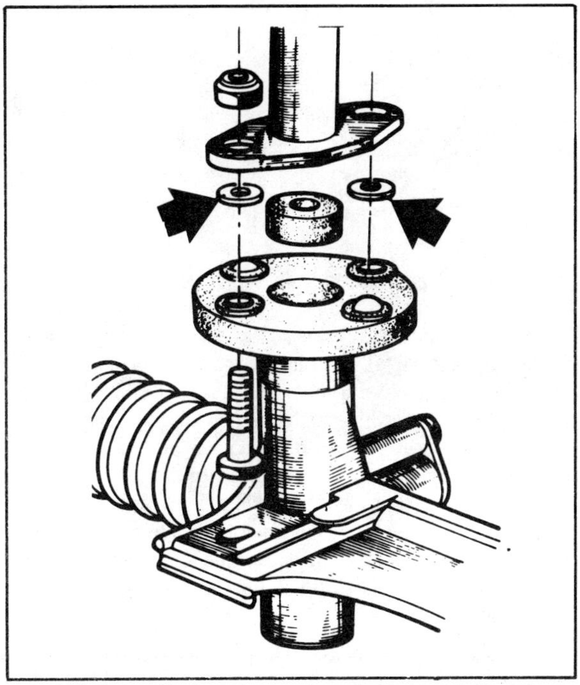

Fig. 14.22 If a modified steering gear is used with the early type of steering shaft, it may be necessary to fit two 8 mm diameter washers, 2 mm thick, as shown, to ensure that the anti-theft mechanism in the ignition switch operates correctly

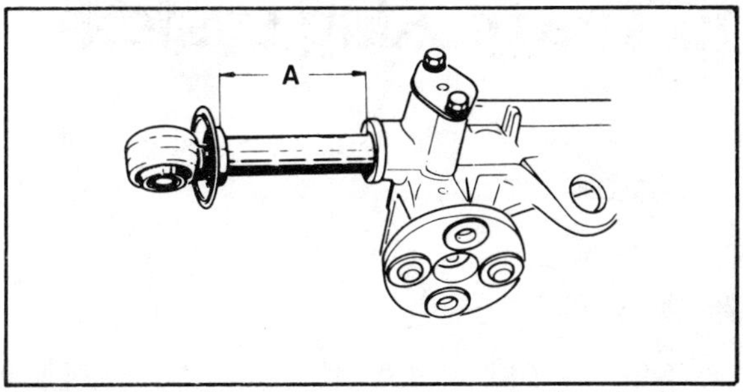

Fig. 14.23 To find the steering centre-point, position the rack end fitting so that the dimension A is 71.5 mm ($2^{13}/_{16}$ in.)

15 The braking system

All models have drum brakes at front and rear, the leading and trailing shoes in each drum being expanded by a single hydraulic cylinder. No servo assistance is provided. A brake-pressure limiter is inserted in the hydraulic pipeline feeding the rear brakes, to prevent premature locking-up of the rear wheels under heavy braking conditions.

While the basic principles of brake servicing are the same for all systems, there are detail differences which must be taken into account when dismantling and reassembling and when ordering spares. The storeman, for example, will want to know the chassis number of your car.

The brake specifications are listed in Chapter 17 and the individual types of brake can be identified from the illustrations of this chapter.

Practical pointers

As with other components of the car, 'repair by replacement' is assuming increasing importance where braking systems are concerned. Service-exchange sets or relined brake shoes from a reputable supplier are a better proposition than attempting to reline existing shoes. Similarly, it is preferable to fit new master and slave cylinders instead of installing new rubber seals in the old components, in which the bores are likely to be worn, scored or corroded. Brake manufacturers, in fact, tend increasingly to supply only new or reconditioned assemblies, instead of repair kits.

This will explain why we have not included in this chapter detailed instructions for stripping or repairing any of the hydraulic components.

Now for one or two useful tips that apply to many of the jobs described in this chapter –

Before disconnecting a brake pipe union, remove the filler cap from the fluid reservoir, place a sheet of thin plastic (which can be cut from a plastic bag) over the opening and screw the cap firmly down on to it. By preventing entry of air into the reservoir in this way, only the minimum amount of fluid will be lost when a union is disconnected. *Don't forget to remove the plastic when the work has been completed* – otherwise the brakes will bind.

Better still, use a special brake-pipe clamp. Most accessory shops sell these clamps, which enable a flexible hose to be clamped-off without risk of damaging the walls of the tube, before a union is disconnected. The use of a clamp will often avoid – or reduce the need for bleeding the system after reassembly.

A Mole or similar self-locking wrench can be safely used as a clamp, provided that two curved pads are fitted to the jaws. These can be made by cutting a short length of 1½ in. diameter metal tube longitudinally and taping the half-sections to the jaws so that the pipe will be pinched between the rounded, outer faces of the tube, without the risk of cutting or crushing it.

The second point is that brake fluid acts as a very efficient paint stripper – so be sure to keep it away from the bodywork. Any drips or splashes should be wiped off immediately and the area washed with water and detergent.

The time factor

A complete check on the braking system can be carried out comfortably in a morning. Typical times for other individual jobs are: fitting new brake shoes to two drum brakes, 1½ hr; bleeding the brakes, 45 min; adjusting the brakes, 20 min per brake.

Routine servicing

15.1 Topping-up the brake fluid reservoir

This is largely a precautionary check. If frequent topping-up is needed, look for fluid leakage from the pipelines, unions or hydraulic cylinders. Since brake fluid specifications change from time to time (to take advantage of improved technology) ask your Renault dealer for the correct grade for your car.

Materials: Correct grade of brake fluid. Methylated spirits. Clean rag, free from fluff.

1 Before unscrewing the filler cap, clean the cap and the surrounding area to prevent grit or dirt falling into the reservoir. Use methylated spirits for cleaning as paraffin or mineral oil could contaminate the brake fluid.

2 Top-up the fluid to within ¼ in. (6 mm) below the threads of the filler cap. If the reservoir has 'Maxi' and 'Mini' or 'Danger' lines moulded on it, top-up to the 'Maxi' level. Never allow the fluid to fall below the minimum or danger marks.

3 Clean the inside of the filler cap and check that the air vent hole is not clogged.

4 If the fluid level has fallen noticeably, ask an assistant to depress the brake pedal firmly while you check all the unions and pipelines for any signs of leakage.

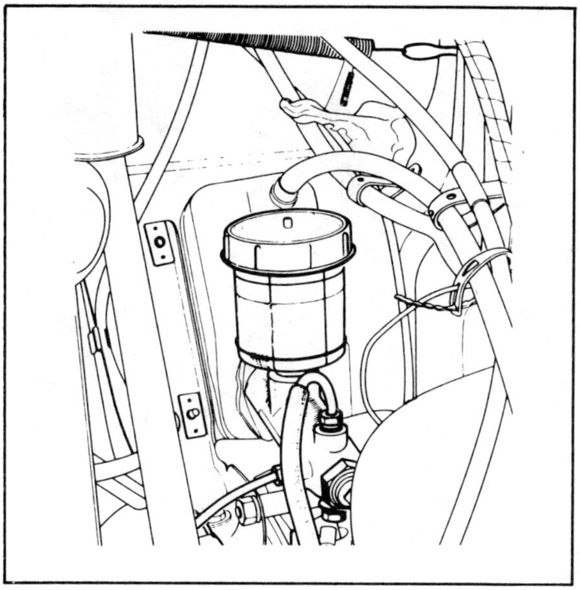

Fig. 15.1 A typical brake fluid reservoir. The fluid level should be kept up to the 'Maximum' mark

15.2 Changing the brake fluid

Brake fluid (and particularly the disc-brake type) absorbs moisture from the air through the vent hole in the reservoir filler cap. Some moisture slowly seeps through the flexible hoses and can also be drawn in past the wheel-cylinder seals. Since this moisture seriously lowers the boiling point of the fluid, 'vapour lock', which can cause complete brake failure, can result when the fluid boils in the wheel cylinders under heavy or prolonged braking conditions. The diagnosis is confirmed if normal braking is restored when the brakes cool down. The water in the fluid also corrodes the internal parts of the hydraulic components. The fluid should therefore be changed after 24 000 miles, or two years, in service. Some authorities recommend a yearly change of fluid.

Obviously, fluid should never be stored in an unsealed container. The old fluid that has been bled from the system must not be re-used.

Materials and Tools: As for bleeding the brakes – see Section 15.3. About ½ litre (¾ pint) of fluid will be needed and this should leave some fluid over for subsequent topping-up.

The fluid is changed by opening the bleed screw on each wheel cylinder in turn, fitting a tube to the nipple, with its lower end in a suitable container, and pumping the brake pedal to expel the old fluid. The process is the same as for bleeding the brakes (Section 15.3) but all the old fluid in the system is pumped out and replaced by new fluid.

15.3 Bleeding the brakes

This is *not* a routine job. It should be necessary to expel air from the system only if any of the unions have been undone or new parts have been fitted, but air can be drawn in past worn wheel-cylinder or master-cylinder seals – in which case renewal of the parts is obviously indicated.

The brake-bleeding procedure is the same as for changing the fluid, but it is necessary only to pump the pedal until air bubbles no longer issue from the bleed pipe. The reservoir must be topped-up at frequent intervals to prevent air entering the system.

A nipple that incorporates a valve (and which ought to be fitted with a rubber dust cover) will be found on each backplate, next to the pipeline union. You will need the help of an assistant to do the job properly if an easy-bleeding device is not used.

To bleed the system –
Materials: Tin of correct grade of brake fluid (see Chapter 17).
Tools: Brake bleed valve spanner. Length of rubber or plastic tube to fit bleed nipple. Container for fluid bled from system. There are also a number of 'easy-bleeding' devices, obtainable from accessory shops, which make brake-bleeding a simple, one-man operation. Axle stand or support block for rear wheel – see above.

1 Attach a rubber or transparent plastic tube to the nipple on the wheel furthest from the master cylinder. Pass the tube through a box or ring spanner that fits the hexagon on the nipple. Submerge the free end of the tube in a little brake fluid in a clean glass jar.

2 Open the bleed screw one complete turn. Your assistant should now depress the brake pedal with a slow, full stroke and then allow it to return unassisted. Top-up the fluid level in the master cylinder reservoir with the fresh fluid. Repeat the pumping strokes after about 5 seconds.

3 Watch the flow of liquid into the jar and continue pumping until air bubbles cease. Tighten the bleed screw while the pedal is held down fully. *Do not overtighten the screw.*

4 Repeat this operation on the other brakes, ending with the nipple nearest to the master cylinder.

15.4 Brake adjustment

Two square adjusting spindles project from the backplate of each brake. The adjuster spindles are prone to seize-up and their flats can be quickly ruined by attempting to turn them with an unsuitable spanner. A special brake-adjusting spanner can be obtained quite cheaply from Halfords and other accessory shops.

To carry out the adjustment –
Tools: Jack. Axle stand. Brake-adjusting spanner.

1 Jack-up and support the wheel on which the brake is to be adjusted. When adjusting a front brake, make sure that the rear wheels are securely chocked and when adjusting the rear brakes, apply the handbrake fully.

2 Turn the adjusters outwards from the centre of the wheel as shown in Fig. 15.2, beginning with the leading-

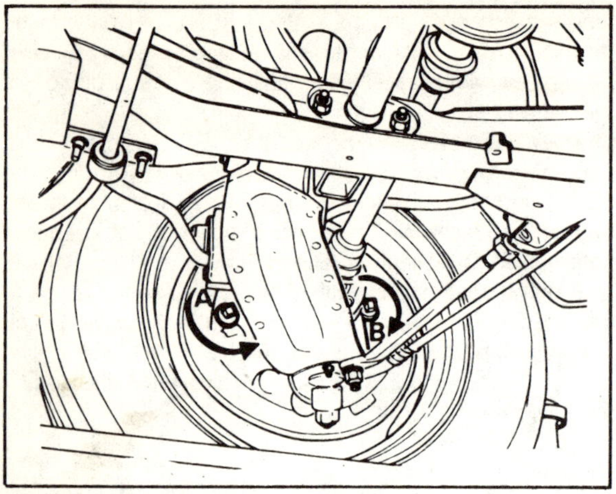

Fig. 15.2 Adjusting the brake shoes. The adjusters should be turned in the direction shown, starting with the leading shoe A and finishing with the trailing shoe B

shoe adjuster, which is in front of the axle on each brake.

3 Since the brake drums usually warp slightly in service, it may be necessary to accept slight rubbing at one or more points during rotation. Otherwise the adjuster would have to be slackened off to such an extent, before the drum was completely free, that excessive travel of the brake pedal would reduce braking efficiency.

4 Spin the wheel, apply the brakes hard and recheck the adjustment.

15.5 Handbrake cable adjustment

Normally, adjustment of the front brake shoes will eliminate any excessive free movement on the handbrake lever. In time, however, the handbrake cable will stretch and it will be necessary to take up the slack by shortening the cable. Be careful not to adjust the cable too tightly, as this will result in the brakes rubbing.

1 On earlier models – see Fig. 15.3 – remove the pin from the fork-end of the brake cable, take up the slack in the cable and reinsert the pin in the appropriate hole. When all this adjustment has been taken up, remove the pin from the fork-end and move the pin in the stirrup piece at the base of the lever up one hole. Then readjust the fork-end.

2 With the later arrangement, release the hooked rod from the hole in the second rod and move it up one hole. When the third hole has been reached, move the pin in the stirrup piece at the base of the lever up one hole and start again with the adjustment at the hooked rod.

3 With either type of adjustment, make sure that the front wheels turn freely and that the brake shoes are applied hard when the handbrake is pulled up by six to eight clicks on the ratchet.

15.6 Removing a front brake drum

The front drums are retained by three countersunk screws and will normally come off without difficulty when the

Fig. 15.3 Handbrake adjustment with a cable-operated mechanismm. 1, normal adjustment at fork end. 2, cable. 3, further adjustment at base of lever

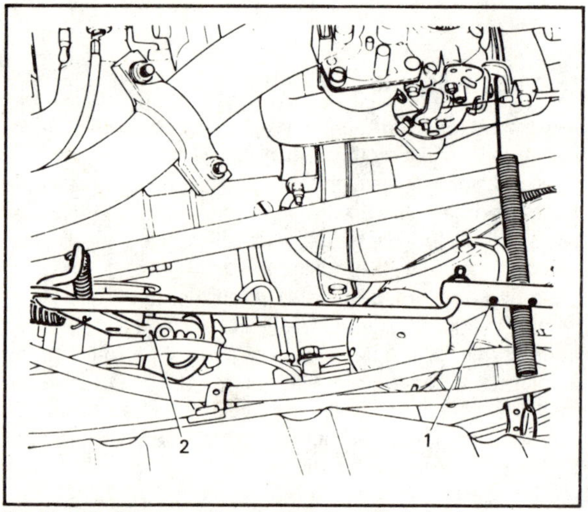

Fig. 15.4 The later type of handbrake linkage. The holes 1 are used to take up small amounts of play and the adjustment at the stirrup 2 is used when the last hole on the tube has been reached

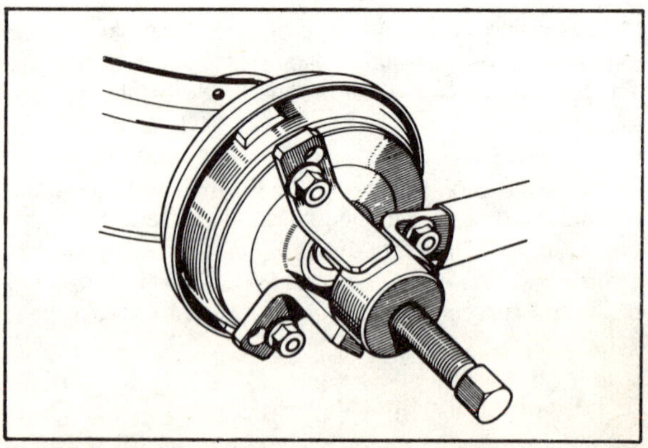

Fig. 15.5 Pulling off a rear brake drum and hub assembly, using the hub extractor T.Av.235

screws have been removed and the brake adjusters have been fully slackened-off – but if they are tight, see item 2 below.

Materials: Penetrating oil or rust-releasing fluid, if needed.
Tools: Jack. Axle stands. Screwdriver. Soft-faced hammer or mallet if required. Brake-adjusting spanner.

1 Remove the front wheel and unscrew the three countersunk screws that retain the drum. If they are tight, soak them with penetrating oil or rust-releasing fluid.

2 Slacken off the brake adjusters and pull off the drum. If it is tight, tap it around the flange with a soft-faced mallet or with a piece of wood interposed between a hammer and the drum. Alternatively, if there are two tapped holes in the drum in addition to the screw holes, screw two 6 mm x 100 thread bolts into the holes so that they will bear against the hub and force the drum off.

15.7 Removing a rear brake drum

The rear brake drums are integral with the hubs and an extractor is usually needed to pull off the assembly. The official tool is T.Av.235. The hub cap can also be difficult to remove, being a very tight fit and Renault dealers use a special tool Rou. 08A.

When the correct tools are not available, however, two alternative methods of withdrawing the drum are described in the instructions which follow.

Tools: Brake adjusting spanner. Hammer, preferably copper- or hide-faced. Steel lever. Special tools: T.Av.235 (see above); Rou. 08-A (see item 2).

1 Jack-up the car and remove the wheel. Slacken back the adjusters so that the shoes are completely clear of the drum.

2 Remove the grease cup from the hub. This is very tight and Renault dealers use a special tool, Rou. 08-A, but the cup can be removed by tapping it out with a wooden or brass drift, being careful not to dent it.

3 Remove the split-pin and the nut locking-plate and unscrew the nut from the end of the stub axle.

4 Draw off the drum by using the special Renault tool, or if this is not available, refit the road wheel and try to remove the drum by pulling on the wheel while rocking it in a horizontal and vertical direction in order to free the hub from the stub axle. Make sure that the car is really securely supported before doing this.

If this method is not successful, some owners use the wheel as an extractor by placing a suitably shaped piece of wood between the centre of the wheel and the end of the stub axle, the thickness of the distance-piece being chosen so that it is just possible to screw the wheel nuts on to the outer threads of the studs. By tightening each nut a little in rotation, it should be possible to pull off the drum. Excessive force must not be used, of course, owing to the risk of distorting the wheel.

5 When reassembling, lightly grease the wheel bearing, refit the drum and adjust the end-float on the bearings as described in Chapter 14, Section 14.4.

15.8 Servicing a drum brake

A drum brake service consists of removing the brake drums, cleaning out accumulations of brake dust and road grit, checking the operating cylinders and adjusters for binding and the cylinder seals for fluid leakage, and renewing the brake shoes if there appears to be any risk of the brake linings wearing down flush with the rivets before the next service is carried out. Special points to look for are seizure of the adjusting screws, seizing of the pistons in the cylinders and binding of the handbrake operating mechanism. These faults are quite common on older cars.

Materials: Paraffin. Methylated spirits. Penetrating oil or rust-releasing fluid. Clean rags. Anti-seize lubricant.

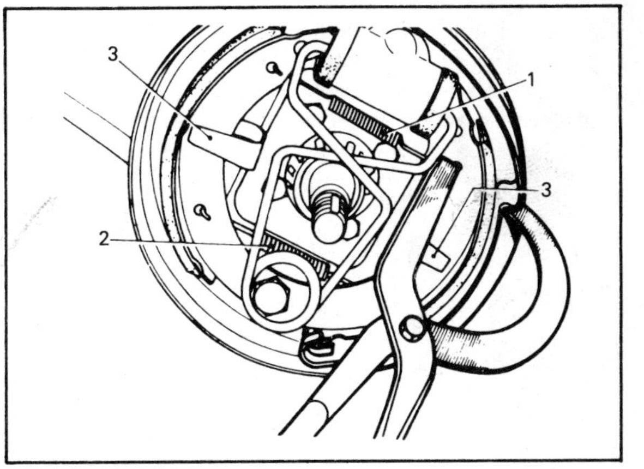

Fig. 15.6 Removing the rear brake shoes. Unhook the return springs 1 and 2 and remove the clips 3. Renault dealers may use the special spring pliers and the piston clamp shown, but these are not essential

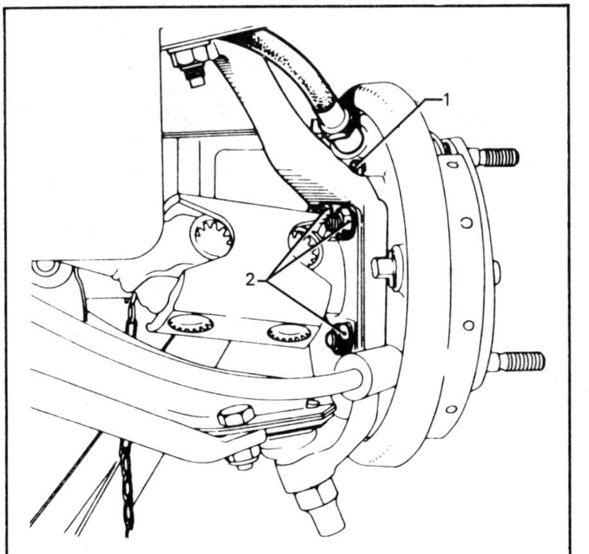

Fig. 15.7 On very early models the brake cylinder bolts 1 cannot be removed until the hub nuts 2 have been unscrewed, but this is not necessary with 1967 and later cars

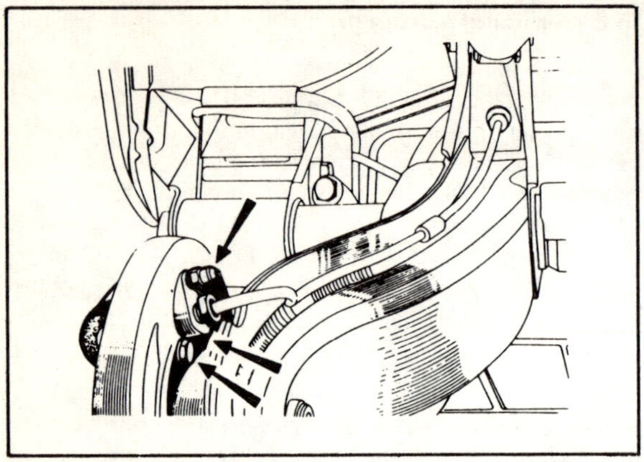

Fig. 15.8 The rear-wheel brake cylinder retaining bolts and bleed nipple are shown by the arrows

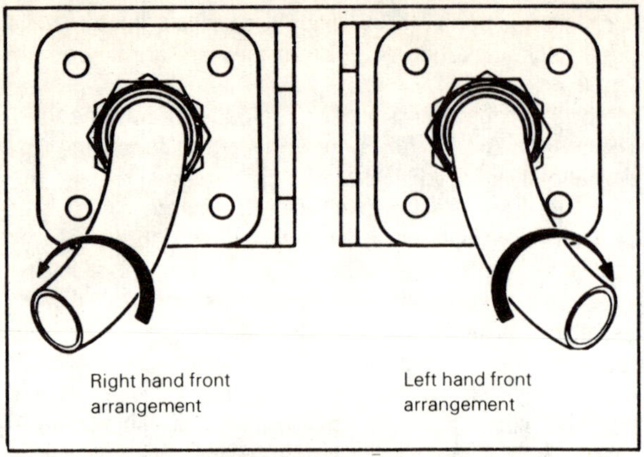

Fig. 15.9 When reconnecting the front brake hoses, turn the end fittings through 1½–2 notches in the direction shown

High-temperature brake grease. For a complete overhaul: Replacement relined brake shoes; set of new pull-off springs; possibly, new wheel cylinders.
Tools: Brake-adjusting spanner. Screwdriver. Pliers. Length of string.

1 Remove the drum as described in Section 15.6 or 15.7.

2 Remove the clips that retain the shoes on the back-plate.

3 Disconnect one end of the brake shoe retracting spring from the shoe, using pliers or a length of rod with a hooked end. An alternative method is to lever the tip of one shoe away from the brake expander, allowing the shoes to be collapsed together and the spring to be disengaged.

4 Tie a length of string around the ends of the brake cylinder to prevent the piston creeping outwards, resulting in loss of fluid and entry of air into the system. Renault dealers use a wire clip but this is not essential.

5 If it is necessary to remove a wheel cylinder, disconnect the brake pipe and unscrew the mounting bolts from the back of the brake backplate. In the case of the front brake cylinders on pre-1967 models, it is necessary to unscrew the four hub retaining nuts before the cylinder retaining bolts can be undone.

6 After reassembling the brake, press hard on the pedal to ensure that the shoes are correctly seated before adjusting the shoes as described in Section 15.4.

15.9 Servicing the brake hoses

The brake hoses should be inspected during routine servicing for any signs of leakage, chafing or general deterioration. They should in any case be renewed after about 36 000 miles or 3 years in service.

Scrupulous cleanliness is vital when removing and refitting the hoses. Always uncouple or couple-up the end which is coupled to the metal brake pipe first and be careful not to twist the hose when loosening or tightening the union. Make sure that it is located so that it cannot rub against any of the suspension components. Check that the steering turns to the full lock in each direction.

If new front-brake hoses are being fitted, the wheels must be hanging free and the hose must be offered up to the support lug without any twist. The end fitting must then be turned through a minimum of 1½ notches and a maximum of two notches in the direction shown in Fig. 15.9.

16 The electrical system

Routine servicing of the electrical system is quite straightforward, calling for no specialized equipment; nor should simple fault-tracing and first-aid measures present any problems. If any serious troubles crop-up, however, it is best to take advantage of the service-exchange scheme operated by your dealer, under which a faulty component is replaced by a reconditioned, guaranteed unit at a fixed charge (this subject is discussed in more detail in Chapter 8).

The time factor

The maintenance checks and simple servicing work described in this chapter do not normally call for pre-planning, minor jobs taking only a few minutes each. Suggested times for more ambitious work are: Removing and refitting the dynamo or alternator, 45 min; removing and refitting the starter motor 45 – 60 min; overhauling a starter motor, 2 hr.

16.1 Battery maintenance

An excellent safety feature on later models is that in the event of a short-circuit occurring, the battery can be instantly disconnected by unscrewing the wing-nut on the negative battery post by a few turns, but never do this when the engine is running, as it will damage the generator.

The tops of the cells must be kept clean and dry, to prevent corrosion of the terminals and leakage of current.

The battery-retaining clamp should be just sufficiently tight to prevent movement of the battery on its mounting. Overtightening it may crack or distort the battery case.

To clean the terminals and terminal posts –

1 Take off the connectors.

2 Scrape any corrosion off the terminals.

3 Replace the connectors and tighten the retaining screws. Smear the terminals and posts with petroleum jelly to protect them against corrosion.

4 Don't overlook the connections at the earthed end of the battery earthing strap, at the starter motor and at the solenoid switch. These connections must be clean and secure.

16.2 Topping-up the battery cells

Check the level of the liquid (the electrolyte) in each cell at weekly intervals and don't allow it to fall lower than 15 mm (just over ½ in.) above the tops of the plates. Bear in mind the following points –

1 Distilled, demineralized or 'purified' water is obtainable quite cheaply from chemists. Tapwater and rainwater may contain impurities that will shorten the life of the battery. In an emergency, water from the drip-tray of a refrigerator which has been defrosted can be used, but *not* the water obtained by melting ice cubes.

2 Never use a naked flame when inspecting the fluid level or allow sparking to occur near the battery when it is being charged. A mixture of hydrogen and oxygen is produced when the electrolyte begins to bubble and if this is ignited the battery can explode.

3 Add water just before the cells are to be charged, to allow the acid and water to mix thoroughly, and to avoid any risk of the water freezing, expanding and damaging the plates and battery case in cold weather.

4 The need for frequent topping-up usually suggests too high a generator charging rate. If one cell regularly requires more than the others, it is probably leaking. Unless the battery is nearly new, or still under guarantee, repairs to individual cells are not usually worthwhile.

5 It should not be necessary to add *acid* to the cells unless some of the electrolyte has been spilt, in which case it would be wise to have a word with your dealer.

6 Finally, remember that the electrolyte is a very corrosive solution of sulphuric acid in water. If any is spilled, wipe it away immediately with a clean wet cloth and then dry the part thoroughly. Household ammonia will neutralize the acid.

16.3 Inspecting and servicing the dynamo

Either a Paris-Rhône or a Ducellier dynamo may be fitted. The two are interchangeable, *but the charging regulator must be of the same make as the dynamo.* If the commutator and brushes require servicing, it is necessary to remove the dynamo and to take off the rear end-plate at the opposite end to the pulley if a Paris-Rhône dynamo is fitted, and the end-plate and body in the case of a Ducellier dynamo.

If the front ball bearing or rear bearing bush is worn, the bearing housings must be changed as complete assemblies.

To dismantle the dynamo –

Materials: New brushes and new end-plate assemblies, if required. Paraffin.

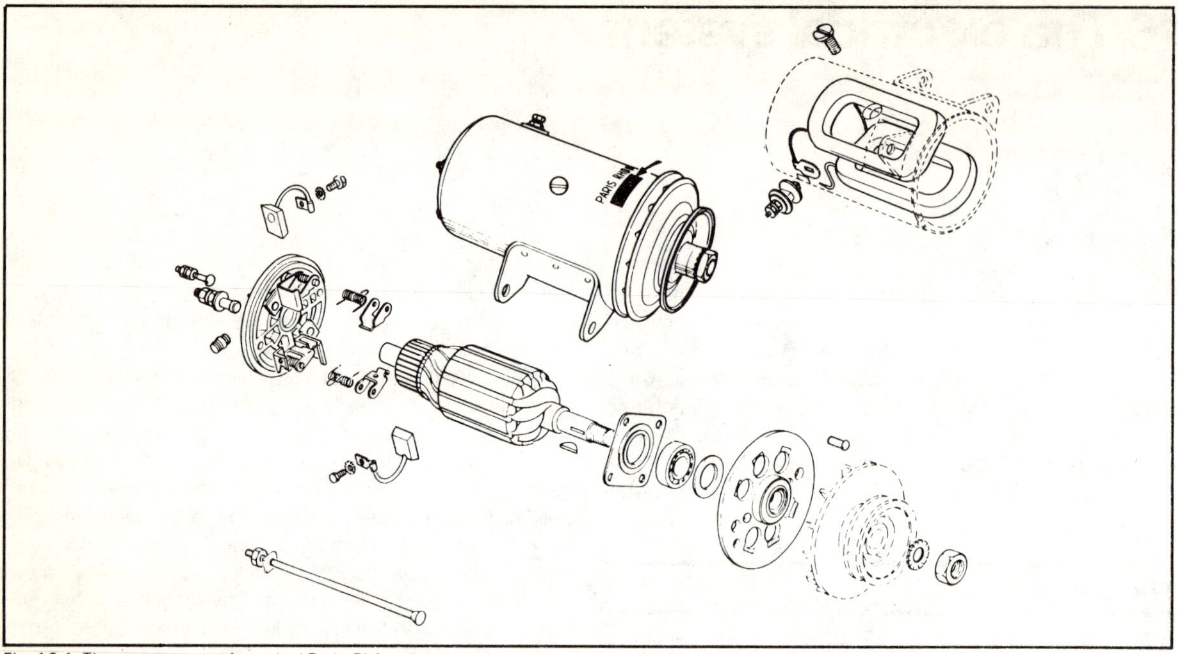

Fig. 16.1 The components of a typical Paris-Rhône dynamo

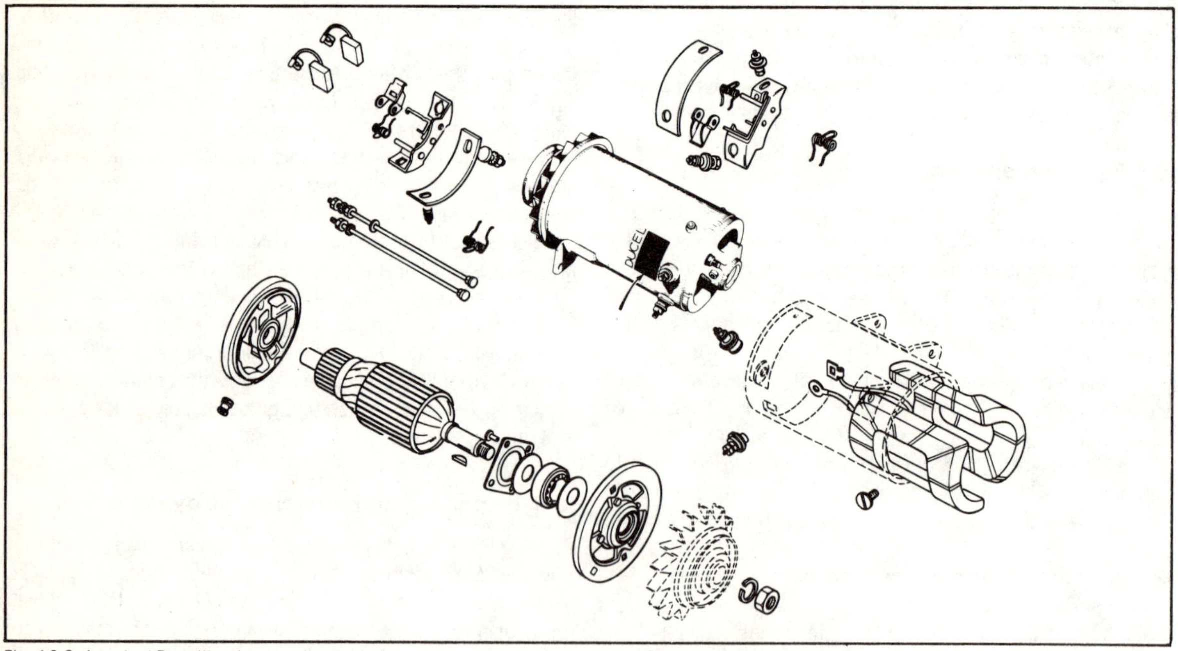

Fig. 16.2 A typical Ducellier dynamo dismantled

Tools: Spanners. Screwdriver. Pliers. Vice.

1 Unlock the pulley nut, holding the pulley in the protected jaws of a vice and being careful not to damage it.

2 Remove the long bolts that pass through the dynamo and take off the rear bearing plate. On a Paris-Rhône dynamo this carries the brushes and to prevent any risk of damaging them, insert two metal strips through the slots in the end-plate to keep them clear of the commutator.

3 Slide the body off the armature, holding the brushes clear of the commutator in the case of a Ducellier dynamo. The commutator, an assembly of copper segments at the end of the rotating armature, and the brushes, can now be examined.

4 Clean the commutator. If it is scored, take it to an

electrical specialist, who will skim it in a lathe.

5 Check that the brushes move freely in their holders. If they stick, clean them and their holders with a cloth moistened with petrol. If they are worn down to a minimum length of 11 mm (about 7/16 in.) for a Ducellier dynamo or 8 mm (about 5/16 in.) for a Paris-Rhône type, renew them. If worn but serviceable brushes are refitted, make sure that they are inserted in their original positions, to maintain the correct 'bedding'.

6 If new brushes are to be fitted, bed them to the shape of the commutator by wrapping emery paper around a cylindrical length of wood or tube which is approximately the same diameter as the commutator and rotating this between the brushes in the opposite direction to the normal rotation of the armature.

7 When reassembling the dynamo, hold the brushes clear of the commutator, using two metal strips passed through the end-plate in the case of a Paris-Rhône dynamo.

8 A new dynamo, or one that has been overhauled, may be de-energized, which means that it will not charge when refitted. To re-energize it, connect it to the car battery, taking a wire from the negative battery terminal to the dynamo body and a lead from the positive terminal to the EXC terminal on the dynamo.

16.4 Servicing an alternator

An alternator requires no routine maintenance, except for keeping the terminals clean and the end-plate free from deposits of dust and grease and checking the driving belt tension as described in Chapter 10. There are, however, several practical points to be remembered when dealing with an alternator which may be overlooked by an owner who has previously dealt with dynamos.

If the battery has been removed, when refitting it, first connect the negative battery terminal to the earth strap and then fit the positive terminal connector. *Never disconnect the battery when the engine is running.*

Care must be taken not to earth the regulator or the 'EXC' wire on the alternator. Never run the engine with the main output cable from the alternator disconnected.

If a charger is to be used to charge-up a flat battery, first isolate the alternator by disconnecting both battery terminals.

If the charging circuit gives trouble, or the alternator requires routine servicing, the work should always be done by a fully-qualified auto-electrician.

16.5 Starter motor servicing

The models covered by this book are fitted with Ducellier or Paris-Rhône starter motors. In both types the pinion is moved into engagement with the flywheel starter ring by a lever which is operated by a solenoid mounted on the motor.

The starter motor should be serviced at reasonable intervals – say at 36 000 miles (60 000 km) – when it should be removed from the car and dismantled, preferably by an auto-electrician, so that the commutator, brushes and the pinion drive components can be inspected and serviced as necessary.

If you decide to do the work yourself, stripping is quite straightforward, but when reassembling the starter it is necessary to adjust the engaged and disengaged positions of the pinion accurately, which calls for the use of the Renault gauge Elé. 17. As an owner will be unlikely to have this gauge it is suggested that when the starter motor has been rebuilt it should be taken to a Renault dealer to have the setting checked. He may also be able to check the torque developed when the pinion is locked; this indicates the efficiency of the motor.

The brushes should be renewed if they have worn down to a minimum length of about 8 mm (5/16 in.)

If the drive is dismantled, fit a new spring locating ring and a new stop to the shaft when reassembling. The stop must cover the snap ring and should be peened over at several points to trap the ring.

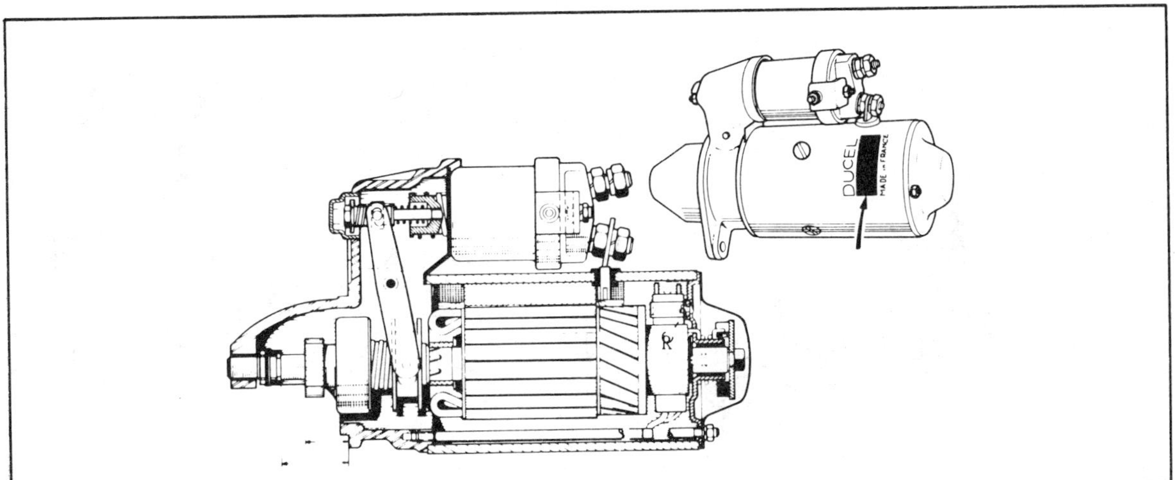

Fig. 16.3 The Ducellier starter motor, in which the pinion is engaged by a solenoid-operated lever

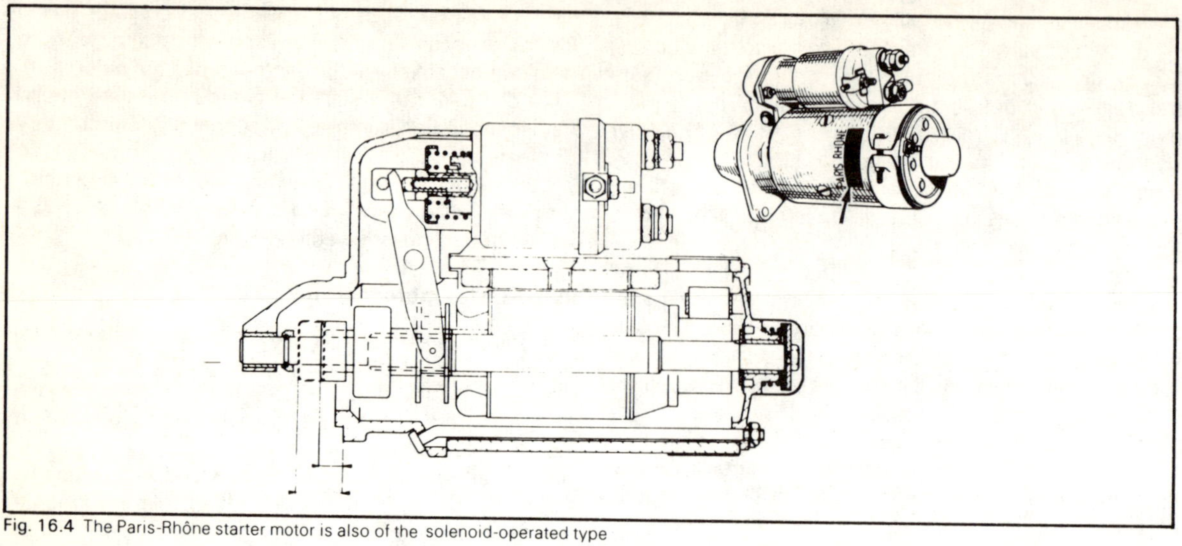

Fig. 16.4 The Paris-Rhône starter motor is also of the solenoid-operated type

16.6 Removing and refitting the starter

Tools: Spanners.

1 Disconnect the battery before disconnecting the main lead and the solenoid wire from the starter solenoid terminals.

2 Take out the two bolts from the flexible coupling on the steering shaft and undo the exhaust pipe clamp bolts so that the exhaust pipe can be turned clear of the starter.

3 The starter motor can then be withdrawn from the front after undoing the two securing bolts.

4 After refitting the motor and reconnecting the flexible coupling on the steering column, check that the steering-wheel spokes are horizontal.

16.7 Adjusting the headlamp beam

It is difficult to align the headlamp beams correctly by hit-and-miss methods of adjustment in the home garage, using aiming marks on the wall. Most service stations, however, have optical beam-setting equipment which enables the lamps to be accurately set. The alignment should be checked with this equipment twice a year if a lot of night driving is done, or at least once every autumn.

The headlamp beam can be raised or lowered by turning screw 1 in Fig. 16.6, and swung from side to side by rotating screw 2. Make sure, however, that the lever beneath the headlamp which controls the height of the beam is correctly set. It should be moved to the left to lower the beam when the car is fully laden and to the right when only a light load is carried.

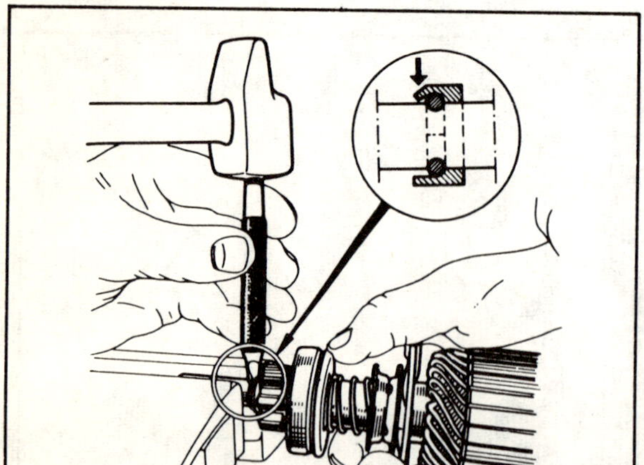

Fig. 16.5 When reassembling the starter pinion, use a new stop and peen it over to trap the snap ring

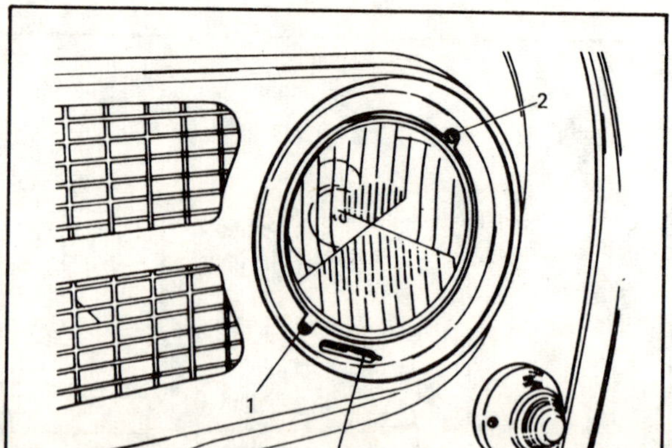

Fig. 16.6 The screw 1 raises and lowers the headlamp beam and the screw 2 swings it from side to side. The lever 3 allows the height of the beam to be pre-set to suit the load in the car

16.8 Removing a headlamp unit or bulb

1 To change the bulb or the light unit on a pre-1968 model, remove the headlamp rim, lift the catch C shown in Fig. 16.7, and remove the unit. The bulb can then be changed by pulling off the connector and lifting the springs that retain it in the reflector. If the reflector has provision for changing the direction of the dipped beam to suit driving on the left-hand or the right-hand side of the road, push the lever to the left for driving on the right and to the right for driving on the left.

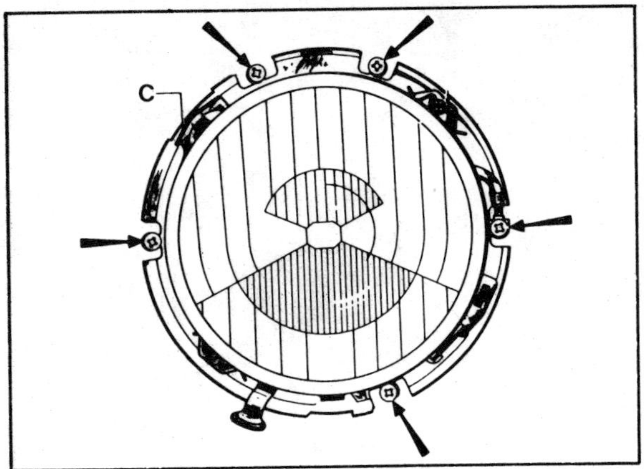

Fig. 16.7 A pre-1968 light unit is retained by the screws indicated and by the catch C

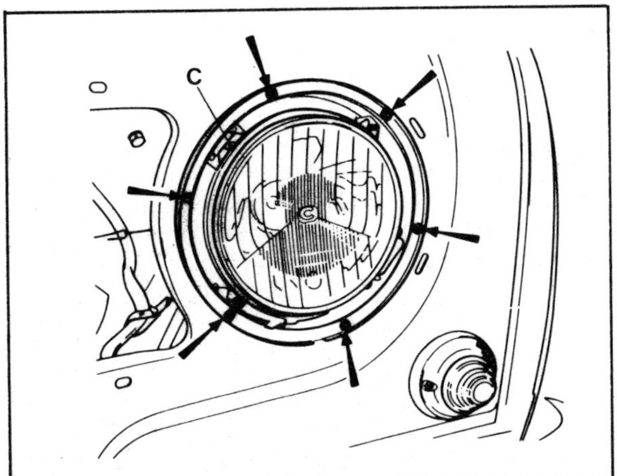

Fig. 16.8 A post-1968 headlamp. The arrows indicate the retaining screws. C is the spring catch

2 To change the light unit on a model from 1968 onwards, remove the radiator grille, lift the catch and remove the unit. The bulb alone can be changed, however, from inside the engine compartment by lifting the two retaining springs on the back of the reflector. On these models, if provision is made for changing the beam for driving on the left or right, lower the lever for driving on the right or raise it for driving on the left.

3 When fitting a new bulb be careful not to touch the glass with the fingers as the slightest trace of grease or moisture will be carbonized by the heat of the filament, reducing the amount of light emitted by the bulb. This is particularly important with halogen headlamps, in which the bulbs run at a very high temperature. Handle the bulb only with a tissue or a clean dry cloth.

16.9 Renewing the side, stop and tail lamp bulbs

Renewal of the bulbs in these lamps is quite straightforward, since the covers are retained by screws, except for some models in which the side lights may be incorporated in the headlamps.

16.10 Changing the instrument panel illumination and warning lamb bulbs

The holders for these bulbs are inserted in the back of the instrument panel, which must be removed in order to change them. The work is not difficult, but on some models it is a little tricky and if you are a novice you may prefer to leave the job to your Renault dealer.

If you decide to remove the panel yourself, work systematically when disconnecting the various switches, cowls and embellishing strips and ease the panel forward

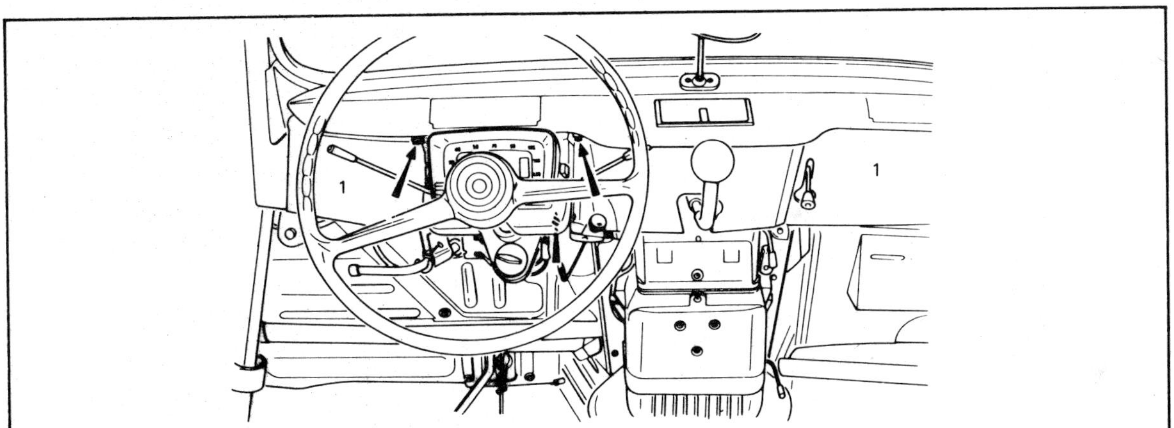

Fig. 16.9 The instrument panel and dashboard fitted to 1965 and 1966 models. The instrument panel is retained by the screws shown by the arrows, but before it can be removed it is necessary to remove the glove compartment panels 1

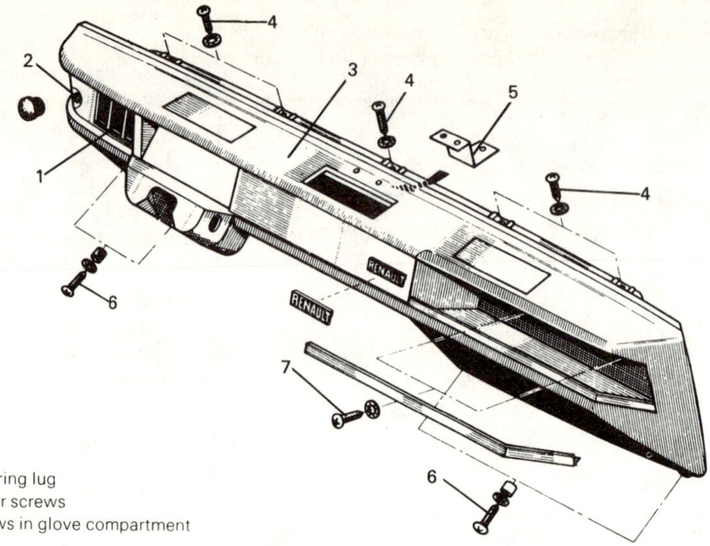

1 Switches
2 Windscreen washer
3 Dashboard moulding
4 Top screws
5 Securing lug
6 Lower screws
7 Screws in glove compartment

Fig. 16.10 The dashboard fitted to later models

far enough to allow the wires to be disconnected (after first marking each wire to ensure correct reassembly) and the speedometer drive to be uncoupled.

1 On models up to 1966, disconnect the battery, remove the two glove compartment panels and unscrew the two nuts which retain the instrument panel. This can then be eased forward and the speedometer cable union can be unscrewed if necessary.

2 On later models, first disconnect the battery and remove the dash panel. Remove the steering wheel, which is retained by three bolts beneath the embellisher, and also the lighting and direction indicator switches and the three switches fitted in the panel and the windscreen washer. Turn the triangular steering column support with one of the corners upwards to make it easier to free the dashboard, which can then be removed by undoing the five retaining bolts from its upper edge, the two screws in the glove compartment and the four screws and spacers from its lower edge. The nuts which retain the instrument panel can then be removed, enabling the panel to be moved forward and the speedometer cable to be disconnected if necessary.

16.11 The windscreen wiper and washer

The wiper normally requires no attention, other than renewal of the wiper blades at least once a year.

If the blades do not sweep a clean arc, wash the rubbers and the screen with a special windscreen detergent such as Trico SR-12 to remove deposits of diesel fumes, which will cause persistent smearing. Always add a wiper-fluid detergent to the water in the washer reservoir, using an anti-freeze type in winter. Do not use ordinary radiator anti-freeze solution, which will damage the paintwork.

16.12 Direction indicators

The flashing indicator lamps are fed with current from a sealed control unit. Failure or erratic action of the indicators may be caused by a blown bulb, dirty contacts in the indicator switch or in the lamp units, or by faulty wiring or a blown fuse. If checks on these points do not reveal any faults, the flasher unit is probably the culprit and must be replaced, since it is not repairable.

The flasher unit is held behind the fascia panel. When removing and refitting it label the leads to match the '+', 'Com' and 'Rep' terminals.

16.13 Testing a faulty brake stop-light switch

On earlier cars the switch is operated by the fluid pressure in the braking system and is screwed into the end of the master cylinder. If it is necessary to renew it, seal the master cylinder by screwing the cap of the reservoir down on to a sheet of plastic in order to reduce the loss of fluid to the minimum. The system should, however, be bled as described in Section 15.3 after the switch has been refitted or a new switch has been installed.

On later models the switch is operated by the brake pedal.

To check the circuit –

1 If the stop lights flicker or do not come on when the brake pedal is depressed, check the lamp bulbs, holders, the wiring and the fuse.

2 If everything seems to be in order, disconnect the wires from the stop-lamp switch, switch on the ignition and touch the terminals on the wires together. If the stop-lamps then light up, either the stop-lamp switch is

faulty or the leads were making poor contact with the terminals on the switch. If the stop-lamps do not come on when the wires are short-circuited, there must be a fault at some point in the wiring or the fuse has blown (see Section 16.14).

16.14 The fuses

Prior to the 1971 models no fuses were fitted, and those provided on later cars vary with the different models.

The fuse-box is attached to the engine bulkhead. It holds four fuses in clips, three of which, rated at 8 amp, protect the instruments, stop-lights, interior lamp, windscreen wiper motor and the heater fan motor. The fourth, rated at 5 amp, serves the direction-indicator circuits.

There may also be a supplementary fuse-box which contains fuses for the headlamp main and dipped-beam circuits. If a radio is fitted, an in-line fuse will be provided in a tubular holder inserted in the feed wire.

A blown fuse can be immediately identified by the break in the metal link. It should always be replaced by a fuse of the same value – never be tempted to bridge the clips with ordinary wire, although household fuse wire of the same rating could be used in an emergency. Always carry a selection of spare fuses.

Simple fault-tracing

There are some simple tests that can be made when it is suspected that the generator is not giving its full charge.

16.17 Testing the generator and charging system

The following tests, for which only a voltmeter is required, are sufficient to show whether or not all is well with the generator and the charging system. A moving-coil type of meter is to be preferred, but any good-quality instrument can be used, as the checks depend on comparative readings, rather than on exact voltages. They are based on the fact that the battery voltage varies according to the state of charge, and is always higher when the cells are receiving a charge from the generator.

To make the test –

1 Clip the voltmeter leads to the battery terminals, making sure that the surface of the metal has been pierced. If the battery is sound and well charged, a reading of 12–12.5 volts should be obtained.

2 Switch on all the lights. The reading should now fall to approximately 11–11.5 volts.

3 Start the engine and speed it up to the equivalent of about 20 mph in top gear, but do not race it. The reading should now be about 13.5 volts, and the voltmeter needle should be steady. If it flickers, there may be a bad contact in the wiring, the generator commutator may be dirty, the brushes may be worn or sticking, or the regulator may be faulty.

4 If voltage readings roughly equal to those quoted are obtained, it can be assumed that the battery and charging system are sound. If the voltage across the battery does not rise by 1 volt when the engine is speeded-up above idling speed, there is a fault somewhere in the charging system, probably one of those just mentioned. If the increase exceeds about 1.5 volts, either the regulator is incorrectly adjusted or the battery is faulty. Do not try to adjust the regulator. Leave this sort of work to a qualified auto-electrician.

16.16 Wiring diagrams

The increasing tendency to separate the wiring looms of modern cars into convenient sections which are coupled together by junction blocks or by non-reversible multi-pin connectors makes life easier for the service engineer and, of course, for the practical owner who wants to replace a faulty section of the loom with the minimum cost and expenditure of time and effort.

When the insulation is damaged or a wire is burnt-out as the result of a short-circuit or a fault in a component, the adjacent wires in the loom are almost invariably damaged, so replacement of the affected section is the only practicable course.

Bearing this in mind, we have included in this chapter and on the back cover of the book, diagrams of the connectors for the components which are likely to be removed for servicing or repair. The colour-coding of the wires should prevent any possibility of incorrect connections, although this is often taken care by the design of the connectors themselves, but the dates quoted are only approximate and different colour codes may be found. As a precaution, record the colour and position of each wire before disconnecting it.

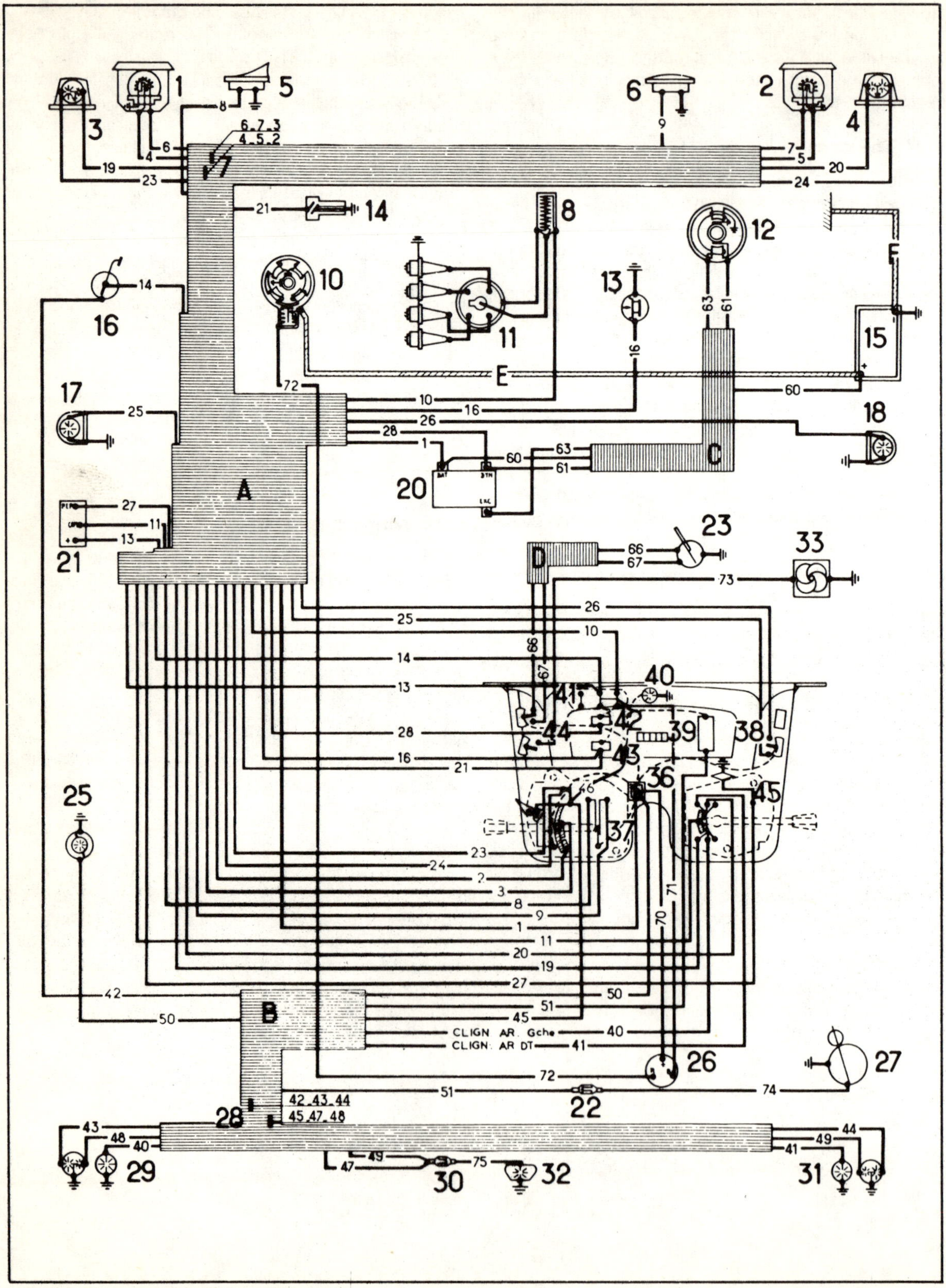

Fig. 16.11 Wiring diagram for 1965 and 1966 models

Key to Fig. 16.11 –

UNITS

1 Left-hand headlight
2 Right-hand headlight
3 Front side lights and left-hand front flasher
4 Front side lights and right-hand front flasher
5 Town horn
6 Road horn
7 Front harness joints
8 Ignition coil
9 Electric choke
10 Starter
11 Sparking plugs
12 Dynamo
13 Oil pressure switch
14 Water temperature switch
15 Battery
16 Stop light switch
17 Left-hand parking light
18 Right-hand parking light
19 Junction on oil pressure switch and electric choke circuit
20 Regulator
21 Flasher unit
22 Junction terminals on fuel gauge circuit
23 Windscreen wiper
24 Instrument panel
25 Interior light
26 Ignition/starter switch
27 Fuel gauge
28 Joints on rear harness
29 Left-hand rear light assembly
30 Junction terminals on feed to licence plate light
31 Right-hand rear light assembly
32 Licence plate light
33 Heater
36 Instrument panel junction plate
37 Combination lighting switch
38 Control block: parking lights and oil pressure warning light
39 Fuel gauge
40 Instrument panel lighting
41 Instrument panel junction plate
42 Charge-discharge warning light
43 Water temperature warning light
44 Control block: heating, windscreen wiper
45 Flasher switch
46 Flasher tell-tale
47 Windscreen wiper switch
48 Heater switch
49 Parking light switch

WIRING HARNESSES

A Front harness
B Rear harness
C Charging circuit
D Windscreen wiper cable
E Battery positive lead
F Battery negative lead

WIRES

Harness	Wire No.	Sleeve colour	Wire colour	Wires connected between items below
A	1	White/blue	Black	20–36
	2	Green	Grey	37–7
	3	Pink	Beige	37–7
	4	–	Blue	7–1
	5	–	Blue	7–2
	6	–	Red	7–1
	7	–	Red	7–2
	8	Violet	Red	37–5
	9	White	White	37–6
	10	Red	Red	41–8
	11	Blue	Blue	45–21
	13	Red	Red	41–21
	14	Red	Grey	41–16
	16	Maroon	Grey	13–43
	19	Violet	Grey	45–3
	20	Maroon	Grey	45–4
	21	Maroon	Green	14–43
	23	Yellow	Red	37–3
	24	Yellow	White	37–4
	25	Violet	Black	38–17
	26	Maroon	Black	38–18
	27	Red	Blue	21–45
	28	Blue	White	20–42
B	40	Violet	Grey	45–29
	41	Maroon	Grey	45–31
	42	Pink	Pink	16–28
	43	–	Pink	28–29
	44	–	Pink	28–31
	45	Yellow	Yellow	37–28
	46	Yellow	White	37–40
	47	–	Yellow	28–30
	48	–	Red	28–29
	49	–	Red	30–31
	50	Blue	White	36–25
	51	Violet	White	39–22
C	60	White	Black	15–20
	61	Blue	Black	12–20
	63	Green	Green	20–12
D	66	Blue	Grey	44–23
	67	Green	Green	44–23
E	68	–	–	15–10
F	69	–	–	15–Ground (Earth)
Single wires	70	White	Black	36–26
	71	Red	Black	26–41
	72	Silver	Black	26–10
	73	Black	Grey	44–33
	74	Violet	White	22–27
	75	–	Black	30–32

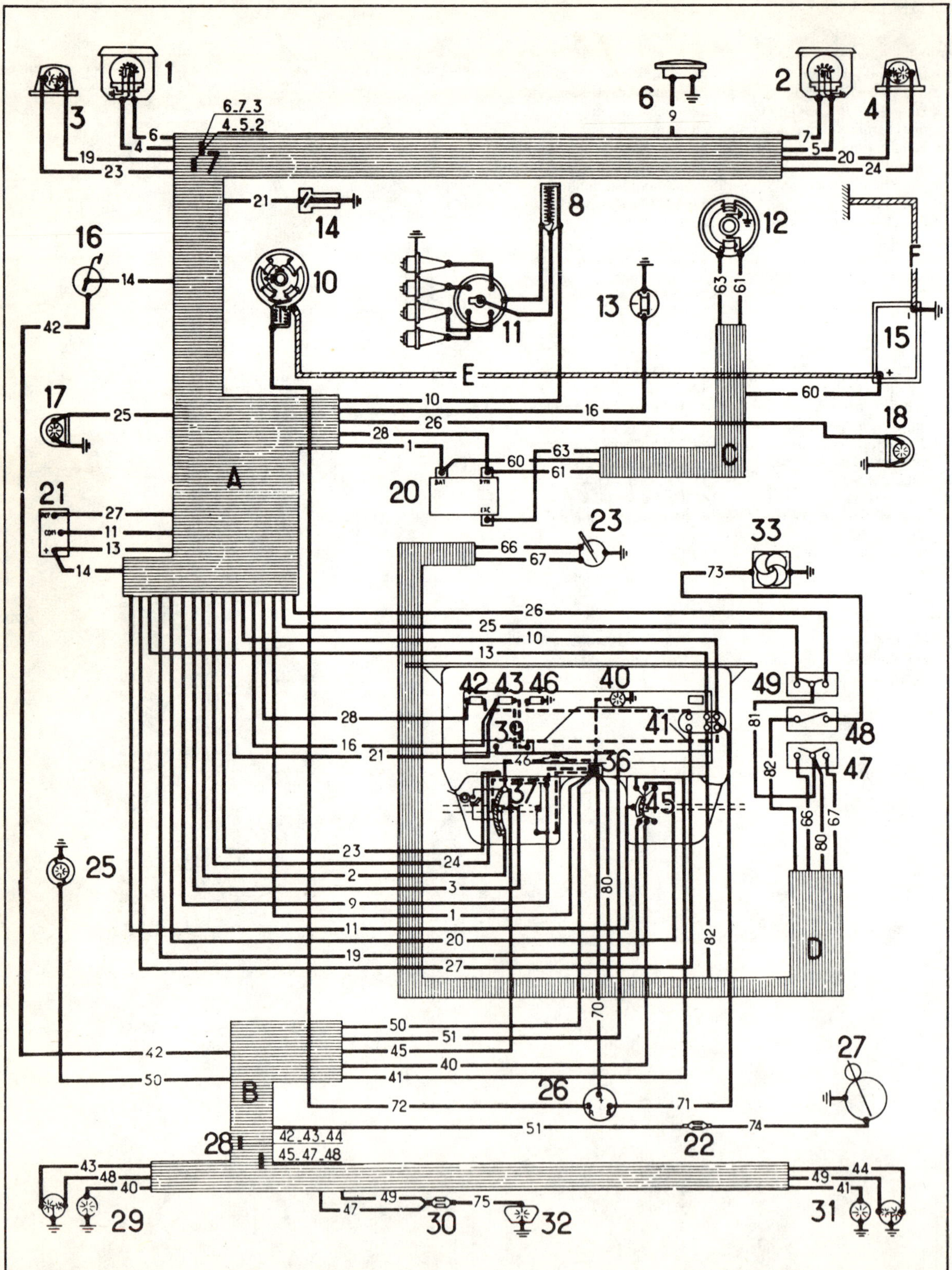

Figs. 16.12 Wiring diagram for models from 1967 to approximately 1971

WIRES

Harness	Wire No.	Sleeve colour	Wire colour	Wire connected between items below
A	1	Clear	White	20–36
	2	–	Grey	37–7
	3	Clear	Beige	37–7
	4	–	Blue	7–1
	5	–	Blue	7–2
	6	–	Red	7–1
	9	Clear	White	37–6
	10	–	Red	41–8
	11	–	Blue	21–45
	13	–	Red	41–21
	14	–	Grey	21–16
	16	–	Grey	13–43
	19	–	Grey	45–3
	20	–	Green	45–4
	21	–	Green	14–43
	23	–	Red	37–3
	24	–	White	37–4
	25	–	Black	49–17
	26	–	Black	49–18
	27	–	Pink	21–41
	28	Blue	Blue	20–42
B	40	–	Grey	45–29
	41	–	Green	45–31
	42	–	Pink	16–28
	43	–	Pink	28–29
	44	–	Pink	28–31
	45	–	Yellow	37–28
	46	–	White	37–40
	47	–	Yellow	28–30
	48	–	Red	28–29
	49	–	Red	30–31
	50	Clear	Blue	36–25
	51	–	White	22–39
C	60	Clear	White	15–20
	61	Clear	Black	12–20
	63	Clear	Green	20–12
D	66	Clear	Grey	47–23
	67	–	Green	47–23
	80	Clear	Pink	36–47
	81	–	Blue	47–49
	82	–	Red	41–48
E	68	–	–	15–10
F	69	–	–	15-Earth
Single wires	70	White	Black	36–26
	71	Red	Black	26–41
	72	Clear	Black	26–10
	73	–	Black	48–33
	74	–	White	22–27
	75	–	Black	30–32

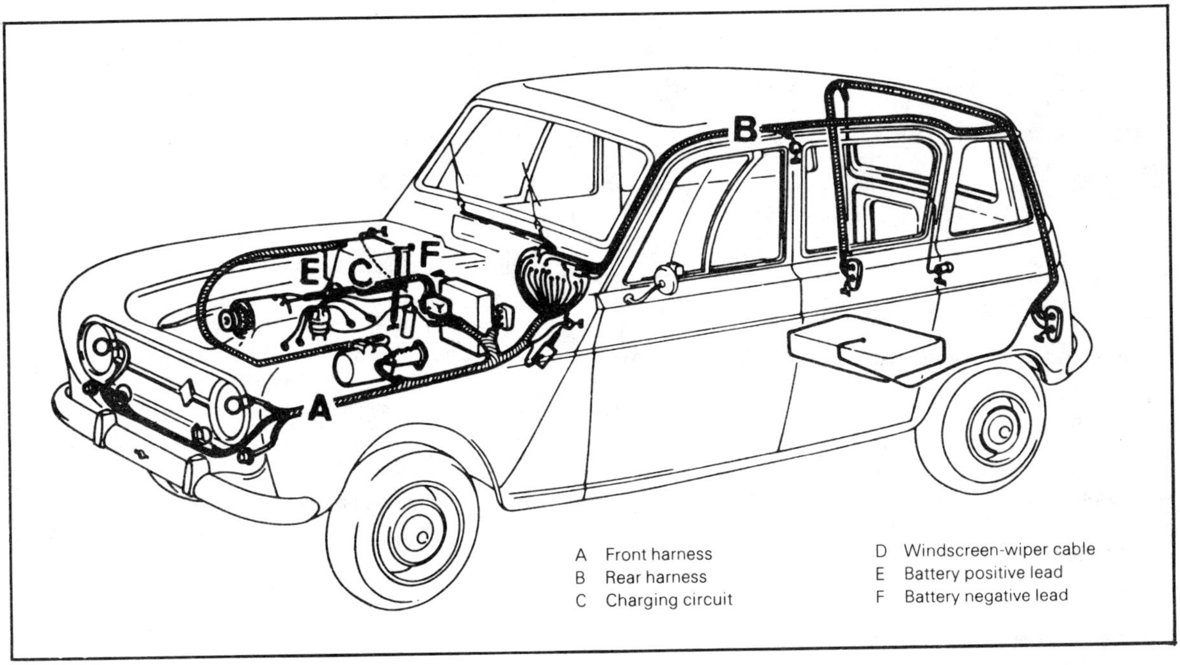

Fig. 16.13 The wiring harnesses. Although this is a left-hand-drive model a similar arrangement is used on right-hand-drive cars

17 Specifications and overhaul data

In this chapter we have included specifications and data which will be needed to carry out adjustments, overhauls and replacements which are within the scope of a d.i.y. owner.

We have avoided giving elaborate lists of fits, clearances and engineering tolerances, since internal and external micrometers, depth gauges and the other precision measuring equipment required to check these, are not likely to be found – or needed – in the average home garage.

As we recommend in Chapter 8, highly-skilled work of this sort should be left to a Renault dealer or to a specialist who is best qualified to handle it. Alternatively, it is often possible to fit a reconditioned, service-exchange component at a cost which shows a considerable saving over the price of a new part.

We make no apology for the fact that in some cases we have used a mixture of metric and Imperial measurements. Since these cars are built to metric standards, measurements in millimetres are often in round figures and can be more easily checked. On the other hand, many owners will have feeler gauges and other measuring tools calibrated in thousandths of an inch or a torque wrench calibrated in pounds feet. We have therefore given the equivalents of the metric measurements, as far as possible to the nearest thousandth of an inch or the nearest pound foot.

When self-locking nuts (stiff nuts) are fitted, these should not be re-used if their self-locking effect has been reduced or if they are of the deformed-thread type and the laquer coating has been affected. They should not be degreased. As a precaution, it is better to fit new nuts.

Top-up and fill-up data

Capacities (approx.)

Fuel tank: up to August 1974	5¾ gal (26.2 litres)
August 1974 on	7½ gal (34 litres)
Engine oil capacity	4½ pints (2.5 litres)
Cooling system (including heater and expansion bottle)	
up to October 1973	8½ pints (4.8 litres)
October 1973 on	9½ pints (5.5 litres)
Gearbox: Type 328, up to September 1967	1½ pints (0.85 litre)
Type 334, September 1967 – August 1973	2½ pints (1.15 litres)
Type 354, August 1973 on	3¼ pints (1.8 litres)

Recommended fuel grade Regular grade, 90–92 octane (2-star in UK)

Oil consumption

A reasonable consumption for a *worn* engine is about 500–750 miles per pint. The figure for a new or reconditioned engine may be as high as 350 miles per pint, gradually improving during the first 2000–3000 miles as the piston rings and cylinder walls bed-in, and eventually becoming negligible between oil changes.

Recommended lubricants (temperate climates)

Engine	Multigrade oil 10W/40, 10W/50, 20W/40, 20W/50
Ignition distributor shaft, contact-breaker pivot, automatic timing control	Engine oil

Gearbox	SAE 80EP
Wheel hub bearings	High-melting-point grease

Engine – see Chapter 9

Four-cylinder, water-cooled, push-rod-operated, overhead-valve, in-line unit, with clutch and gearbox mounted ahead of engine.

The type numbers of the engines covered by this book are given below and we have used these to identify the different units where necessary.

800-01 845 cc engine fitted to models before October 1973.

800-05 Detoxed (anti-pollution) engine fitted to 1974 and later models (October 1973 onwards). Similar to 800-01, apart from anti-pollution carburettor and air filter, aluminium-tin main and big-end bearing shells, the fitting of an external oil filter and larger cooling system capacity.

Technical specifications – engine

Capacity	845 cc (51 cu in.)
Cylinder bore	58 mm (2.284 in.)
Piston stroke	80 mm (3.150 in.)
Compression ratio	8:1
Power output (DIN): 800-01 engine	27 bhp at 4700 rpm
800-05 engine	34 bhp at 5000 rpm
Firing order	1, 3, 4, 2

Engine lubrication

Oil filter: 800-01 engine	Gauze filter in sump only
800-05 engine	Screw-on replaceable canister beneath petrol pump
Minimum oil pressure, engine hot:	
at idling speed	17 lb/sq in. (1.2 kg/cm^2 or bars)
at 4000 rpm (50–60 mph in top gear)	34 lb/sq in. (2.4 kg/cm^2 or bars)

Engine maintenance and repair

Valve/rocker clearances: Hot	Inlet, 0.18 mm (0.0075 in.)
	Exhaust, 0.25 mm (0.010 in.)
Cold	Inlet, 0.15 mm (0.006 in.)
	Exhaust, 0.20 mm (0.008 in.)
Crankshaft end-float	0.05–0.25 mm (0.002–0.010 in.)
Camshaft end-float	0.06–0.14 mm (0.002–0.0055 in.)
Cylinder head – maximum bow on seating face for gasket	0.05 mm (0.002 in.)

Torque-wrench settings	lb ft	Nm
Cylinder-head securing bolts: cold	45	60
hot	48	65
Main bearing cap bolts	45	60
Connecting rod big-end cap nuts	26	35
Flywheel fixing bolts	35	45

Cooling system – see Chapter 10

Type	Pressurized, sealed system, with expansion bottle. Engine-driven fan
Pressure in system	13 lb/sq in. (0.9 kg/cm^2 or bar)
Thermostat: type	Bellows type fitted in outlet from water pump
opening temperature	Marked on flange – normally 85°C (185°F)
Anti-freeze solution	This must be of a suitable type to prevent corrosion of the engine and heater matrix, and the special Renault coolant should therefore be used. This is particularly important for later cars which have aluminium heater matrices.

Carburettor and petrol pump – see Chapter 11

Carburettor: 800-01 engines	Solex 26 DIS5 or Zenith 28IF – Mk V05-069
800–05 engines	Solex 32 EISA4

Standard jet settings should not be changed without consulting a Renault dealer

Petrol pump	Mechanical diaphragm pump operated by a cam on the camshaft

Ignition system – see Chapter 12

Sparking-plug type	Champion L87Y or plugs of other makes having equivalent heat range
Sparking-plug gap	0.024–0.028 in. (0.6–0.7 mm)
Distributor	Ducellier or SEV-Marchal
Distributor rotor rotation	Clockwise
Contact-breaker points gap	0.016 in. (0.4 mm)
Dwell angle	57° ± 3°

Static ignition timing

The initial ignition setting depends on the automatic advance curve of the distributor. The reference number is stamped on the side of the distributor body.

Advance in degrees, or measured on flywheel before tdc mark –

800-01 engines. Models up to 1971, distributor advance curve A46. 1974 models onwards, distributor advance curve R284	6°+ 1° 10mm ± 1mm (25/64 ±3/64 in.)
800-01 and 800-05 engines. 1972-73 models, distributor advance curve R252	0° ± 0° 0 ± 1.8 mm (0 ± 5/64 in.)

Clutch, gearbox, drive shafts – see Chapter 13

Clutch type	Single dry plate. Early models, coil spring 1969 models onwards, diaphragm spring

Clutch cable adjustment, free-play at operating lever	2½–4 mm (3/32–5/32 in.)
Gearbox: changes in types fitted	
1965 models	3 forward speeds fully synchronized (type 328)
1968 models (September 1967 on)	4 forward speeds fully synchronized (type 334)
February 1972	Type 334, but without starting handle dog
1974 models (October 1973 on)	4 forward speed fully synchronized (type 354)

Suspension, steering, wheels and tyres – see Chapter 14

Suspension	By torsion bars at front and rear

The steering geometry and front-wheel alignment differ on early and late models and must be checked with the special jigs and gauges held by a Renault dealer. This is not a d.i.y. job.

Torque-wrench settings

	lb ft	Nm
Front stub axle nut	90	120
Upper ball joint	26	35
Bottom ball joint	37	50
Steering arm ball joint	26	35½
Suspension upper and lower arm hinge pins	28	37
Castor tie-rod	30	40

Wheels and tyres

The tyre pressures given below are average figures only. The latest recommendations by the manufacturers of the tyres fitted to your car should always be checked, as there are sometimes variations in the pressures recommended for different makes of tyre. Most garages and tyre specialists should have this information.

Wheel size	13 in.
Tyre size	135–13 radial ply
Tyre pressures: Normal use, front	20 lb/sq in. (1.4 kg/cm^2 or bars)
rear	23 lb/sq in. (1.6 kg/cm^2 or bars)
Fully laden, or continuous fast cruising, front	21 lb/sq in. (1.5 kg/cm^2 or bars)
rear	26 lb/sq in. (1.8 kg/cm^2 or bars)

Braking system - see Chapter 15

Front and rear brakes	Hydraulically-operated drum brakes, with leading and trailing shoes at front and rear, and pressure-limiting valve in rear brake pipeline
Drum diameter	Prior to 1967 models: front, 180 mm; rear, 160 mm 1967-72 models: front, 200 mm; rear, 160 mm 1973 models onwards: front, 200.25 mm; rear, 160.25mm
Handbrake	Cable-operated, working on front shoes
Brake fluid	Conforming to SAE 70 R3 or higher specification

Electrical system – see Chapter 16

Type	Negative terminal of battery earthed
up to September 1970	6-volt system
1971 models (Sept. – Oct. 1970 on)	12-volt system
Generator: up to October 1975	Dynamo
October 1975 on	Alternator

Weights and measures – approx.

Overall length	12 ft 1 in. (3.683 m)
Overall width	4 ft 10½ in. (1.486 m)
Overall height, unladen	5 ft 1 in. (1.549 m)
Ground clearance, laden (under anti-roll bar)	6⅞ in. (175 mm)
Turning circle, between kerbs	32 ft (9.75 m)
Weight	13¾ cwt (700 kg)

Metric conversion tables

Inches	Decimals	Milli-metres	Inches to millimetres		Millimetres to inches		Fahrenheit & Centigrade			
			in.	mm	mm	in.	°F	°C	°C	°F
1/64	0·015625	0·3969	0·0001	0·00254	0·001	0·000039	−20	−28·9	−30	−22
1/32	0·03125	0·7937	0·0002	0·00508	0·002	0·000079	−15	−26·1	−28	−18·4
3/64	0·046875	1·1906	0·0003	0·00762	0·003	0·000118	−10	−23·3	−26	−14·8
1/16	0·0625	1·5875	0·0004	0·01016	0·004	0·000157	−5	−20·6	−24	−11·2
5/64	0·078125	1·9844	0·0005	0·01270	0·005	0·000197	0	−17·8	−22	−7·6
3/32	0·09375	2·3812	0·0006	0·01524	0·006	0·000236	1	−17·2	−20	−4
7/64	0·109375	2·7781	0·0007	0·01778	0·007	0·000276	2	−16·7	−18	−0·4
1/8	0·125	3·1750	0·0008	0·02032	0·008	0·000315	3	−16·1	−16	3·2
9/64	0·140625	3·5719	0·0009	0·02286	0·009	0·000354	4	−15·6	−14	6·8
5/32	0·15625	3·9687	0·001	0·0254	0·01	0·00039	5	−15·0	−12	10·4
11/64	0·171875	4·3656	0·002	0·0508	0·02	0·00079	10	−12·2	−10	14
3/16	0·1875	4·7625	0·003	0·0762	0·03	0·00118	15	−9·4	−8	17·6
13/64	0·203125	5·1594	0·004	0·1016	0·04	0·00157	20	−6·7	−6	21·2
7/32	0·21875	5·5562	0·005	0·1270	0·05	0·00197	25	−3·9	−4	24·8
15/64	0·234375	5·9531	0·006	0·1524	0·06	0·00236	30	−1·1	−2	28·4
1/4	0·25	6·3500	0·007	0·1778	0·07	0·00276	35	1·7	0	32
17/64	0·265625	6·7469	0·008	0·2032	0·08	0·00315	40	4·4	2	35·6
9/32	0·28125	7·1437	0·009	0·2286	0·09	0·00354	45	7·2	4	39·2
19/64	0·296875	7·5406	0·01	0·254	0·1	0·00394	50	10·0	6	42·8
5/16	0·3125	7·9375	0·02	0·508	0·2	0·00787	55	12·8	8	46·4
21/64	0·328125	8·3344	0·03	0·762	0·3	0·01181	60	15·6	10	50
11/32	0·34375	8·7312	0·04	1·016	0·4	0·01575	65	18·3	12	53·6
23/64	0·359375	9·1281	0·05	1·270	0·5	0·01969	70	21·1	14	57·2
3/8	0·375	9·5250	0·06	1·524	0·6	0·02362	75	23·9	16	60·8
25/64	0·390625	9·9219	0·07	1·778	0·7	0·02756	80	26·7	18	64·4
13/32	0·40625	10·3187	0·08	2·032	0·8	0·03150	85	29·4	20	68
27/64	0·421875	10·7156	0·09	2·286	0·9	0·03543	90	32·2	22	71·6
7/16	0·4375	11·1125	0·1	2·54	1	0·03937	95	35·0	24	75·2
29/64	0·453125	11·5094	0·2	5·08	2	0·07874	100	37·8	26	78·8
15/32	0·46875	11·9062	0·3	7·62	3	0·11811	105	40·6	28	82·4
31/64	0·484375	12·3031	0·4	10·16	4	0·15748	110	43·3	30	86
1/2	0·5	12·7000	0·5	12·70	5	0·19685	115	46·1	32	89·6
33/64	0·515625	13·0969	0·6	15·24	6	0·23622	120	48·9	34	93·2
17/32	0·53125	13·4937	0·7	17·78	7	0·27559	125	51·7	36	96·8
35/64	0·546875	13·8906	0·8	20·32	8	0·31496	130	54·4	38	100·4
9/16	0·5625	14·2875	0·9	22·86	9	0·35433	135	57·2	40	104
37/64	0·578125	14·6844	1	25·4	10	0·39370	140	60·0	42	107·6
19/32	0·59375	15·0812	2	50·8	11	0·43307	145	62·8	44	112·2
39/64	0·609375	15·4781	3	76·2	12	0·47244	150	65·6	46	114·8
5/8	0·625	15·8750	4	101·6	13	0·51181	155	68·3	48	113·4
41/64	0·640625	16·2719	5	127·0	14	0·55118	160	71·1	50	122
21/32	0·65625	16·6687	6	152·4	15	0·59055	165	73·9	52	125·6
43/64	0·67185	17·0656	7	177·8	16	0·62992	170	76·7	54	129·2
11/16	0·6875	17·4625	8	203·2	17	0·66929	175	79·4	56	132·8
45/64	0·703125	17·8594	9	228·6	18	0·70866	180	82·2	58	136·4
23/32	0·71875	18·2562	10	254·0	19	0·74803	185	85·0	60	140
47/64	0·734375	18·6531	11	279·4	20	0·78740	190	87·8	62	143·6
3/4	0·75	19·0500	12	304·8	21	0·82677	195	90·6	64	147·2
49/64	0·765625	19·4469	13	330·2	22	0·86614	200	93·3	66	150·8
25/32	0·78125	19·8437	14	355·6	23	0·90551	205	96·1	68	154·4
51/64	0·796875	20·2406	15	381·0	24	0·94488	210	98·9	70	158
13/16	0·8125	20·6375	16	406·4	25	0·98425	212	100·0	75	167
53/64	0·828125	21·0344	17	431·8	26	1·02362	215	101·7	80	176
27/32	0·84375	21·4312	18	457·2	27	1·06299	220	104·4	85	185
55/64	0·859375	21·8281	19	482·6	28	1·10236	225	107·2	90	194
7/8	0·875	22·2250	20	508·0	29	1·14173	230	110·0	95	203
57/64	0·890625	22·6219	21	533·4	30	1·18110	235	112·8	100	212
29/32	0·90625	23·0187	22	558·8	31	1·22047	240	115·6	105	221
59/64	0·921875	23·4156	23	584·2	32	1·25984	245	118·3	110	230
15/16	0·9375	23·8125	24	609·6	33	1·29921	250	121·1	115	239
61/64	0·953125	24·2094	25	635·0	34	1·33858	255	123·9	120	248
31/32	0·96875	24·6062	26	660·4	35	1·37795	260	126·6	125	257
63/64	0·984375	25·0031	27	690·6	36	1·41732	265	129·4	130	266

How to read the remaining tables in this section

Read the 'tens' in the first or last column and the units along the top. Eg, to convert 25 feet to metres read down to 20 and across to 5 = 7·62 m.

Feet to Metres

(ft) *(m)*

	0	1	2	3	4	5	6	7	8	9	
—		0·305	0·610	0·914	1·219	1·524	1·829	2·134	2·438	2·743	—
10	3·048	3·353	3·658	3·962	4·267	4·572	4·877	5·182	5·486	5·791	10
20	6·096	6·401	6·706	7·010	7·315	7·620	7·925	8·230	8·534	8·839	20
30	9·144	9·449	9·754	10·058	10·363	10·668	10·973	11·278	11·582	11·887	30
40	12·192	12·497	12·802	13·106	13·411	13·716	14·021	14·326	14·630	14·935	40
50	15·240	15·545	15·850	16·154	16·459	16·764	17·069	17·374	17·678	17·983	50
60	18·288	18·593	18·898	19·202	19·507	19·812	20·117	20·422	20·726	21·031	60
70	21·336	21·641	21·946	22·250	22·555	22·860	23·165	23·470	23·774	24·079	70
80	24·384	24·689	24·994	25·298	25·603	25·908	26·213	26·518	26·822	27·127	80
90	27·432	27·737	28·042	28·346	28·651	28·956	29·261	29·566	29·870	30·175	90

Square Inches to Square Centimetres

(sq. in. or in.²) (cm²)

	0	1	2	3	4	5	6	7	8	9	
—		6·452	12·903	19·355	25·807	32·258	38·710	45·161	51·613	58·065	—
10	64·516	70·968	70·420	83·871	90·323	96·774	103·226	109·678	116·129	122·581	10
20	129·033	135·484	141·936	148·387	154·839	161·291	167·742	174·194	180·646	187·097	20
30	193·549	200·000	206·452	212·904	219·355	225·807	232·259	238·710	245·162	251·613	30
40	258·065	264·517	270·968	277·420	283·871	290·323	296·775	303·226	309·678	316·130	40
50	322·581	329·033	335·485	341·936	348·388	354·839	361·291	367·743	374·194	380·646	50
60	387·098	393·549	400·001	406·452	412·904	419·356	425·807	432·259	438·711	445·162	60
70	451·614	458·065	464·517	470·969	477·420	483·872	490·324	496·775	503·227	509·678	70
80	516·130	522·582	529·033	535·485	541·937	548·388	554·840	561·291	567·743	574·195	80
90	580·646	587·098	593·550	600·001	606·453	612·904	619·356	625·808	632·259	638·711	90

Cubic Inches to Cubic Centimetres

(cu in. or in³) (cc or cm³)

	0	1	2	3	4	5	6	7	8	9	
—		16·387	32·774	49·162	65·549	81·936	98·323	114·710	131·097	147·484	—
10	163·872	180·259	196·646	213·033	229·420	245·808	262·195	278·582	294·969	311·356	10
20	327·743	344·130	360·518	376·905	393·292	409·679	426·066	442·453	458·841	475·228	20
30	491·615	508·002	524·389	540·776	557·164	573·551	589·938	606·325	622·712	639·099	30
40	655·486	671·874	688·261	704·648	721·035	737·422	753·809	770·197	786·584	802·971	40
50	819·358	835·745	852·132	868·520	884·907	901·294	917·681	934·068	950·455	966·843	50
60	983·230	999·617	1016·004	1032·391	1048·778	1065·166	1081·553	1097·940	1114·327	1130·714	60
70	1147·101	1163·489	1179·876	1196·263	1212·650	1229·037	1245·424	1261·811	1278·199	1294·586	70
80	1310·973	1327·360	1343·747	1360·134	1376·522	1392·909	1409·296	1425·683	1442·070	1458·457	80
90	1474·845	1491·232	1507·619	1524·006	1540·393	1556·780	1573·168	1589·555	1605·942	1622·329	90

Pounds to Kilogrammes

(lb) *(kg)*

	0	1	2	3	4	5	6	7	8	9	
—		0·454	0·907	1·361	1·814	2·268	2·722	3·175	3·629	4·082	—
10	4·536	4·990	5·443	5·897	6·350	6·804	7·257	7·711	8·165	8·618	10
20	9·072	9·525	9·979	10·433	10·886	11·340	11·793	12·247	12·701	13·154	20
30	13·608	14·061	14·515	14·968	15·422	15·876	16·329	16·783	17·237	17·690	30
40	18·144	18·597	19·051	19·504	19·958	20·412	20·865	21·319	21·772	22·226	40
50	22·680	23·133	23·587	24·040	24·494	24·948	25·401	25·855	26·308	26·762	50
60	27·216	27·669	28·123	28·576	29·030	29·484	29·937	30·391	30·844	31·298	60
70	31·751	32·205	32·659	33·112	33·566	34·019	34·473	34·927	35·380	35·834	70
80	36·287	36·741	37·195	37·648	38·102	38·855	39·009	39·463	39·916	40·370	80
90	40·823	41·277	41·731	42·184	42·638	43·091	43·545	43·998	44·452	44·906	90

Index